Memoir Madness

Driven to Involuntary Commitment

Jennifer Semple Siegel

Copyright © 2012, Jennifer Semple Siegel

ALL RIGHTS RESERVED. No part of this book shall be reproduced or transmitted in any form or by any means, electronic, mechanical, magnetic, photographic, including photocopying, recording, copying or pasting on the internet, and/or by any information storage and retrieval system, without prior permission of the author and publisher. No patent liability is assumed with respect to the use of the information herein. Although every precaution has been taken in the preparation of this book, the publisher and author assume no responsibility for errors or omissions. Neither is any liability assumed for damages resulting in the use of the information contained herein.

This work of non-fiction is based on the author's memories and perceptions of a specific life event. Others associated with the author may have different perceptions of the same events.

Some names and/or minor characteristics of real persons have been changed to protect their privacy. Nicknames have been used for some real persons, most notably, Stoney. Names of some places have been changed, for example, The Crystal Ship and Denise's Diner.

For coherence and literary purposes, some passages have been compressed, expanded, or shifted. Some scenes and dialogue have been recreated. The time lines (late 1968 to May 9, 1969; April 2002; and August 2004 and later) are accurate, and the facts of the case are correct, including the amount of time the author spent in Cherokee, Iowa.

Events for which the author has no documentation and/or memory of exact dates have been presented as flashbacks.

For her late grandparents' first person narratives, the author has referred to interview summaries contained in her hospital records—interviews conducted and summarized by her psychiatrist (and other hospital personnel). The author has also relied on her personal knowledge about these people who raised her. The recreated third person narratives are the voices the author remembers, and may not reflect the memories and viewpoints of her family. Chapter 54, the scene in the Sioux City police station, is a possible scenario that occurred between the author's grandfather and the police matron and is based on textual clues contained in her Informant Report ("Special Insert," after Chapter 55). While paperwork for her hearing was being filled out, she was locked in another room.

Minor factual errors, albeit unintentional, are the author's alone.

About MEMOIR MADNESS...

CHRISTMAS EVE, 1968: history is made as Apollo 8 astronauts deliver their Christmas message from orbit around the moon.

On earth, at The Crystal Ship, a rock and head shop near Hollywood, California, 18-year-old Jennifer Semple listens to the iconic broadcast and, through the fog of drugs, ponders the future.

In the ensuing days, the girl experiments with LSD and other drugs; juggles a crumbling relationship with a notorious drug dealer; and tries to make sense of life at 2001 Ivar Street, a Hollywood, California, flophouse—where hippies, drug dealers, freaks, strippers, groupies, college students, Jesus Freaks, counterculture gurus, drag queens, rock stars and wannabe rocksters, svengalis, and con artists converge during one of the most volatile periods in history.

Jennifer's grandfather (and guardian) coaxes her into returning to Sioux City, her hometown:

"To get your head on straight," he says.

After a series of blowups with her grandparents, she, still considered a minor by Iowa law, is dragged into the Iowa court system and involuntarily committed to the Cherokee Mental Institute in Cherokee, Iowa.

While incarcerated, she corresponds with Jeff, a new boyfriend in Pennsylvania, and also interacts with other patients: Wolfie, a psycho-path who preys on other patients; Penny, a 17-year-old unwed mother; Carrie, a teen cutter with strange obsessions; Joyce, a young married mother enthralled with "10 ways of suicide"; Drew, a young man facing a stiff prison sentence for possession of marijuana; and D.J., a 42-year-old mentally challenged man and 25-year resident of Cherokee.

Eventually released from the institution, Jennifer flees Iowa and settles in Pennsylvania, where she still lives today.

As young Jennifer narrates her late 1960's memoir, how will the older and wiser memoirist, now voluntarily returning to Cherokee as a visitor, reconcile that painful time in her history with her current ordinary life as a wife, mother, grandmother, writer, and teacher?

Memoir Madness

Driven to Involuntary Commitment

*

Jennifer Semple Siegel

*

Author's Other Books (Amazon Author Central)
www.Jennifer.BanMyBook.com

*

Photographs, artwork, and other extras:
www.photos.MemoirMadness.com

*

✌ **Ban My Book Publishing**

www.BanMyBook.com

*

For more information:
Jennifer@BanMyBook.com

ISBN-10: 0-9886242-3-0
ISBN-13: 978-0-9886242-3-8

Cover Image

"The Turret"

Created from an August 2004 Photograph:
Cherokee Mental Health Institute
And a photo of the Moon (NASA)

Cover Design:

Jennifer Semple Siegel

Dedication

To
The Patients
of
Cherokee Mental Health Institute
Who were, are, and will be committed,
For frivolous reasons,
Against their will.

If the doors of perception were cleansed then everything would appear to man as it is: infinite.

—*William Blake, "The Marriage of Heaven and Hell"*

...The world as it appears to me is my creation, and for it I must assume responsibility. Given, as the bricks out of which I can build a universe, is a chaotic kaleidoscope of colors, shapes, sounds, moods, hopes, fears, joys, pains, ideas, movements... Out of this anarchy, I organize a world for myself. I subdue the disordered shapelessness into a world by choosing one out of an infinity of possible structures.

—*Peter Koestenbaum, "Existentialism: Philosophical Anthropology"*

To die before you've reached the sky is tragedy–the sky is always an inch away from our fingertips–no matter *how* high we may reach.

—*Jeff A. Brown*

Table of Contents

Prologue: Caged 1
February 19, 1969 3

I. Going to Cherokee 5
1. Christmas Eve, 1968 7
2. Blue Moon 14
3. Wallich's Music City 22
4. New Year's Eve, 1968 25
5. Dee Dee: Rescuing Jennifer 28
6. The Mission Hotel 32
7. Dee Dee: Angel Kisser 35
8. Rudy and Hitching the Strip 40
9. Rudy's Pad 46
10. Cops 49
11. The Luckiest Hand 51
12. Downers 53
13. Dee Dee: The Bribe 60
14. Sold Out 64
15. Carlos the Doorman 67
16. Crazy 71
17. The Hungry Tiger 73
18. On the Edge 76
19. Ice Queens 78
20. Pressure 81
21. Dee Dee: Tell Her What She Wants to Hear 82
22. Mo: A Bad Feeling 84
23. Goodbye, Hollywood, You Bitchin' Town 86
24. Kiss the Sky 89

25. Mother's Call   91
26. Devils Dance in Me   93
27. Tick Tock   96
28. Dread   104
29. Mo: Bitter   105
30. Icy Chill   106
31. The Birthday Party   107
32. Crash   110
33. Just A Nice Girl   112
34. Flashbacks   114
35. Dear Peter   118
36. Inaugural   122
37. A Suicide   123
38. Jobs   125
39. Running with Wolves   130
40. Purgatory or Hell?   133
41. A Letter from Jeff   134
42. Merry-Go-Round   140
43. Mo: Incorrigible   142
44. Turn On   143
45. Mo: Why So Angry?   145
46. The Annotated Angry List   147
47. Mo: Regrets   151
48. This is War   154
49. Mo: "That Hippie"   155
50. Threats   158
51. Donnybrook   161
52. Dee Dee: Informant   163
53. Circling   165
54. A Possible Scenario   167

II. *Verdict*   **171**

55. Mo: Relieved   173

Special Insert: 175
   Informant Report   177
56. Dee Dee: Double Generation Gap   179

III. *Driven*   **181**

57. Driven to Forget and Escape   183
58. State of Denial   185
59. Ignited   186
60. Convergence   189
61. Urgency   191
62. To Cherokee   194

IV. *Cherokee*   **195**

63. February 19-28, 1969   197
64. Main Street   209
65. The Miami Incident   212
66. Rock God   213
67. Reality   215
68. What If?   218
69. March 2-5, 1969   221
70. To West Cedar Loop   230
71. March 6-7, 1969   234
72. Admission   237
73. March 7-14, 1969   239
74. March 15-17, 1969   253
75. Intruders   263
76. His Place: A Toilet Service   265
77. Shadows   268
78. March 17-21, 1969   271
79. The Sundial   279
80. March 22-31, 1969   281
81. April Fool   293
82. Mel's Room   295

    83. April 2, 1969   298
    84. Logic   301
    85. April 2-15, 1969   303

V. Leaving Cherokee   337
    86. April 16-30, 1969   339
    87. May 1-6, 1969   357

VI. Released   367
    88. A Journey Ends   369

VII. Final Diagnosis   375
    89. May 9, 1969   377

Epilogue   379
    A Final Update   381

Special Thanks & Apologies   391

About the Author   393

Acknowledgments, Sources, and Notes (Chronological)   395

Works Cited and Consulted (Alphabetical)   403

Prologue

Caged

February 19, 1969

Caged.

    I was caged.

    Then driven.

    Driven to Cherokee.

    Driven to involuntary commitment.

    Caged.

    Caged. A hazy memory of riding in the back of a police car. Two shadows in the front seat, the county sheriff and a female escort.

    Patsy Cline's "Crazy" buzzing from a tinny transistor radio.

    Outside, the Iowa landscape bleak: cloudy and cold, condensation and frost riming the windows, piles of dirty snow dotting the countryside.

    I, cargo. Caged in the back of a police car.

    Destination: Cherokee's other place, an outline on a hill.

    Shifting, crossing my legs...

    Please, can we stop?

    Hot and steamy inside.

    Shivering, teeth rattling...

    Please...I have to go!

    Hear something, George?

    Naw, nothin' important.

    Laughter.

    Caged cargo has no voice.

Madness has no voice.
Listen, crazy girl...
Two voices: *We have come to take you away, ha, ha...*
"I'm crazy, crazy..."
Fragments, crazy-quilt impressions, acid flashbacks...
I, crazy?

I

Going to Cherokee

1

Christmas Eve, 1968

(Ninth Revolution Around the Moon)

85 hours, 44 minutes, and 58 seconds into the Apollo 8 mission, astronauts James Lovell, William Anders, and Frank Borman broadcast photographs of Earth from lunar orbit.

The vast loneliness up here on the moon is awe-inspiring...makes you realize just what you have back there on Earth," says Lovell. "The Earth from here is a grand oasis in the big vastness of space."

"We are now approaching lunar sunrise," Anders says. "For all the people back on Earth, the crew of Apollo 8 has a message..."

In the beginning God created the heaven and the earth...

(Santa Monica, California)

I'M SPRAWLED OUT in the work room with Levi, a clerk at The Crystal Ship and a drug dealer on the Strip.

My old man Stoney drops stones into a rock polisher.

Duane and Pi, owners, arrive to lock up for the holidays.

The Crystal Ship sells semi-precious gems in the rough, crystals, polished rocks, pipes, beaded jewelry, incense, rolling papers, and drug paraphernalia.

"You gotta hear this," Pi says, clicking on the radio. "The astronauts..."

*

And the earth was without form...

"That is *so* fucking far out," Stoney says, shutting off the polisher.

...And God said, Let there be light: and there was light.

President Kennedy's promise of landing men on the moon before 1970...will it really happen?

...God divided the light from the darkness.

Imagine! Men circling the moon, 250,000 miles from earth, something I'll never experience–except in my own head.

...called the light Day...

Levi rolls a joint and lights up. "To Apollo 8!"

...the first day.

"Yeah!" Stoney says.

...God made the firmament...

We all take tokes, except Pi, who's seven months pregnant.

...and it was so.

The shop now closed, we hover around Duane and Pi's radio, to wonder what Earth looks like from outer space.

...God called the firmament Heaven.

Duane takes the last toke. He hands the roach to Levi, who eats the evidence.

...Let the waters under the heavens be gathered...

"Yummmm," Levi says, "Priceless."

...and it was so.

"Yeah, like not getting busted in my own shop," Duane says.

"I have a present for everyone," Levi says.

...God saw that it was good.

"Not wrapped. Sorry." Levi offers each of us a blue tab of acid.

...from the crew of Apollo 8...a Merry Christmas...

"Blue Moons, the best shit on the market. Merry F. Christmas!"

...and God bless all of you...

"Now we can all split," Duane says, turning out the lights.

...on the good Earth.

"Far fucking out!" Stoney says.

*

(2001 Ivar Street, Hollywood, California)

Blue Moons.

Black dots from the linoleum rise up and float, planets bursting into blue, red, yellow, green, purple, orange.

Birthing galaxies...

Does God feel the same awe?

A blazing light: *I* am the creator of these galaxies, responsible for billions—

My fault should they go bad...My fault.

Oh-my-god. I am God.

I must destroy life, before it spreads viruses.

A butterfly net appears. My mission: capture these galaxies, trap them in a cosmic jar, smother them before they destroy their Creator.

They will destroy, just as we have our God.

Is God dead?

Define "dead."

Is God Death itself?

To believe is to die.

Is Death God?

Why not?

Who is God?

How.

When is God?

Past.

Does He possess a butterfly net?

Kaleidoscope light???

What color is God?

The essence of light.

What is essence?
The color of God.
What is God?
Why night?

Black, slick water, first smell, like old rubber boots, first smell, primal scent, tangy licorice love drizzling my body.

Luscious rum balls.

Velvet sugar, past boil, butter lust, savored again and again and again.

Is God dead?
To believe is to die.
Is God Death itself?
How.
Is Death God?
The color of God.
Who is God?
Why not night?
When is God?
If not now, never.
Does He need a butterfly net?
The color of essence.
What color is God?
Dead.
What is essence?
Kaleidoscope sky???
What is God?
The Man.
The Man.
The Man.

WHAT IS THAT?

A siren.

Stoney?

The room wavers—nothing has substance.

How can nothing have substance? Can something have nothing? What *is* nothing, anyway? If it has a name, then it has to be something; nothing would not have a name, if it were truly nothing. Are there empty spaces in something, nothing places to hide? My head spins—a million nothing places, black licorice dots swirling around and around.

Two sirens.

Stoney? Stoney? Oh, Stoney...

No one exists but me.

I know that now.

I am truly alone.

All you people are clowns, and clowns are not real; therefore, you were not, are not, and never will be.

Stoney...

Why are you smiling?

Yellow haze flows when you whisper, Winesap apples when you sing "White Rabbit," orange flames when you shout.

"Fuck you!" Orange and blue flames blast from your lips, tickling my thighs.

Blink. Blue butterflies flutter from your eyes, flicker, land on my triangle—pure geometry.

Yes, fuck me.

You ram a needle into your pulse—amber liquid whooshes through arteries to your heart to veins, from heart, back through your circulatory system, every branch, down to the smallest capillary, racing through your body, upstream to your brain, down river to your fingertips, flowing down to your toes, looping around and around...

You light up, a star burst covering the sky with flashes: red, gold, white, green, purple, blue, silver...then fading, whirling diamond chips, crackling and descending, descending, descending, disappearing behind ocean waves.

Your eyes, paisley.

Your heart, a rainbow.

Your body: granite, a quake.

An Odyssey in 3-D.

You come. A single red rose blooms.

I catch petals as they drop, wine red and smooth, cold as polished stone.

Stoney.

Oh, Stoney.

Warm as barberry oil.

Your solidity: a trick...

You cannot be.

Three sirens. The police!

No, just me in you.

Yes.

Stoney fizzles, soft as a mother's breast.

THE ROOM ZIGZAGS, we congealing to the floor.

I move, even as my legs melt into the dead dots.

The room has turned to sea.

I have grown gills.

I am back in a mother's womb, only she is *not* the mother I knew–this Mother is all wise–

Blue Moon Mother.

Blue Moon hurtles me through the galaxy...

WE ZIP through one million galaxies, head filling with sights, sounds, aromas, music, tastes, textures known only to a God.

She *is* the galaxy.

She is my God–

I am Her Daughter.

I *am* the Child of God.

2

Blue Moon

December 1968

(Tenth Revolution Around the Moon)

Christmas Day, 89:22:34. On the far side of the Moon and out of radio contact with Houston, Apollo 8's Service Propulsion System (SPS) has been ignited to accelerate it out of lunar orbit.

At 89:34:16, radio contact has been re-established with the crew.

89:34:25. Astronaut Lovell: "Please be informed there is a Santa Claus."

(Hollywood)

*F*AR OUT BLUE MOONS.

Stoney and I don't come down until after three—we crash for a few hours. Then, about seven, we go to Cecil's Stand for cheeseburgers and fries.

Later we exchange presents—he gives me a jade ring and a petrified wood ashtray in psychedelic colors; I give him a blue rock. Both from The Crystal Ship. I'm not sure what he likes.

After we open our presents, we argue about his being too wild when we play. He wrestles too goddamned rough sometimes, today getting me into a hammerlock and flipping me on my back. Something snaps–my back hurts like hell.

"You jerk," I say, "You could've broken my back."

"Shut up, bitch, stop your squawking."

We exchange more words. Don't I have the right not to be injured?

We calm down.

"Let's not wrestle anymore."

Stoney has an unfair advantage.

"That's cool," he says.

I think he understands; he apologizes, anyway, promising not to be so rough. We'll see.

The two of us look like hell. I *feel* like hell.

We go to bed early and make love, and rap about our acid trips.

Weird. I thought we had connected last night, but we didn't, not really. We were on separate trips.

Stoney only remembers shooting heroin and balling.

For me, it was so much more.

STONEY LEFT 45 MINUTES AGO for San Francisco, to score some acid. We decided it would be best if I stayed behind–save money to buy a van.

It's so cold in here, no heat, no one to keep me warm. I wish I could have gone with Stoney. He says he'll be back, at the latest, by tomorrow evening.

I can't wait. I'm so alone; no one's around anymore. Pam went back to Arizona for the holidays, and Big Brother (Jeff) split weeks ago. Why did he just up and leave? Not even a goodbye kiss. I don't understand why his going back to Pennsylvania was so important. He talked about it, but I never thought he'd actually do it.

Now that Stoney's away, I've been thinking a lot about Jeff. He's a puzzle. If he were here, I'd find him and invite him over; we'd sit up all night and rap about music, movies, and books.

He's really bright, but sometimes he talks over my head, with all that philosophy stuff. He should go to college, do something important with his life, not bum around like Stoney and me, go to college at USC or UCLA and still be a part-time hippie.

I wrote him a letter, begging him to come back.

What does Pennsylvania have that California doesn't?

I've no wish to go back to Sioux City–I'd rather stay here by myself, in this smelly, dirty dump, a strange pad, bright blue paint, hardly any furniture. Our first day here, I turned on the tap and whoosh! Water, water, everywhere, a missing pipe. What a mess; we're only going to stay here another month. I didn't want to move out of the dorm until after Christmas, but Miss Miller said Pam and I had to get out by the first of the year; we decided to split early, on December 1. Horton and Miller kept hassling us; they hated Stoney and Jeff and their smoking in the sitting room (la, de, da). And Stoney was forced to move out of The Crystal Ship–Duane paranoid about Stoney's stash.

We three pooled our money together for this place, though Pam stayed back at the Dorm. Why did she kick in if she's not going to live here?

Now I'm flat broke, no job; I quit two weeks ago–well, I just stopped going. The bank has probably figured out I'm not coming back.

I bounced a check last week. I had no choice–Percy, a friend, needed help, though he turned out not be such a good friend, but a rip-off artist and bullshitter. He claims he has sex with rich and famous queers for money and needed a loan to get a dose for the clap. Said he got it from Liberace. Gross.

Percy spent the money, *my* money, on new boots and a cowboy hat. He did buy me breakfast, though.

Far fucking out.

STILL WAITING FOR STONEY, but it's early yet. I just got up–I slept 14 hours straight. So tired...I just crashed in the middle of writing a letter to Jeff.

I'm going to cut back the dope—wish Stoney would too. He can be difficult, especially when he's high. He's careless with his dope, leaving it all over the apartment. The other day, when I picked up a newspaper, weed and seeds fell all over the floor, and I had to pick it all up by hand. What if the cops come? We'd never flush that shit down fast enough.

God, I'm so worried about him—he's bringing back a lot of acid, hiding it in his coat lining. I think the heat is onto him—it's only a matter of time before the cops nail him. We might both end up in jail, and that would *really* freak my grandparents out.

> *147:00:42. On December 27, Apollo 8 splashes down in the Pacific Ocean. The U.S.S. Yorktown is on scene for the rescue: the astronauts on board by 12:20 p.m. (EST), the Apollo capsule by 1:20 p.m. (EST).*

STONEY'S BACK. He shows me 500 tabs of STP bought from his San Francisco source. I've never seen so much acid.

We drop some Blue Cheer—yeah, I *am* going to put down for good—just one more trip...

Stoney undresses; we try making love, but it just isn't happening. On the way home, he visited some dealer friends and shot up heroin. God, I hate that stuff. How can anyone enjoy shooting up a drug that makes you stupid? Heroin addicts just lay around, drooling and slurring their words—no fun at all, human door stops, always passed out.

Once the acid kicks in, I no longer care about screwing Stoney—I'm off on my own trip, a bummer...enter the King of Schlock...Slip, slip, slip into Bobby Goldsboro hell, a world of clowns.

Stoney's drug dealing friends show up; everyone's a clown, I'm in a roomful of clowns, red cheeks and noses, white pan-caked faces, all in clown costumes, with ruffles around their necks, hands, and feet. Big curled up shoes and psychedelic wigs the color of rainbows, and they're all singing "See the Funny Little Clown," some cart wheeling all over the place, others balling up bread bags, setting them on fire, and dropping the sizzling balls to the rug.

Smoke and burning plastic fill the air.

Even the naked clowns still wear their shoes, ruffles, and wigs, even as they make love with other clowns...

I'm just a spectator.

STONEY AND I look at a VW van. I found my old savings passbook from Sioux City: cool! I still have $136.14 left. We need two or three hundred yet. If we don't get the van, then maybe I'll use the money to visit Big Brother in Pennsylvania.

I love Stoney, but I'm sick of being stoned all the time. If I'm not wired, I'm in a daze, always tired and feeling shitty. And the dope is getting scary; last week, we smoked some grass cured in embalming fluid. I passed out.

No more dropping acid three and four times a week. On Christmas Eve, I almost flipped out on that blue shit; ever since, I've been having flashbacks. Having a good time for 12 hours or so is one thing, but freaking out when I haven't dropped anything is totally scary. It's freaky when you're at work and start tripping for no reason.

I'm glad I quit that stupid job—I hate that bank and those stuffy people; I don't give a fuck about who gets a loan for a Toyota or Ford.

After we look at the van, Stoney drops me off at the apartment and leaves to score some mescaline for New Year's, says he'll be back in an hour or so.

John Steinbeck died about a week or so ago [December 20], and I just found out. I liked *The Grapes of Wrath*, even though I had to read it for high school.

STONEY DIDN'T COME HOME last night. I worry that he's been busted, so I hunt all over Hollywood and Santa Monica for him. I even check with the fuzz down at L.A. County.

I find him hanging out at The Crystal Ship, flirting with his ex-old lady Syndi, she hanging all over him. She's a skinny chick with short red hair, in a pixie style popular about three years ago, all doe-eyed, and looks about 15. But there's nothing innocent about her; she's fucked half of Hollywood, and I wouldn't put it past her to have another go-round with *my* old man.

"You better not be screwing that bitch!" I yell.

I shove Syndi away from Stoney.

Stoney pushes me away. "So what if I am?"

We get into a huge argument, right in the shop, and stay at it until he shoves me smack into the wall. I lose my balance; Stoney grabs me, steadying me to my feet.

"Fuck you!" I push him away. "You're an asshole!" I stomp out of the shop.

I storm back to the pad and sulk–trying to think up things to make his life miserable. I could kill that bastard.

An hour later, he drags himself through the door and apologizes, says he ate some strange mescaline that made him sick; he passed out at the shop and couldn't move. Says he didn't fuck Syndi: "No way!" he says. "Took me months to get rid of that slut."

I believe him. I still want to sock him, though I'm glad to see him safe. But then he ruins our good karma.

After the bad mescaline, you'd think he'd be a bit reluctant to use any more dope, right? Wrong. He pours those 500 tabs onto the table, counts out 13.

"I wonder what would happen," he says, holding them out in the palm of his hand, "If I dropped every last stinking one of these?"

"I wouldn't try it," I say. "Probably kill you."

"I'd have one helluva super trip."

"Maybe your last trip."

"The ultimate trip!" Then he pops them into his mouth.

"No!" I try prying open his mouth, but it's too late–he's already swallowed the tabs.

He grabs a Coke from the refrigerator and guzzles it. "I'm on my way to the *best* trip of my life!"

"Oh, shit!" What am I going to do? Call an ambulance? I can't call an ambulance; there's too much dope in this place– after the doctors pumped his stomach, we'd each get about 50 years...

Stoney laughs. "Jesus, Jennifer, you're *such* a drag."

God damn. If he's willing to risk his life for the ultimate trip, then who am I to stop him? I'll stay here, pop some bennies, keep watch on him all night, and if he gets to a critical stage, I'll get Rudy from downstairs to help me out; he'll know what to do without ringing in the heat.

Stoney slips into some strange trance-like state; he doesn't move, but his eyes and muscles twitch like crazy, and his carotid artery looks like it might pop out of his neck. Yet when I put my ear to his chest, his heartbeat sounds regular, though I don't know exactly what constitutes a normal rhythm. Though his face is puffy and little redder than usual, he doesn't seem to be dying. He's even smiling–something cool's happening in there, so who am I to ruin a perfectly good trip?

Okay, so Stoney blows some circuits; he's done that already–what's a few more?

While I watch him, the mail arrives–a letter from Jeff. Cool letters, a bit over my head. But he's groovy and sensitive–I doubt if he would drop 13 tabs of acid.

God, just look at Stoney–that shit's got to be eating up his brain cells.

Strange. I love him, but I don't always like him. We don't do regular things together. Yeah, we drop acid and, sometimes, make love, but he leaves me alone a lot–does his own thing– and, at times, he can be hateful and mean. Then he does stupid crap like dropping 13 tabs. I wish he were more like Jeff, not do so much dope, but some of the time, he's very sweet and gentle.

Then there's Jeff...When he was still here, we did a lot of fun stuff together–we laughed and carried on like two kids, ran around the strip.

Haven't I known him forever?

No, only since October.

3

Wallich's Music City

October 1968

(Hollywood)

*I*T WAS AFTER EIGHT, a crisp evening.

Rick was *still* missing.

Damn him. A total jerk.

I kicked at the ground, scuffing my shoes on the pavement. If he weren't so cute...

"Hey, Eleanor, would you turn up your radio?"

From my left, a male voice, not too deep, with a funny accent I've never heard before. I turned; a strange dude sat next to me, tapping his right foot, left foot on the wall, knee tucked under his chin. A homemade cardboard badge, with "Rent-a-Cop" written in Magic Marker, safety-pinned to his hat. He wore a plaid shirt, denim jacket, and bellbottoms, the outfit worn and ragged, the pants baggy. Long light brown hair, thin and a bit scraggly. Horned-rimmed glasses, thick lenses–probably almost blind without them.

Not too spectacular–not even a good pickup line.

"I'm not Eleanor. She's my roommate. I'm Jennifer."

"Oh. Sorry. But could you still turn up your radio?"

"It's Eleanor's radio," I said, turning it up as loud as it would go.

"Hey Jude," my favorite Beatles song, wafted out of the

speaker.

Paul McCartney sings like an angel, and I don't care if the lyrics are about shooting heroin, as some people seem to think.

"That's why I thought you were Eleanor. I recognized the radio." A kind smile, showing perfectly white teeth, but one front tooth slightly overlapping the other. He looked older, about 25. "So you're Jennifer. I should have looked at the chick, not the radio."

"That's okay."

"No, not okay. Sorry about the mistaken identity. Call me 'Virgil,' but my real name is 'Jeff.'"

Maybe not so strange and definitely not a pervert. On the street, one never knows.

"Well, then. I'd better call you Virgil, because my family and friends back home call me 'Jeff' all the time. It's been my nickname forever."

He laughed. "So how does a girl get a boy's nickname?"

"My cousin couldn't say 'Jennifer'; he called me 'Jeffer,' which got shortened to 'Jeff.' So I got stuck with it. How'd you get your nickname?"

"I made it up. I needed a street name, and I'm a Virgo. Seemed logical."

"I didn't think you looked like a Virgil."

"Well, you don't look like a Jeff, either."

We both cracked up, laughing at the silliness of it all.

Usually, I feel so awkward when meeting new people, but I felt totally comfortable around this guy.

Rick never showed up, but it didn't matter; I had a groovy time rapping with Jeff; he was funny and smart. He was from East Berlin, Pennsylvania, in L.A. only about a month, hitchhiking cross country because he wanted to see the world. Now he was homesick.

His birthday was a few weeks before mine. At first, I didn't believe he was my age, but he showed me his driver's license;

he seemed so much older, but in a good way, not at all like Establishment. He lived on Hudson Street, where he rented a room from some chick who agreed to give him cheap rent in return for some babysitting. His favorite Beatle album: *Sgt. Pepper*, but *The Magical Mystery Tour* followed a close second.

Maybe I'd see him again.

We exchanged phone numbers.

4
New Year's Eve, 1968

(Hollywood)

*T*HE WINDOW OPENS TO THE FREEWAY.

As the sun slips behind a hill, I lean forward and breathe in. The air, still unseasonably warm, foreshadows a chill, the specter of the diminishing year only hours away.

2001 Ivar Street, our space odyssey.

A drab, stucco apartment building next to the freeway, end of the line for a few acid heads, speed freaks, heroin addicts, prostitutes, and crazies with guns. At first, living here was kind of fun, but now I'm tired of dealing with freaks skirting the edge.

I'm scared. I'm afraid of getting killed by Rudy, an old freak with no front teeth; he lives downstairs and always packs an iron in his bell bottoms. I'm afraid Tessa, that spade chick a few doors from Rudy, will end up stabbed or shot to death. I've never seen so many mean-looking dudes going in and out of the apartment next to hers. Tessa's so strait-laced, and those creeps bug the hell out of her, pounding on her door, baiting her. Maybe I shouldn't care what happens to her, but I do. I'm not that stoned.

Death is too final, too real.

I'm so tired; I drop five bennies, just to get pumped up for the New Year.

Ever since he dropped yesterday, Stoney's been acting

weird. Thirteen tabs of STP. I thought he was going die; he slipped into unconsciousness, face twitching like an epileptic's, head puffed out like a balloon. I was afraid to call the ambulance, there was so much dope in the place–still is–so I watched until he opened his eyes. I can't put my finger on it, but he hasn't been the same since. He keeps talking weird shit, like spreading his wings and flying out our second-story window.

He scares me.

THERE'S GOING BE A BIG BLOWOUT at the Mission Hotel tonight. Free dope. You name it, someone'll have it. As we leave for the party, Stoney's face is still puffy, his eyes dull. Like, maybe his brain was sucked out of his head–like a yolk from its shell. We haven't made love in days, and at first, we made love all the time. My first time, three weeks ago; imagine, an 18-year-old virgin. At first, I thought Stoney loved me, he wanted me all the time. Then he started shooting Horse and dropping tons of acid and whatever else he could get his hands on. It doesn't matter what he drinks, smokes, drops, snorts, or shoots, just so he's on another plane. Now just another broken down freak, gone out of control. He zips up his jeans.

We're through.

"What's going to become of us?" I ask.

He looks up at me, his eyes half closed, mouth hanging open, drool running down the corners. "Huh?"

I want to throw up.

Maybe I'll meet some friends at the party–too bad Jeff's not here, but maybe Eleanor or Mel will be there. I could use a good friend now, a shoulder to cry on.

I can't depend on Stoney anymore.

WE HITCH A RIDE to the Mission. A straight couple from San Jose picks us up.

The wife tries luring me away from Stoney, promising me a hot meal and warm bed, salvation. Sure. Like I really want to spend New Year's Eve with Perry Como and his old lady. She assumes I'm 14; if I keep my mouth shut, maybe she'll give me some bread.

Just before we hop out of the car, the woman slips me a twenty.

"Get yourself some help," she whispers.

I stash the money into my pocket and calculate how much weed it'll buy.

THE MISSION'S A JOINT, but it's happening tonight. Every room's filled with at least four people. The two-dollar rooms are five bucks because of New Year's, but we know just about every freak here. I'll find a place to party and crash.

Stoney's on his own.

On the first floor, we stop off in a room; heroin addicts shoot up. As Stoney ties off a rubber strap around his arm, makes a fist, and taps for a vein, I leave. He'll be out for the rest of the night. I go from room to room, taking a toke here and a toke there, keeping my eyes open for familiar faces.

On the second floor, I find Mel, Eleanor, and Julius Caesar, an old freak decked out in a Roman soldier costume appropriated from 20th Century Fox.

We sit on the bed, rapping. I admit I'm sick and tired of all the dope and heroin addicts crashing at the pad; I just want to go home, maybe even back to Iowa…

5

Dee Dee: Rescuing Jennifer
New Year's Eve, 1968

(Sioux City, Iowa)

*W*HAT A MESS.

Jennifer's been missing about a week; my sister-in-law Hazel hasn't heard from her in ages.

The doorman at Hazel's building said that a few weeks ago Jennifer and some long-haired hippies tried to talk their way into Hazel's apartment while she was in Las Vegas. Jennifer told him some cockamamie story about leaving something behind and wanting to pick it up, but the doorman didn't buy it–he was sure they were there to steal. He wouldn't let the hippies in, but agreed to accompany Jennifer to the apartment, where she glanced around and announced, "I can't find it; I must've taken it with me," and left.

I can't believe that a child of mine would steal, especially from a relative. This can't be my little girl–it must be the drugs driving her to such despicable behavior.

SEEMS SO LONG AGO when we took that little girl away from Mary Lou. Back in '57, we had no choice but to go out to L.A. and get Jennifer and the baby out of that situation. Neighbors called, said those kids were running wild, Robin not even two yet, Jennifer her only caretaker. Plus, Mary Lou's drinking and her fights with Stan escalated, becoming loud and violent–the police called several times.

Then we found out two months after the fact that the girls had been run over by a truck. Thank God, they weren't seriously hurt, but it was only a matter of time before they'd be injured or worse.

We decided to go out, see for ourselves. We didn't tell Mary Lou we were coming–too easy for her to lie.

Stan's a decent man, but our Mary Lou proved to be too much of a handful.

In L.A., with Stan's help, Olive and I rented, on a month-to-month lease, a furnished two-bedroom apartment in the same building, and settled in.

After 1:00, we visited Mary Lou, obviously hung over. She looked twice her age, not the 26-year-old woman we loved and raised, her skin yellow and lined, makeup smeared, ratty hair bleached blond with dark red roots.

"What do *you* want?" She lit up a cigarette, her hands shaking.

We had some words–not very nice.

We found Robin in her crib, her pajamas sopping wet; the smell was overwhelming. I wouldn't treat a mangy dog that poorly. She played with her stuffed bunny, talking to herself.

Amazing what kids will tolerate.

"Where's Jennifer?" I asked.

"Where do you think, asshole? In school."

"No lip," Olive said. "Your father just asked a simple question."

"Who needs this?" Mary Lou asked.

"Why does everything we say have to result in fighting and name calling?" Olive said.

My wife wasn't helping; sometimes, it's better to ignore the nastiness and move on.

"How does she get home?"

"She walks. Do I *look* like a taxicab?"

I wanted to slap her, but it was more important to pick up Jennifer, get her settled into our apartment, at least for the time being.

"I wasn't judging. I just want to meet her, that's all."

Mary Lou mumbled the name of the school and gave me some rough directions.

Mary Lou agreed to allow us temporary custody of Robin. Olive took her to our apartment to bathe and feed her; I went to meet Jennifer.

I spotted her about two blocks from home, walking with a boy her age.

They held hands.

"Jennifer," I whispered. I didn't want to frighten her; she might not recognize me right away. For a seven year old, two years is a long time.

She continued walking.

"Jennifer." A little louder now.

She paused, but didn't answer.

"It's Dee Dee, honey," I said, invoking my family nickname.

"Oh, oh, oh!" she said to the boy. "It's my grandmother, I mean, my grandfather. You're really here." She took my hand, and tried to steer me to the middle of the block to cross.

"She's afraid to cross at the crosswalk," the boy said. "But at the jaywalk, she ain't."

"Don't worry," I said, gripping her hand. "You'll be safe with me."

It's a promise I've tried like hell to keep.

I DON'T HAVE A GOOD FEELING about this situation. We should have done something about Jennifer when we were out in October, but she assured us she was doing fine, although she admitted to experimenting with pot last summer. Said she was through with all that, and she looked okay, so we didn't intervene—she was working, after all, her employers pleased with her job performance. She caught on fast; they were thinking of sending her to school for more training. But now she's walked off the job—hasn't called in—nothing. Mr. Chauncey, her supervisor, says her performance has dropped off; he, too, is puzzled by her sudden odd behavior. Then there's the overdrawn checking account, the bad checks. She'd saved a lot of money. Is someone else draining her account dry?

Apparently, she's moved out of the dorm and into some hippie apartment building, God knows where, and no phone. She refuses to tell Hazel or Mary Lou her address, and sporadically shows up, all bedraggled, dirty, and barefoot, looking pathetic and hinting for money and food.

I have no choice. I must fly out and find her.

6

The Mission Hotel
New Year's Day, 1969

(Los Angeles)

I am the god of hell fire, and I bring you Fire...
—"Fire," The Crazy World of Arthur Brown

WE'RE STILL RAPPING as smoke fills the room—I start coughing and gagging.

The damn place is on fire!

"Let's get out of here!" I scream at Mel, Eleanor, and Caesar as they disappear into the smoke. "Where are you? Help me, I've gotta get out!"

A chorus of screams.

Somewhere, I find my last bit of strength; I jump off the bed and run blindly around the room. But I can't see anything now; the room is dense with stinging smoke.

I've got to get out!

I stick my head out the window and take a deep breath. The clammy air feels good, but fires spread fast, like that Chicago fire that killed 99 school kids when I was eight. Firefighters found the little kids, dead and stiff in their desks, still holding pencils above charred pieces of paper; will they find my charred body in this room, stretched out on this grungy bed?

I don't want to die! Will I have to jump?

The concrete slab below looks far away. How many bones will I break? Could I even die?

People scream and cry as they grope their way through the hallway. I start out the window, but halfway out, something clicks–maybe that guardian angel I've forgotten–

I'll take my chances in the hall. As I grope for the door, I trip over Caesar. I kick him. "Get the hell up!"

He groans and raises himself up, so I figure he'll be okay, and why should I care anyway?

My so-called friends left me here to die.

In the hall, blinded by smoke, I drag my fingertips along the wall as I navigate toward the stairs; I can't get air into my lungs. Stumbling down the stairs, I hold my breath. The walls don't feel hot.

Where are the flames?

Suddenly, I'm outside; I can't get enough of the cold air into my lungs, and my chest heaves back and forth. My lungs, hurting like hell, fill with air; I hack and cough, and everyone's coughing up their guts. On the street, Stoney is passed out, flat on his back, and–

Oh-my-God-he's-dead!

–But he moans. Caesar, Eleanor, and Mel stand over him, cajoling him to get up–how did he get out, drugged up like that?

"You made it," Eleanor says–as if my escape were of minor consequence.

Cops, hundreds of them in gas masks, rush into the Mission Hotel, their guns drawn.

"What the fuck?"

The Preacher Man, who, an hour ago, was shooting up heroin with Stoney, says, "Tear gas, Jennifer. A goddam police raid. Can you imagine such stupid shit?"

I'm relieved no one's burned up, but then I'm goddam

pissed off because of the window. I would've jumped out the goddam window, the goddam fucking window....

7

Dee Dee: Angel Kisser

January 1969

(Sioux City)

I'LL NEVER FORGET that first time we rescued Jennifer–

So innocent back then, not the pill-popping, marijuana smoker I'm hearing about now.

I couldn't believe how much love I felt for that kid–I'd thought that well had dried up long ago. I'd given up trying to raise decent kids. Oh, I suppose George and Colleen have turned out okay, maybe a few bumps along the way, and Dick and I have become close in recent years, but it hasn't been easy.

Mary Lou's another matter–I don't know if she'll ever be right...

I love my kids, but I've got to admit: when Olive pleaded with me about getting Jennifer and Robin out of that situation, my gut locked up.

I'm too old and tired for this!

But one doesn't turn away family, especially defenseless kids, so, of course, when my son-in-law Stan called, we drove out immediately.

That day, when she was walking home from school and holding hands with that boy–William, I believe–I knew we were doing the right thing.

I had to leave California shortly after Christmas–I still

owned National Industries and had to get back to work.

I didn't want to go.

The thought of leaving Jennifer behind, even temporarily, made me ill. I didn't feel quite the same about the baby, but Jennifer and I had a history–she'd lived with us, off and on, from birth until she was five, when we thought Mary Lou, newly married to Stan and pregnant with Robin, had finally pulled her life together.

Jennifer didn't want me to leave, either.

"I want to go to Sioux City with you and see snow!" she said, sobbing.

I promised her she'd be joining us there soon, though maybe not in time for snow.

But I wasn't sure if we'd win custody–judges almost always rule in favor of the mother, no matter how lousy.

I flew back to Sioux City, leaving the car with Olive. After the judge's decision, I'd fly back and drive back with Olive and, hopefully, Jennifer.

Stan had already taken the baby to Arkansas.

I doubt if she remembers now, but I wrote her two letters–to let her know I hadn't forgotten.

I still have copies–I keep carbons of everything I write:

THURSDAY

Dear Angel Kisser:

> I haven't seen you for a long time. Maybe you and Mo can come home soon. I looked all over the neighborhood for Old Sport and can't find hide nor hair of him. Maybe he doesn't live here anymore. The other day, I saw a spalpeeny dog around Otoe St. with a round ball on his nose and a curly tail. He was jacking around and following a little girl. He was acting like Old Sport but his feet were dirty and his hair wasn't

combed and he hadn't washed his teeth so I knew it wasn't old Sport. I asked the little girl to tell me his name. She said it was Old Ortspay and that he was always following her. She said he followed her to school and wanted to sit in a seat just like Old Sport and pretend to read and the teacher hit him on the bare rudy and run him out. She said she didn't want an old dirty dog like that in her school. Then he went all over the neighborhood and tried to get in the houses and nobody would let him in. He was cold and wet and hungry but he was such a spalpeen nobody cared. Then he saw a little dirty girl who lives in a dirty house and her name is Efferjay and he followed her home. What do you think? Her mamma let the dirty old thing in out of the cold and fed him some Pard out of a dirty dish and gave the old jerk a dirty pillow with the name "Ortspay" on it to sleep on. And do you know what? The old spalpeen liked it. I was glad the dirty old thing found a place to live. But I'm kind of mad at him for pretending he was "Old Sport."

Colleen has a dog named Speenart. He is big as a mule but you will like him. And when you come home you can visit them.

Saw Timmy the other day–he had a cowboy hat on.

It is warmer here now. It has been awful cold.

Not much snow. The streets are all dry. See you soon.

                    Love
                    Dee Dee

I've always loved telling stories—maybe a little preaching thrown in, but it doesn't hurt to include a lesson or two.

Mostly, I wanted Jennifer to know she was wanted and loved. A few days later, another letter with a reinforcement story:

SATURDAY NITE

Dear Angel Kisser

I looked all over and I couldn't find Old Sport anywhere. Maybe he went away to school. I'm getting the house nice and warm and clean for you and Mo so all you have to do is move in. There is some snow out side and is snowing a little now. The weather is nice and fresh. Tell Mo that I finally went to work. I made a door hood to-day and Monday I have to make 10 awnings. Your bed is still here—it didn't run away. Why don't you have Mo tell you about the bed that ran away?

Did Mo ever tell you about the lazy cat she had when she was a little girl? When Mo was a little girl she had a pretty cat but it was lazy. The other cats all went out to the field to catch mice and caught themselves a nice mouse but Mo's cat was just too lazy. She just laid around in the sun and was hungry all the time and she kept getting thinner and thinner and skinny but she wouldn't go out to catch a mouse. Mo tried every way to her to go out and work for her dinner but she was so lazy she would rather be hungry. Finally she got so skinny and weak she couldn't even catch a mouse if she tried. So do you know what Mo did? She went out to the field herself early in the morning and worked all day and finally caught enough mice for a nice mouse dinner and brought them in to the lazy old thing and her cat gobbled them up. Just like Old Sport with his Pard. And every day for a long time Mo went out and caught a nice mouse dinner for the lazy old thing and finally the cat got big and strong and fat and healthy and Mo said, "Now look here, cat, you are strong again and if you want to eat from now on you will have to catch your own mice." After that she went out every day and hunted mice with the rest of the cats. She had learned her lesson. Ask Mo she will tell you all about her lazy cat.

Hurry up and come home and you can meet Colleen's dog–his name is Speenart.

Love Dee Dee

I don't know if Olive ever told Jennifer about her lazy cat, but I sure had a lot of opportunities to tell her other stories; at the last minute, Mary Lou realized she was unable to care for her children. She signed the papers allowing us temporary custody. We had California's permission to take Jennifer back to Sioux City.

I flew back to California; the three of us drove back–one of the happiest times of my life.

I've watched Jennifer grow up–all too fast. She's inherited my storytelling gift; if she can get herself off all those drugs and away from all those no-good hippies, maybe she can pass down this gift to her children and grandchildren.

8

Rudy and Hitching the Strip
January 1969

(Hollywood)

STONEY PULLS HIMSELF TOGETHER and announces he's hitchhiking to New York City to sell those 500 tabs of acid—minus 13 tabs.

I beg him not to go—hitching cross country is too dangerous. Cops, rednecks, thieves, killers, all just waiting to arrest, beat up, roll, or even kill someone careless like Stoney.

Devil-may-care Stoney. I've never met anyone who was so slapdash with dope.

"This shit's so hot on the east coast," he says. "And I can make a killing."

"I wish you wouldn't go."

He sighs. "I have to."

I cry as he sews 487 tabs of STP into the lining of his coat.

He kisses me goodbye. "I'll see you in two weeks."

"Will you?"

"Don't worry, I'll be back."

I WISH STONEY would make money a safer way. Is acid really more profitable in New York?

Stoney's dealer friends scare me—they're either narks or connected with bikers and the mob; they throw around a lot of bread, a bit too cocky for all the dope they hold.

I want nothing to do with those bozos, told them up front they're not welcome when Stoney's away. So far, none of those bad-asses have showed up. No way do I want this pad turning into a flophouse for drug addicts and felons.

After Stoney leaves, I start hanging out with Rudy–nothing sexual; he's too old, two front teeth missing. I love Stoney and would never cheat on him.

Rudy, Pam's occasional old man, lives downstairs, his apartment always filled with chicks lounging around. Some of them live there, but most just hang out. Some of them earn bread by turning tricks.

I'd never do that; I'd find a regular job first.

SOMEONE POUNDS AT THE DOOR; I glance at the clock: 9:00 a.m.

"Go away," I mumble, rolling over and burrowing deeper.

"Rise and shine, Sunshine Girl!"

Who else but Rudy?

"It's too early. What do you want?"

"I want to show you something."

Right. I hope Rudy doesn't go perverted. He's got nothing I'd want to see. "No way!"

"C'mon, Jennifer, let me in. It's cool. I'll explain."

"Okay, okay. I'll be there in a minute." I roll out of bed, grumbling, and quickly jump into my bra, socks, jeans, shirt, and shoes. No way do I want Rudy leering at me in my pajamas.

I open the door. Rudy's not his usual disheveled self; he wears pressed, though faded and worn, brown slacks, and a gray flannel shirt. His long hair is hidden, tucked into a cap, his beard neatly trimmed. He wears a bridge–Rudy with front teeth.

His pistol, hidden in the cuff of his right sock, bulges

slightly. "Let's go," he says.

"What's with the straight dude act?" I ask.

"You'll see." He leads me down the steps, into the street, and underneath the freeway overpass, toward Hollywood Blvd.

An old man, dirty and disheveled, pisses against the concrete wall leading into the overpass tunnel.

"Where are we going?"

"You, my chick, are going to help earn us some bread." He steers me through the tunnel.

"Like hell I am." I pull away.

He laughs. "I don't mean balling johns–that's much too tacky for the likes of you."

"Then what?"

"I'll explain over coffee; no one should toil before their morning fix."

Over coffee, eggs, and doughnuts at Cecil's Stand, Rudy explains that I have the right look: pathetic waif.

"You should take advantage of your gift, earn mucho bread."

Why does this sound more and more like a variation of turning tricks?

"Most street chicks look so tough they could hard boil an egg just by staring at it, but you...," he says with genuine admiration, "you could part straights from their dough just by batting those baby blues and giving those saps a sob story. Hummm...you might not even need the sob story." He stares into space and rubs his chin. "But the story can't hurt."

New Year's Eve: the woman from San Jose who slipped me a twenty when I hadn't even asked. "I see."

"You'll need a way to earn some dough–that loser boyfriend of yours isn't going to be much help."

"He's coming back," I say. "And he's going to have over $10,000."

"If he doesn't get busted."

"No way—"

"Jennifer, we both know that Stoney's a one-way ticket to the slammer. He's careless with his dope and reckless about the characters he hangs with. You want to go down with him?"

Rudy's right. "No."

"Okay, then. Let's get started." He stands up, hikes up his slacks, and rubs his hands together.

"What are we doing?"

"We're going to hitchhike for money."

"Hitchhike?"

"You heard right."

He leads me to a crosswalk, where cars stop a lot, and sticks out his thumb. Immediately, a middle-aged couple in a lime-green Pontiac with tail fins stops.

"Ah, perfect, a married couple," Rudy whispers as we head for the car. "Just observe and listen—you'll get the hang of it."

"Howdy, folks," Rudy says. "A fine day for a ride. How far you going?"

"Farmer's Market," the man, a small dude with big round glasses and a flattop, says.

"Good, good. I have to pick up some oranges for my wife here." Rudy nods toward me. "Jenny has leukemia."

The woman, large and round like a beach ball, turns around and studies me. "Oh, my," she says, her face going flush.

I droop and sigh.

"The doctor at the free clinic says she should eat plenty of fresh fruit. Takes the edge off her treatment."

"Well, you're going to right place," the woman says.

"It's been rough, being out of work and all—"

The man's face—dubious and wary—reflects back to me from the rear view mirror.

Yes, we need the sob story, after all.

"—But things are looking up, finally," Rudy says with relief.

"Oh?" the man says.

"Yes, on Monday, I start my new job at McDonnell Douglas. Good money and benefits, $3.47 an hour to start."

"Long Beach," the man says.

"That's right," Rudy says.

"Good employer. You'll get back on your feet fast."

"Well, that's the plan. But here's the deal. The job starts on Monday, but I won't get paid until the following Monday."

"If you asked, maybe they'd give you an advance," the woman offers.

"I asked," Rudy says mournfully. "But they don't give advances to new employees. Too many con artists landing jobs, getting advances, and then not reporting for work, so honest folk like me suffer."

"Look," the woman says as she digs through her purse and pulls out two twenties. She wiggles around and hands them to me. "Take this money, and buy yourselves enough groceries until your first payday."

"Thank you," I say in the tiniest voice I can muster. "God bless you." Tears run down my cheeks; although our story is a lie, I *am* sad, because, somewhere in the world, it probably *is* true, and maybe I'm taking money from a real cancer patient.

The car pulls up in front of Farmer's Market; we hop out.

"Thank you, folks," Rudy says, giving the man a firm handshake. "You'll be rewarded in the hereafter."

We blend into the crowd, putting distance between ourselves and our benefactors.

"You're a natural," Rudy says, hugging me.

We spend the next three hours hitching for money; not everyone bites—one guy even orders us out of his car—but it doesn't matter; we've cleared $75.65, an amazing $25.00 an hour.

As a reward, Rudy takes me to the Tick-Tock Restaurant for a late lunch, where I order a Coke, cheeseburger, French fries, and an ice cream sundae.

But he gives me none of the bread.

"Good job, Jennifer," Rudy says as he inhales a chunk of sirloin steak. "But never hitch by yourself–too many rip-off artists and perverts out there."

I'll try to remember that.

RUDY TURNED STONEY AND ME onto this pad, apartment #12, the loneliest place on earth. Rudy might be a dirty old man who spends his days screwing chicks half his age, but he helps pass the time.

I first met Rudy just before my eighteenth birthday when Pam dragged me to one of his famous parties.

9

Rudy's Pad

October 1968

(Hollywood)

$\mathcal{E}$LEANOR, PAM, DERRICK, MEL, and I hitched to Ivar Street.

Rudy, a friend of Pam's, was throwing a big, blowout party, with some super grass and acid.

I knew to stay away from the acid, though—Mass the next day with Mo and Dee Dee, who had arrived the day before to check up on me.

Rudy's pad was filled with psychedelic posters and black lights. In the middle of the living room, a large hookah filled with wine held court on an old coffee table, heads taking hits from it whenever they felt like it, Rudy refilling the bowl with grass and relighting it whenever the dope ran low. The wine gurgled with each hit.

Rock music rumbled throughout the apartment: Jimi Hendrix, Cream, Beatles, Doors, Canned Heat, Grass Roots.

Rudy handed out tabs of Blue Cheer—I pocketed mine, for my own birthday blast.

One rule of the street: never refuse free dope.

I stayed away from the juice—I didn't need Mo smelling booze all over me—but I took several hits from the hookah; she'd just think I'd been smoking cigarettes, although I hadn't smoked tobacco since last summer.

Pam was right—that *was* super grass—

I'm floating, all warm, like I'm wrapped up in a hazy, purple blanket.

Arthur Brown's "Fire" blasted through the speaker; everyone stopped to listen.

Pam and Rudy, sitting lotus-style in a corner, were kissing and feeling each other up. Half undressed, they rose, Rudy's prick exposed and very large. As she followed him into the bedroom, she turned to me and winked. "Don't wait for me."

Derrick and Eleanor, deep into an intense acid conversation, ignored everyone else. I turned to Mel; he was cute, but he, too, was flying high on acid, studying his fingers as if they were galaxies and shaking out his red curls. He wrote something in the air with his finger—he was seeing trails, happy trails, probably something glittery or musical, definitely brilliant colors.

I hit on the hookah and passed out.

Eleanor shook me; it was light out.

I struggled to consciousness. "What time is it?"

"About 8:00." She was still tripping, but pretty much at the maintaining stage, where dealing with the straight world wouldn't freak her out.

Mass at 11:00! "We should go," I said, jumping up.

"Yeah, I'm meeting my dad for breakfast."

She didn't have to worry about her dad; he already knew she did acid, even approved.

Derrick, passed out on the sofa, snored like an elephant honking.

"You make it with him?"

"Nah. It was too strange."

"Where's Pam?"

Eleanor nodded toward the bedroom.

"Still?"

"Still. Beat about six other chicks to the punch. Dude's popular."

Man, I don't see it. He's got to be the most unattractive man in the world, a pockmarked face, two front teeth missing, rank body odor.

Pam swore he's 29, but he's at least 40, if not older, with that thinning grizzled hair and wrinkled face. He must be one helluva stud in bed.

"You think we should say something to Pam?"

Eleanor laughed. "Pam can take care of herself."

AT THE DORM, I jumped into the shower and allowed the hot water to rinse away the stink of weed.

By 10:00, ready to face my relatives.

Maintain, Jennifer, maintain.

It's just the paranoia.

10

Cops

January 1969

(Hollywood)

I HEAR FROM LEVI that Stoney might not come back, at least any time soon.

Evidently, New York, cop wise, is super cool right now. L.A.'s too hot.

Levi's right. When I get home from Cecil's, two cops wait outside the pad.

"We're looking for Stoney."

"He's not here."

"May we look around your apartment?"

I might appear innocent, but I'm not stupid. "I don't think so."

The two cops look at each other meaningfully. "Well, you pass along to Mr. Stoney we've got our eye on him," one says as he gives me his card. "If you got any information, give us a call."

I drop the card into my coat without looking at it.

"If you cooperate, we'll see what we can do for you."

A threat.

"Nothing to tell."

Please, God, please don't let my voice doesn't betray my terror.

"You think about it."

After the cops leave, my knees turn to rubber. I'm lonely and sad without Stoney, and also scared shitless the cops will get a warrant and raid the pad. God knows what Stoney's left stashed without my knowledge.

The cops'll find it for sure, and *I'll* get busted for possession, not Stoney.

How could he leave me in such a predicament?

11

The Luckiest Hand

August 2004

(Delta Flight #5883 to Omaha, Nebraska)

J WOULD NEVER SEE STONEY AGAIN.

I have no pictures of him, and yet his image remains grooved in my mind—my first real love, however ill-conceived.

Shortly after we parted, I drew a picture of him from memory. I needed to take something from that relationship, to make sense of that whirlwind month.

I still have that drawing, found in 2012, hidden among my papers.

Seems odd now, but I never knew much about him: where he came from; his parents; where he was born and where he went to high school; his thoughts; his real politics (though we all pretended to be liberals); his religion; and his hopes, dreams, aspirations.

I don't even know if the full name he gave me was genuine or fake.

In 1969, this is what I knew about Stoney: he liked rocks, rock music, and dope; he was born February 2, 1948 (or maybe 1949), making him an Aquarius; and he was tall and handsome in a dangerous sort of way: large amber eyes, slightly slanted, with long dark eyelashes; porcelain skin; and dark wavy hair, cut fairly short—above his shoulders.

He reminded me of the smooth-talking, slick version of the devil.

This is what I now know about Stoney: he didn't like or respect women very much.

The day he split for New York, I was dealt the luckiest hand of my life.

12

Downers

January 1969

(Hollywood)

JUST MY LUCK, having the cops show up like they did, looking for Stoney.

What has he done, anyway? Must be bad.

I stumble downstairs to Rudy's pad and pound on the door.

Rudy, his usual sloppy self, opens the door. Several girls sit around smoking dope, munching chips and pretzels.

Words won't come. Instead, I bawl.

A skinny and a chubby girl argue over a pair of red silk underpants, something about the chubby one borrowing them and stretching them out.

"How am I supposed to turn tricks in baggy panties?" the skinny girl shouts.

"Knock it off, Linda," Rudy shouts over the din. "You don't need panties for what you're going to do. Johns don't give a fuck about underwear. Just squat and screw. Better yet, suck."

Linda growls and slides the panties on anyway. She shakes her finger at the chubby girl. "You stay out of my things!"

The chubby girl gives her the finger and stomps out the front door.

"Women," Rudy says, shaking his head. He turns to me. "Now, what's the problem?"

The story spills out. "I'm going to get busted!"

"Look, Jennifer, they're not after you. You're nothing to them–they want Stoney, and they think you've got information."

"They've threatened me!"

"Yeah, that's what cops do when they ain't got shit."

"I'm scared. I can't go back to that pad."

"Okay, okay. Just crash here for a few days, 'til the heat's off."

"Thanks."

"Phoebe!" Rudy snaps his finger to one of the girls on the floor. She jumps up. "Get Jenny here a cup of tea, with lots of sugar."

"Okay." Phoebe disappears into the kitchenette.

"Oh, that's okay, I don't want anything."

"It'll be good for you, calm your nerves."

I don't even like tea much–but I don't argue when Phoebe serves me the steaming cup.

I take a sip; the tea is super sweet, with a bitter aftertaste. I set it down. "I don't want it."

"It's a special kind of tea from Mexico," Rudy says, picking up the cup and pushing it back to me. "Supposed to help you relax. C'mon, drink up."

Reluctantly, I drink, but this has got to be the most appalling tea I have ever tasted–why does Rudy insist I finish it?

A few minutes later, a flash: the room swirls; I'm dizzy, can't keep my eyes open.

That bastard spiked it. Downers, lots of them–not a damn thing I can do, except go with it, sleep it off...

Hope I don't O.D. and die like my mother's best friend Cee...

...I SLIP IN AND OUT OF CONSCIOUSNESS—not like acid. Downers render you stoned and stupid. Acid blasts you into alternate universes—this shit immobilizes.

I'm flat out on Rudy's sofa, unable to move—awareness slowly returning. I'm conscious of time passing, but how much, I don't know: a minute, an hour, a week—it doesn't make much difference; I'm not going anywhere until my body says I can.

I catch bits and pieces of conversations, mostly petty bickering among the girls, fighting over Rudy, some disappearing into his bedroom.

I can't imagine...

Two girls not invited into Rudy's inner sanctum get into a cat fight, scratching and biting each other, nearly falling on top of me.

In slow motion, Rudy reaches for his right pant leg, hikes it up, and grasps the pistol from his sock. He raises it into the air and aims for the front window. He cocks the trigger.

Pulls it.

B-O-O-O-M!! C-R-r-r A c K-k-k . . .

A lick of fire escapes from the barrel.

I follow the bullet; in slow motion, the cylinder hangs in midair before creeping over my head, arcing slightly and traversing across the room, eventually shattering through the window as if it were ice, shards exploding, clinking like cubes in a glass.

Everyone freezes.

Smoke swirls out of the barrel. "That's enough, girls," Rudy says softly, re-cocking the pistol, aiming dead on at the two chicks.

I've got to drag myself away, even if I'm tossed into the slammer for the rest of my life. Better than dying here with a bunch of crazies, gun fanatics, sex perverts, and drug addicts...

I black out...

"The Loco-motion" blares from a speaker, and Tessa's deep chocolate voice accompanies Little Eva's: "Come on, baby, do the loco-motion..."

Tessa sings along as she stands at the sink, washing dishes–

I'm sacked out in her roll-away bed, tucked under clean sheets.

"How'd I get here?"

Tessa's apartment is three doors down from Rudy's.

"Ah, you're awake. I found you propped up in front of my door when I got home from work–could barely move you. What's with you, girl?"

I offer the short version of Stoney's splitting and events at Rudy's, making sure that Tessa, totally anti-drugs, knows I didn't take the downers willingly.

"Girl, you were right to get out of there. That guy's a nut cake."

"I don't remember coming here."

"It all has to do with your subconscious–" Tessa is a Psych major at UCLA–"the will to survive is deeply ingrained. The mind can propel the body away from danger, even if you're paralyzed."

"Thank you," I say, my eyes growing heavy again.

Tessa wipes her hands on a dish towel. "Just trying to help a lost girl." She pulls the sheet straight. "I got to study now. Just sleep it off. I'll fix something after you shake the dope off."

Drifting in and out of consciousness, I'm safe, warm in the womb of Tessa's guest bed.

I roll out of bed about noon, starving; Tessa fixes me a breakfast of bacon, eggs, home fries, toast, orange juice, and coffee, which I consume like I've never had such an luxurious meal.

I'm still a little groggy, but at least I'm functioning.

"Sorry about barging in on you like that." I finish my third cup of coffee. "Thanks for the food—I haven't eaten so good in weeks."

"Just get yourself some help and away from all these losers."

"I've put down acid for good."

"Well, that's a start."

I feel safe here, but I can't stay—I'd be risking getting Tessa busted, and she's as straight as they come—one of those people everyone likes because she's real about the straight life. She chooses straightness, not because her mother, school, church, or country told her to.

"I want to make something of myself," she once said. "Make my people proud of me, show white America a thing or two positive about the Negro race."

I'd absolutely die if she got busted because of me.

I help her wash up the dirty dishes and strip the bed—I offer to do her laundry, but she says, "That's okay. I'll do it later."

That's my cue to leave.

I sneak past Rudy's place, and go back to apartment #12, where I take a quick shower, put on clean clothes, and gather some extra underwear and tops.

I'll hide out at The Crystal Ship for a few days.

Maybe Stoney will be back soon.

THE CRYSTAL SHIP didn't exactly work out as I had hoped. Duane said, as Stoney's old lady, I was too hot. Said the cops were nosing around the shop, so I couldn't stay.

"I'll keep a low profile."

"Sorry, Jennifer. Can't risk it."

Then Levi said I could crash with him in his panel

truck–he's got a mini-pad all set up, complete with a double mattress, a lamp on battery, books, and even a dresser. "You can use the bathroom in The Crystal Ship, but only when Duane's not around," Levi said. "Then you can hang out all you want."

"He's *so* paranoid."

"He's just being a dick."

Levi might buy the shop–Duane's wife Pi just had a premature baby girl; he wants to develop a more stable business than a head and rock shop.

Another head going straight.

Last night, I made it clear that we weren't going to have sex. "You're just a friend, Levi."

"There's nothing wrong with screwing friends," he said.

"Sorry. I'm spoken for."

"Well, if you're waiting for Stoney, forget it. He won't be coming back for a long time."

I still don't want to fuck Levi.

Hard to believe, but less than six weeks ago, everything was so fantastic–an entire new life with Stoney stretching out before me.

*

"Well, have you decided?"

"Almost. Just one thing."

"Name it, beautiful girl."

That we live together for a week or two before we...you know–"

"Fuck." Stoney rubbed his chin. "Hmmm..."

I whispered, "I'm still a virgin."

"Oh, man, that's so far out."

"I want to make sure we're compatible."

"That's cool. I can do that."

"I'll give notice at the Dorm tonight."

*

Seems a lifetime ago now.

I'm afraid Levi's right about Stoney not coming back.

LEVI'S BEEN DATING PAM, off and on, but he swears no woman will ever tie him down.

"Don't you love Pam?"

"She's cool, a good lay, but nothing special. I got my life, she's got hers–you know she's been hanging out with Rudy again."

"I thought that was over?"

"Who knows? I don't tell her what to do, she doesn't tell me."

I don't understand these people who make sex such a casual thing; I don't want sex just for sex's sake. If I offer my body to someone, it's because I want to be intimate with *that* person, no one else.

Levi has 101 arms. Horny bastard. I'm tired of fighting off his advances. Even Rudy understood "no," but Levi will try mounting anything with a cunt.

No choice–I have to go back to Ivar Street–nowhere else to go.

I'll go back to the apartment, clean it up, and scour every nook and cranny for hidden stashes. Flush it all down the toilet. Then, even if the cops do come, they won't find any shit around.

Once I get my head together, I'll figure out my next move.

13

Dee Dee: The Bribe
January 1969

(Hollywood)

IT DOESN'T TAKE LONG to find Jennifer's Ivar Street flophouse.

Apparently, the hippie community is small and not too loyal—I find a grubby longhair who knows where she lives. I bribe him—he's missing two front teeth—to tell me her address. When I go there, I find she hasn't been home for three days.

Jesus, I hope I'm not too late; if she's dead in a gutter, it will kill her grandmother and maybe me, too. But my informant assures me he's seen her around town, that she's been living in a panel truck for the past three days—God knows why; this dump might not be much, but it's better than the back of a truck. I give the informant twenty bucks with a promise of another if he lets me know when she returns while I stake out the place. We've agreed: the hippie will raise the American flag when she has returned—no honor among thieves. Jennifer may think these thugs are her friends, but they'd sell her up the river for a song, and they have.

But I'll do whatever it takes to get her back to Sioux City and the help she needs.

I don't know how long I can sit out here in the car, borrowed from my sister-in-law Hazel, who's absolutely livid with Jennifer. She'd rather wash her hands of this child, but I can't. I feel responsible for whatever has happened. We shouldn't have allowed her to come out to California—it was too much freedom too soon. But I thought she could handle it. Hazel and Mary Lou should have kept better tabs on her.

I'm amazed at how the days in January, even in California, can be cold and raw; it doesn't help I'm fighting a bad case of the flu. I just want to go back to Hazel's and flop into bed.

Fortunately, I have to wait only about an hour. As the flag inches up the pole, I move fast, as fast as a 68-year-old man can move. I walk up some outside steps to her apartment.

I pound on the door; Jennifer orders me to go away. She has apparently seen me from the window.

"I just want to talk, honey," I say.

"Leave me alone."

"I've come a long way to see you."

She opens the door, and peeks through the crack. "What do you want?"

"I just want to visit with you."

She opens the door and motions me in but doesn't look directly at me.

I feel her shame.

She appears thinner than when I last saw her just a few months ago, all around unhealthy, her hair long and stringy and dirty. She smells bad.

The place is a mess—clothes, papers, and garbage strewn about. Dirty dishes, obviously days old, are piled on a table and on the stove. The walls a ghastly dark blue, and barely a stick of furniture, only a table and chairs in the kitchen, in the bedroom, an old mattress without sheets.

Where I come from, only the lowest of the low live this way.

"Are you alone?" I ask.

She nods. "My boyfriend's in New York."

"I see."

"I don't think he's coming back." She bursts into tears.

I take her into my arms, although the smell almost kills me. "Well, Angel, he can't be much of a boyfriend, now can he?"

"I love him," she says, sniffling.

"I know, but there will be others."

She stiffens in my arms and pulls away. "I'll never love again. Never!"

I have made some progress here and don't want to blow it, so I say nothing as she continues to rant about how awful men are. Soon she settles down.

"I'm sorry the place is such a mess," she says, picking up the dishes on the table and stacking them in the sink. She grabs a dirty rag, wets it, and swishes it around on an old Formica table. "I wasn't expecting company. You want some coffee?" She dumps some grounds, obviously days old, from the strainer into the sink.

"Ah, no thanks. I, uh, just had some."

"I think we're out anyway."

"Tell you what: let's go back to Auntie's. You can get a hot shower, some clean clothes, and a hot meal."

"No!"

"I promise, no tricks."

I have to tread lightly, gain her trust. Later, I can worry about getting her back to Sioux City.

"I'm not leaving," Jennifer says. "I'm paid here until the end of the month."

It takes about 20 minutes to convince her into coming with me, but she agrees.

She gathers a few things to take with her. As we leave the flophouse, the hippie I have bribed reminds me I still owe him twenty bucks.

Although I say nothing, I make sure Jennifer sees me peeling off a twenty and paying him.

She must understand: she means nothing to these people;

they'd sell her—and their own—souls for a few measly bucks and some dope.

14

Sold Out

January 1969

(Canoga Park, California)

I'VE SPLIT THE PAD, now at Mom's.

This morning, when I got back to the apartment from Levi's, Dee Dee was waiting for me; the place was a mess–he was definitely grossed out.

That pad was never a palace, but Stoney and his creepy doped-up friends didn't help matters much, leaving dirty dishes, garbage, and clothes all over–like I'm their mother–and burning plastic bags and letting them drop to the floor, just to see what would happen. Like you couldn't predict the burn holes in the carpet.

I was going to clean up, but when Dee Dee appeared out of the blue, my plans changed.

Rudy sold me out. Now Dee thinks all hippies are snitches–made a big show of paying him off. Rudy would sell out his mother.

Stoney's still in New York City, but I don't think he's coming back, and maybe it's just as well. I don't think he's capable of loving anyone, he's so screwed up. He lifted my jade ring and petrified wood from The Crystal Ship. Some Christmas presents. I shouldn't talk–the other day, I lifted some jeans, but I don't like how I felt afterwards–like I had dirty hands.

I'm not going to live with another man out of wedlock; the next boyfriend will have to marry me. I met a guy two days ago; I thought we were just friends, but he made it very clear what he wanted. "No, I'm not ready for that yet. Besides, I have the clap," and he let it go.

Still, I feel so *used*.

When will I get Stoney out of my head?

Those two dicks coming to the apartment really freaked me out, but, now, at least, the heat's bearing down on Rudy. Shooting off that gun didn't exactly lower his profile–thank God no one got hurt from that stupid stunt. Just rattled the whole building. Even the other crazies think Rudy's gone too far.

Those cops warned me they'd be back, though. I don't want to end up in jail, but Stoney's headed there, and I could go down with him.

I'VE PUT DOWN ACID–never again. I've been clean for almost a month–well, since a few days after Christmas. Maybe I'll go to college, do something important with my life, maybe not. I still love getting strung out on bennies–

I'm not ready to go completely straight.

Dee Dee asked me about spending a few days with Auntie, but she's such a bitch, always nagging me about one damn thing or another, reminding me that I'm allowed at her la-de-da penthouse only because I'm family and, in any case, I'd better toe the line because my presence there is conditional.

Furthermore, I'm a slut.

She pointed downward out her window, told me, in no uncertain terms, "There's the street, and you can be back on it faster than a blink."

With Auntie, everything she offers has a hook. She's worse than Mo.

Besides, we got into a big fight about Carlos, her doorman, who blabbed about the stupid caper I tried to pull last November, when she was away.

15

Carlos the Doorman
November 1968

(Hollywood)

JEFF, STONEY, DENNY, PERCY, PAM, and I were wandering around on the strip, bored, when Percy, sniffing his armpit, said, "I sure could use a shower."

I was flying high on bennies; earlier, Stoney had given me a roll, and I dropped five of them. "My aunt's in Vegas," I said. "You can use her shower."

The second the words tumbled out, I regretted them.

I wasn't so worried about Jeff, Stoney, or Pam–they were okay–but Denny and Percy, bad scenes, were not to be trusted. Percy would steal anything not nailed down, and Denny would leave a mess and not give a shit.

"Oh, cool! Let's go."

What could I do? I couldn't take the invitation back–not without seeming like a total jerk–and The Dorm was out of the question.

Imagine old Horton running into naked guys in the shower; she'd probably faint at the sight of their soaped-up dicks...

Jeff took me aside. "You sure your aunt would be okay with this?"

"I don't know." I paused. "Probably not."

"Be careful," he said. "Percy's a rip-off artist."

A knot in my stomach. I couldn't afford to do anything that would get Auntie all pissed off. If anything was lifted, my ass would be grass—

I may even end up back in Sioux City.

"I'll stay outside," Jeff said.

"That's cool."

If there had been a cool way to keep everyone out, I would've done it.

My friends chattered the entire way to Auntie's.

What am I going to do?

At the door of Auntie's building, Carlos was on duty. In his uniform, a red satin suit with gold accessories and a blue pill box hat with three gold cords wrapped around it, he looked a little like an organ grinder. He was small and swarthy, big ears and a jaw line like a monkey's.

Damn. He knew and trusted me and would probably let us all inside the apartment.

I tried signaling my distress to him. "Hey, Carlos," I said with a false lilt, "Could you let us in my aunt's apartment?"

"What for?" he asked in a high pitched voice. His question gave me the out I needed.

"I left a dress behind. I want to pick it up."

He looked me and our group over. "Hmmm...." He rubbed his chin. "I doan know."

"I really need that dress."

Carlos considered my request. "Tell you what," he said in a thick Spanish accent. "I let you go." He waved my friends away. "But not deez others."

I looked at the guys, trying to signal "Sorry" to them.

"Okay."

"I go too, okay?"

"Sure." I've always liked Carlos—when I visit Auntie, he always jokes and kids around with me—but, now, he was all business. I was grateful.

In the elevator, Carlos apologized profusely. "Señora Lewis pays d' rent, so I muss be careful. Ees my job, si?"

I patted him on the shoulder. "It's okay, Carlos, I understand."

On the eleventh floor, Carlos unlocked Auntie's door; we entered the apartment, bathed in the night lights of Hollywood. Cigarette, perfume, and whiskey odors still hung in the air, familiar smells, reaching far back into my childhood. He switched on the foyer light.

"I left it in here, I think." As I opened the hall closet, Carlos was right there beside me.

"Escoose, pleze, Jeneefer, but I muss tek care."

I couldn't believe Carlos would think I'd steal from my own aunt, but there he was, stuck to me like a cockle burr.

"Okay." I rooted through the closet, looking for a dress I knew wasn't there. "Maybe it's in the bedroom."

Carlos, wearing an unfamiliar deadpan on his face, nodded and followed me into the bedroom.

I made a big show of going through Auntie's closet. "Damn. I must have left it at my mom's." By now, he must've realized my deception.

Does he think I'm here to *steal?*

I wish I could have explained how my big mouth got me into this fix, but I didn't think he'd believe me–not at that point. Maybe if I had explained while we were riding up in the elevator, we would've had a great laugh, and all would've been okay, Carlos and I standing outside the apartment for a few minutes, telling each other silly jokes like we always did.

"Yeah, now I remember–it's at my mom's."

"Okay, Mees Semple, we go, and I lock up."

"Thanks, anyway, Carlos."

As he locked the door, he was tightlipped. We didn't speak as the elevator descended to the ground floor.

Jesus.

16

Crazy

January 1969

(Canoga Park and Hollywood)

AUNTIE HAS BLOWN EVERYTHING out of proportion; I'd never steal from family or friends, or anyone else, for that matter. I still feel icky about stealing that pair of jeans last month. But Auntie doesn't believe me and is *totally* pissed off about my invading her apartment.

"It's a good thing Carlos is a smart doorman," Auntie said. "Otherwise I'd be on my way to the poorhouse."

No point in trying to prove my innocence. So I asked to stay with my mom, get away from the sniping witch. Mom's not happy with me, but at least she has the sense not to hassle me. Besides, what can she say? To shape up and get my head on straight and lead a normal life?

Still, she's bumming now; her best friend Cee killed herself in November–took 40 Valium. I suspect Cee meant to be found unconscious, but, alas, Tia, her house mate, worked late and found her dead instead. So I'm trying not to upset Mom any more.

Dee Dee wants me to go back to Sioux City; I don't have a good feeling...he insists he just wants me to come back for a few weeks, and then I can go anywhere I want. I definitely don't want to go back to Ivar Street, but Sioux City? If I do go, it will only be for a while, to figure out my next move and visit friends.

Maybe I'll go to Pennsylvania to visit Jeff.

It's just too crazy at Mom's, my four-year-old brother running around like a wild animal, and Mom moping around, mourning Cee's death. To keep my strange brother calm, Mom mixes weed in his food, a lot of good that does. That kid was born wild, runs around in circles, crawls the walls, and jabbers incessantly–but not anything anyone can understand.

Back at Auntie's.

Even Dee Dee thinks her mouth runs off too much. "Give the kid a break," he says. A lot, coming from him.

We've called a truce of sorts; for now, Auntie has backed off.

But it won't last. She gets all bent for the silliest reasons–you'd think she'd save the effort for the really important issues, like world peace. Instead, she's busy trying to control everyone else's behavior–petty stuff.

When Mo and Dee Dee came out in October, a week before my birthday, Auntie took us out for Sunday dinner and nearly made us all crazy. Then there was Mo and all her preaching and ultimatums, and Dee Dee and his choice of boiled lobster.

I, still on the tail end of a trip.

17

The Hungry Tiger
October 1968

(Hollywood)

We ended up at the Hungry Tiger.

Auntie was pissed off because I ordered a cheeseburger, fries, and milkshake.

"This is a *fish* place," she said, all huffy. "Why not try something different, like a nice trout or salmon fillet?"

What was the big deal, anyway?

I wanted a cheeseburger, not some smelly fish.

Dee Dee picked out a lobster from a tank; when the cooked creature arrived, still with its eyes staring at us, all red and boiling, I thought I'd puke. He had to crack open its shell with a mallet and then pick at its insides with a tiny fork and pull out some white flesh, which he dipped into melted butter.

Ugh. If I were the spirit of that lobster, I'd come back and exact my revenge on everyone responsible for my current state.

Auntie delicately sliced into her red snapper, no breading, her sides a salad, and pan fried potatoes.

Mo cut her fried halibut into pieces, alternating her bites between cole slaw and baked potato.

I dug into my cheeseburger and fries, which I ate with my fingers.

Auntie rolled her eyes and shook her head.

Mo kept looking at me funny.

"What?"

"You don't look so good, a bit thin and pale."

"Well, if you had to eat that crap at the dorm, you'd be thin, too."

Auntie stabbed her fish with her fork. "It's perfectly adequate food for a young working girl."

"If you like liver three times a week."

"It's good for you," Mo said, chewing her fish. "It's on all the new diets."

"You and your diets," Dee Dee said.

"I hate liver," I said. "I wouldn't eat it if I were starving to death."

"Young people are so picky these days," Auntie said.

Mo leaned over and drilled right into my face. "You're not getting any sleep. You'd better not be cattin' around."

"Lay off," Dee Dee said. "Let the kid eat in peace."

"The bed's lumpy, but I'm getting used to it."

No point belaboring the bed issue–Auntie would just jump in about the old days, sleeping on straw mattresses in drafty barns.

"If I hear you're taking that LDS and hanging out with hippies," Mo said, shaking her fork at me, "you'll come home so fast your head'll spin."

"It's LSD," I said.

"Whatever it is, just stay away from it."

"Yes, ma'am."

"And don't take that tone with me."

Last summer, I had made the mistake of admitting to smoking weed, and I hadn't heard the end of it yet: every letter and phone call filled with dire warnings of eternal damnation and threats of being yanked back to Sioux City.

"And stay away from that marijuana. And no shacking up with dirty hippies."

I nodded, watching a residual paisley drift over Mo's head.

Dee Dee, clenching his fork, stabbed that poor, messed-up lobster with a vengeance.

Jesus, would this meal ever end?

18

On the Edge

January 1969

(Hollywood)

I STILL HAVE NIGHTMARES about that lobster who suffered such a cruel fate.

Pam's finally back from Arizona—she's coming over tomorrow; we had a long talk on the phone.

She's back at the dorm, and Horton's still digging for information: "Did you know that Jennifer has taken that *awful* LSD?"

Pam said, "Oh, really?"

That's far out. That old lady once gave me a stern lecture. "Watch those dirty hippies," she said. "They'll give you V.D. and other strange diseases."

Why should the old bag care, anyway? I'm not at DePauw anymore, so what I do or don't do is no longer her business, though I sure could use some bennies right now.

When my grandfather leaves, I'll resume normal life.

Stoney was cheating on me, though not with Syndi; I should have figured it out when he stayed out all night and didn't come home until morning. God, I'm so stupid!

Eleanor, my ex-roommate, and I had a long discussion about men and how they're after one thing and one thing only.

She's still in high school; she's supposed to be living with her dad, but he doesn't have room for her, so she lives at the dorm. She actually went on a double date with him and Rosa, who also lives at the dorm.

How weird is that?

I can't imagine double dating with *my* grandfather.

Yuck!

Pam and I are going to L.A. County Hospital on Saturday for physicals and some birth control pills.

It's about time for both of us. We talked about this way last fall–I thought Pam would've done that already, but, no.

19

Ice Queens
November 1968

(Hollywood)

"Bummer," Pam said as I walked into our room.

Noon.

And I was still high from Mel's Halloween party last night at the Mission.

"I saw Syndi going down on Mel," Pam said. "I can't believe you went to his room after that."

The tail end of an acid trip, everything still bright, senses sharp and edgy. "No big deal. It's not like he loves her or anything."

"Wow, you've changed your tune."

"We had a long talk."

"Did you–?"

"No."

All my life, I've been taught to treat my body like a temple, not to allow boys to touch me in certain places or go too far, a rule so ingrained, I wonder if I'll ever be able to make love.

Am I frigid?

I've read about frigid women, in Aunt Colleen's *True Story*, ice queens who never thaw, who can't climax–what an odd word.

Better than that old-fashioned "crisis":

When Anastasia came to her crisis, she shouted out her lover's name, much to her husband's chagrin.

I was only 13 when I read about poor Anastasia and her chagrined husband—I had no idea what crisis meant in that context. A mysterious code, maybe.

I didn't know what "chagrin" meant, either.

"Do you think women of our generation are upsetting nature's delicate balance by screwing around?"

Pam stared at me like I'd just recited Greek poetry—in Greek. "Come again?"

"I mean, I've been taught all my life to wait for marriage…"

"That's Establishment, honey."

"But what if our parents are right, that we should wait for the right guy? I wouldn't want to get pregnant by the wrong guy. Maybe it's against nature not to choose carefully."

"That's why we have The Pill."

"I'm not on The Pill."

"Neither am I," Pam said.

"Jesus! You'd better get your ass down to the Clinic—before you have Rudy's or Levi's baby."

"I'm using foam."

"That's just great, Pam. You'd better use The Pill; it's more reliable."

"I feel funny about going to the Clinic, like they'll think I'm sleeping around…"

"Jesus Christ, chick—you *are* sleeping around."

"I don't want my parents to find out."

"They'll find out if you get knocked up, and no one's around to claim the baby."

"Maybe I won't get pregnant—maybe I'm sterile."

"I don't get you, woman."

"If I get pregnant, it'll be Levi's or Rudy's. No more spade guys. That would *really* freak my parents out."

"I can't see Rudy as a dad. Maybe stick with Levi for now."

"Rudy's a better fuck–"

"Yeah, he's been around longer."

"–Though Levi's getting there."

"I'm horny," I said. "I wished I would've screwed Mel. I'm tired of waiting."

"Well, don't wait. Go find him, tell him you're primed."

"He's meeting an old friend today."

"Oh, oh."

"It's not what you think," I said. "Let's smoke a joint. Mel gave me a dime bag."

Pam checked her watch. "I guess, but better make it fast. I'm meeting Jeff at two."

"Jeff Brown?"

"Yeah. He's all mopey. Saw you go into Mel's room."

"He knows Mel and me are hot." I rolled three tight joints.

"Jeff's got a thing for you."

"We're friends, that's all." I lit up one of the joints. I loved smoking weed when I was coming down from a trip–like landing gently on the ground instead of crashing nose down. I took a toke and passed it to Pam.

"Well, I'm going to give him a little comfort."

I grabbed Pam by the shoulders. "Please, nothing casual, okay?"

She pulled away. "What's it to you?"

I didn't know how to explain Jeff's morality; he's looking for love, not an easy lay.

Pam can't give him love.

"He's, ummm, complicated."

"He's a guy."

How could I tell her that Jeff was the complete opposite of Syndi?

20

Pressure

January 1969

(Hollywood)

To this day, I'm sure Jeff doesn't really want a casual thing.

I want to ask the clinic doctor about my back; on Christmas Day, Stoney and I were fighting; he scrunched me in this weird position, and my back just snapped. It hurt like hell, and it still hurts a little.

Dee Dee is really pressuring me about going to Sioux City. I just might go. I miss Jeff, and Sioux City puts me just that much closer to the East coast.

Besides, I wrote Jeff that if he doesn't get his ass back to California, I'll hitchhike to East Berlin, Pennsylvania.

21

Dee Dee:

Tell Her What She Wants to Hear

January 1969

(Hollywood)

*F*OR THE PAST FEW DAYS, I've soft pedaled around Jennifer.

I convinced her to move from that rat trap; actually, I think she's relieved to get away from there, what with its vermin and dopers. We packed up her meager things—we left behind the boyfriend's belongings and junk—and brought her stuff back to Hazel's.

She and Hazel are at each other constantly, Hazel laying on the guilt, reminding her of her immorality and shocking behavior, and Jennifer jumping on her for being an old stick-in-the-mud. I wish Hazel would stop it; her constant goading hurts my chances of getting Jennifer back to Sioux City. I don't care what Jennifer's done. It's over, time to look ahead.

She has admitted to using LSD and other drugs regularly and how the boyfriend had hitchhiked to San Francisco to buy dope and is now in New York to push it. What is this world coming to when kids think they have to take drugs to have a good time? Living with a drug dealer. How low can a person go, selling drugs to children?

I ask Jennifer to come with me to Sioux City, just for a visit, to get herself squared away, that she'll be free to come and go as she wishes. She assures me that it's over between her and this Stoney character, but she's been talking on the phone with some other hippie and mumbles about going to Pennsylvania to visit him. I'm heartsick she'll run away, and we'll never see her again; still, I use the Pennsylvania deal as a lure to get her home; once in Sioux City, we can figure out our next step.

My best hope: she'll come to see things our way, the right way, and it won't be a problem.

But know this: I'll tell her anything she wants to hear, just to get her home.

I don't feel guilty.

22

Mo: A Bad Feeling

January 1969

(Sioux City, Iowa)

WHEN WE WENT TO CALIFORNIA to visit Jennifer in October, I had a bad feeling. Things didn't seem right–she looked different–but she assured us everything was fine, and not to worry.

At her birthday party, she said she had smoked some pot last summer but she didn't do it anymore, and she wasn't messing with any boys.

Still, I let her have it good. I told her in no uncertain terms that if we got any reports of drugs or fooling around, she'd have to come back home and get counseling. We should have dragged her back then, but Harley said we should pull back and allow her to find herself.

A lot of good that did. Quite frankly, Hazel and Mary Lou didn't keep close enough tabs on her. Hazel's so busy running all over the world, how could she ever be expected to know what's going on right under her nose? And Mary Lou, with all that old drinking and catting around, how could she ever instill good, Catholic morals in an impressionable teenager?

And when Cynthia came to me with a filthy letter from Jennifer, mailed way back in November, I just about died, it was so shocking and filled with dirty stories about hippies and drugs. Why that girl waited until January to come to me with this, I'll never know. I gave Cynthia a serious piece of my mind, too, and told her mother about how long her daughter sat on this letter. Why, Jennifer could have been dead by now, for all of her poking and foostering around.

"I'm sorry, Mo," Cynthia said. "Jennifer's my best friend. I didn't want to betray her..."

"All the more reason..."

"I had to think about it."

"Humph!"

"I thought she'd get over it, come home, and when she didn't, I got scared." Cynthia sniffled and sobbed. "I'm such a snitch."

I don't get it–a true friend will help, even when it hurts, and not look back.

"Please. Don't tell her."

I see no reason to keep this from Jennifer–someday, she'll thank Cynthia for saving her hind end.

Harley said he had no choice but go to California and bring her back. But when Hazel told me how awful that brat has been behaving and the state of that hovel she was wallowing in, well, I thought maybe we should let her "do her own thing," as they say these days, and leave her to fend for herself, come what may.

But Harley was adamant. "We spent 11 years raising this kid–you want to give up *now*?"

I admit, he raised a good point, but, still, I don't have the energy for all that old fighting any more.

Mary Lou whipped it out of me long ago.

I finally just had to let my daughter go, bury my grief.

23

Goodbye, Hollywood, You Bitchin' Town
January 1969

(Hollywood)

DEE DEE'S BUGGING ME in the worst way–says I have three choices: go to my mom's, Auntie's (no way), or go back to Sioux City. He's really acting scary, and Auntie's turning up the heat.

I'll pass on Auntie's and Iowa, thank you.

I'm going stir crazy in this joint. I want to go out for a walk, but Auntie says no.

"You just want to go and see those damn dirty hippies," she says.

Yeah, she's right. Even so, she and Dee Dee can't keep me locked up forever. Only a few more days of this shit, and I'm splitting into the unknown, though I found out that Dee Dee *can* make me go back to Sioux City, being that I'm under 21. Bummer. It's okay for a boy of 18 to be drafted and dodge bullets in Vietnam, but when he gets home his parents can force him to live anywhere they want, even against his will.

One positive: if Dee does make me go, it will be a shorter distance to Pennsylvania. And he'll think I'm going back to Hollywood–instead, I'll be headed in the opposite direction.

I miss Jeff in the worst way. I wrote and told him so. Pam's still putting the moves on him. God, I hope he doesn't fall for her games. She's sweet but shallow, a new boyfriend every day–Jeff gets too hung-up, and she'll break his heart. Pam showed me a letter he wrote while he was on acid, and I've never seen him write stuff like that–totally incoherent.

Mo tells everyone I need a psychiatrist; God, she's so out of it. If everyone who turned onto acid went to a shrink, half the fucking nation would be on the couch.

As soon as Dee leaves, I'm going to hitch cross country–why not? Pam and I were going to take the Greyhound to East Berlin, but it's $145.00 round trip, and I don't have that kind of money. I'll get a map of the U.S. and stick my thumb out.

If Jeff can hitchhike, so can I.

I'll play Dee Dee's little game; I'll stay in Canoga Park. Then when he leaves, I'll split for Pennsylvania.

Screw Hollywood.

> *There is only a short time left before Jehovah will destroy this wicked system of things.*
> —The Watchtower

GOODBYE, HOLLYWOOD, you bitchin' town.

I leave tomorrow evening for Sioux City, not that I have much of a choice.

I'm coming back, but not to Hollywood. Maybe I'll hang out in Pasadena–gotta stay out of Hollywood for a while. It's too hot, what with all the drugs. I've learned from my experiences with Stoney and Rudy and the gun; someone could've been killed.

You know what really makes me sick? That I chose Stoney over Jeff–he said it kind of hurt him when he saw me with Stoney, but I didn't think too much of it then. In my last letter, I asked Jeff if it was too late for us.

"If it is, I will say no more," I wrote. "No matter what,

though, if Stoney comes back, I'm *not* going back to him."

If Jeff doesn't feel the same way, I hope I haven't ruined our friendship by blowing off my mouth. I asked him about coming to Pennsylvania, for maybe about a week.

Mo is hysterical; I told Dee Dee that if she lectured me on morals, I'll simply leave, and I will, too. When I talked to her on the phone, she kept firing off a list of what I could and couldn't do.

"You're not shacking up with any dirty hippies," Mo said.

I heard Peter will be in Sioux City at the same time I'm there.

Bad news. I'm not sure I can face him after what I have done, dumping him in that Dear John letter while he was in Vietnam.

Maybe I can avoid him totally.

Tomorrow at this time, I'll be in the sky, on the way to Sioux City.

I wanted to wait until Saturday or Sunday, but Dee Dee says we have to leave tomorrow.

I don't know what *his* hurry is–it's not like he has a job or anything.

I have a bad feeling about this trip.

24

Kiss the Sky

January 16, 1969

(United Airlines, Flight #266, on approach to Denver, Colorado)

'Scuse me while I kiss the sky
—"Purple Haze," Jimi Hendrix

I HATE FLYING, especially when I'm going somewhere I don't want to be. Last summer, it wasn't so bad flying to California–somehow, the prospect of crashing to earth and becoming part of a smoldering heap doesn't seem so likely when you're going somewhere fun.

But I'm headed for Sioux City, in the dead of winter, my grandfather snoring next to me, my grandmother lying in wait for me at the Sioux City airport.

I can't wait.

We're approaching Denver–I hate landings the most–then we get to do it all over again where we'll catch our connecting flight to Sioux City.

A nighttime flight.

Just get this bucket of bolts safely on the ground!

We're flying in a figure 8, stacked somewhere over Denver, my stomach lurching, in sync with the winding and curving of the plane.

Why did I agree to this trip, anyway? I'm 18, for God's sake, a woman now.

Though being 18 floats you in a no-man's land of not-quite-adulthood, 18 to 20, a purgatory of conditional freedom: be good, get married, or fight in Vietnam, don't make waves...

Don't drop acid and live with your drug-dealing boyfriend. Exile to Sioux City: my sentence for not conforming to Establishment rules. I was so naïve back in October, when I turned 18.

Enduring the entire afternoon with my family and their friends didn't seem so bad: the reward of true adulthood awaiting me, a final shedding of parental rules.

25

Mother's Call

October 1968

(Hollywood)

MOTHER CALLED ABOUT 2:00 A.M.

I grabbed the phone before it awakened everyone, including Mrs. Horton, that old busybody. I knew it was Mom even before she spoke, the only person I know who calls in the middle of the night, rip roaring drunk.

"Jevfer?"

"Yes, Mother."

"How'd you know it wush me?" Her petulant, little girl voice.

"I read your mind."

Mom's into all that Edgar Cayce and astral projection stuff.

"Shee? You shouldn' pooh-pooh the shupernat'ral."

"Okay, I won't."

She called to warn me, in her slurriest voice: Mo and Auntie had cooked up a surprise birthday party; my quiet celebration with my grandparents and great aunt would now be a full-blown affair with some of my California relatives and friends of Auntie and Mom.

Great. A fucking circus.

Anytime my family gets together, it *is* a circus, filled with fussy and feuding relatives.

"Act bijchin' shurprised."

I assured her I'd *be* surprised.

Mom kept me on the phone for the next hour, lamenting her lousy life, and complaining about my brother Sidney, Larry (my stepfather), and having to deal with Mo.

Better her than me.

Mom was angry with her best friend Cee, but it wasn't clear why. If it was a man thing, I didn't *want* to know. Mom's affairs have always baffled me.

As she slurred her way through the early morning, I muttered "um" and "un-huh," at appropriate intervals, drifting in and out of consciousness. Still, I was glad to be warned about the surprise.

Mom passed out; I knew because she snored in my ear.

She'd be out for the night.

In the morning, Mo probably found her slumped over the dead phone.

I quietly hung up.

Far out! I'm 18!

26

Devils Dance in Me

August 2004

(Delta Flight #5883
On Approach to Omaha, Nebraska)

I YEARN TO UNDERSTAND my mother, but I doubt if I ever will.

I Googled her as Jan Durrell, her professional name. Mary Lou "Marilyn" Semple Carson Kraft Whalen was a burlesque dancer who performed under the Durrell name.

On "Java's Bachelor Pad," a full body pinup of Mary Lou, scantily clad in a red feather bikini and high heels, her short hair platinum, adorns the cover of *Devils Dance in Me*, by Lee Shepard (Chariot Book, 1963), accompanied by the blurb, "Her body ruled her brain. She lived in a town where female flesh was willing, waiting–and dirt cheap."

A pulp fiction cover.

Her pose, by today's standards, is mild: Jan Durrell, head haughtily tossed in the air, her chest thrust forward, legs slightly apart, right hand on lower hip seems to dare the men gawking at her to try any funny stuff.

Even knowing what my mother was, I'm still shocked by the pinup.

She's my mother, for God's sake.

OF FOUR DEFINING EARLY EVENTS in my life, Mary Lou dominates three.

One: Mother's chronic alcoholism. In 1979, Mary Lou died of liver failure–a slow suicide. She was just 48, five years younger than I am now. To this day, her shadow trails me–as if she's tapping on my shoulder, begging forgiveness. It's difficult, though–probably why she continues to plead–but my inability goes beyond her lifestyle choices.

I would forgive for that.

Two: Robin, my younger sister, and I being run over by a truck. Mary Lou was in bed when it happened–hung over. Robin and I escaped unharmed, at least physically, though, at six, I got a crash course on the concept of death. Experts insist the age of reason comes later, but I know better; it comes when it's awakened.

Three: Robin and I being raised apart, she in Arkansas, I in Iowa. I'll always feel a profound sadness and loss and, yes, anger. If only Mary Lou had reconciled her life, my grandparents would not have been forced to choose between raising Robin and giving her up.

MOM, if you were alive, I would tell you: your own mother carried the guilt of that decision to her grave. As I grow older, I understand why Mo and Dee Dee gave up my sister, though knowledge doesn't lessen pain. It only affects how I choose to forgive; she did what she thought was best and made a decision that offered little clarity of hindsight.

But it was the wrong decision. Thirty years later, in 1987, when I finally reunited with Robin, how could I blame her for preferring ties with her Arkansas kin? She remembers nothing about Mother or me, so how could she possibly love us?

Mother, your part in this drama is unforgivable. I'm still working on forgiving Mo and Dee Dee, now also long dead. Perhaps this year's trip to Sioux City will be one leg in that process.

I concede that you had little to do with Cherokee, defining event four; by this time, you were remote from my life.

But you should know that I'm about to undertake one of the most important journeys of my life. I'm going to the Woodbury County Courthouse, obtain my commitment records, and accept whatever they reveal.

I might even go to Cherokee again.

27

Tick Tock

October 1968

(Hollywood)

"**W**HEN ARE YOU GOING to the big family shindig?" Pam asked.

"In about 45 minutes."

"Far out." Pam rolled a fat joint and fired up. She took a toke and passed it to me; still in my pajamas, I sucked in the sweet, blue smoke, and passed the joint to Eleanor.

Auntie will soon stop by to pick me up for the party.

Pam, taking pity on me, sacrificed some of her precious Gold.

Eleanor took one more toke. "Gotta meet my dad and Rosa for lunch." They had just returned from Big Sur the previous night. Ooh, la, la. Officially, Rosa still lived at the Dorm, but she'd been sleeping over at Mr. Firestone's pad.

"I know they're fucking like jackrabbits," Eleanor once said, rather cheerfully. "But he'll never marry her."

I wonder if Rosa knew that.

"See you guys tonight. Lotsa luck at the parental b'party." Eleanor grabbed her black leather jacket and flew out of the room.

I can't imagine my grandparents doing anything like jackrabbits.
Totally mellow.

Pam and I finished the joint; I rushed for the shower, washing off the stink of weed.

As I brushed my hair and slipped on my bellbottoms, Pam announced Auntie's arrival.

Seated in the parlor, Auntie was tapping her fingers lightly on the arm of the big sofa.

I've never met anyone so much in a hurry. She's rolling in money and has never worked, at least in my lifetime, yet she bustles around and lectures everyone in the family on the importance of hard work and all her tribulations–when has *she* ever experienced any hardships in her pampered life? Uncle Harry, considerate soul that he was, dropped dead one day, leaving Auntie a small fortune.

"You're late," she said, eyeing me up and down. "Couldn't you dress any better?"

"I dress up all week," I said.

"Well, you look like a bum."

No point answering. Without speaking, we got into her car, a white two-door Ford Mustang, convertible, black top. A brass plate on the dash announced, in script, "This car was manufactured especially for Hazel Lewis."

Auntie started up the car and pressed a button; the roof opened and folded under.

As we sped down Hollywood Boulevard, she lit up a Parliament and blew the smoke out the side. Her iron-gray hairdo didn't move an inch. "That girl was still in her pajamas."

"What girl?"

"That little tart at the dorm."

"You mean Pam?"

Auntie shrugged.

"It's Saturday. A lot of the girls hang out in their PJ's."

"Well, it's downright immoral."

There must be a special place in hell for people who don't

dress before noon.

We slipped inside the Tick-Tock Restaurant, where about 15 people jumped up and yelled, "Surprise!"

I tried to act surprised.

The only relatives there: Mom, Larry, the two kids—Sid on a harness leash and baby Arliss in Larry's arms—Mo and Dee, and Auntie. The others comprised of friends. Mom's group: Cee, her son; and her roommate Tia. Auntie's group: Bob and Andy, who, I think, are queers, but I like them anyway; Katherine; Vesta and Swede.

Growing up, I always liked Auntie's friends; they always pampered and made much of me, like I was a big deal, the only kid to come into their lives, so it was kind of cool to see them. When I was 12, I had a huge crush on Bob and Andy; I couldn't decide which guy I liked best, so I liked them both. Back then, I didn't know anything about queers, but I don't think it would have mattered anyway; they're such big flirts and very handsome, both with large sensitive brown eyes. Katherine is a stitch, a wicked sense of humor.

We once traveled together on the train, from Omaha to Los Angeles, and she kept me entertained with stories—made up, of course—about the other passengers. She gave them all names, but the only one I remember is "Floating Butt," given to a fat lady because her rear was so big it shook when she walked.

Vesta, who keeps her jet black hair in a Veronica Lake style, and Swede, a large blonde man with a ruddy complexion, are known for their extravagant gifts—my birthday no exception: $50.

Mom's friends, on the other hand, are just plain weird; Cee was probably my least favorite person there. Pam may be a little loose, but she's soft-spoken and good-hearted. Cee was slutty, crude, loud, bitchy, and gross looking. She wasn't ugly, just harsh looking, like she'd been around the block a lot, straw hair and leathery skin. She smoked constantly, much to Mo's dismay. Tia, her roommate, shy and nervous and oddly jealous of Mom, hung onto Cee as if she were afraid Cee would slip away from her grasp and never come back. Cee's son, with his almond brown eyes and black curly hair, was eight, going on 21.

He's going to be a wild one.

Still mellowed from the Gold, I felt remote; this gathering seemed like a more muted version of the previous week's strained dinner at the Hungry Tiger–the presence of others softening the blow of Auntie's chronic disapproval and Mo's lecturing.

Dee Dee melted into the group–just present, not saying much.

Mom was only slightly sauced, more hung over and tired from her marathon phone conversation with herself. I couldn't believe how small she seemed. When I was young and still living with her, she had loomed large in my life, a volatile presence about to explode. But she's only about five feet tall and, maybe, 110 pounds. Her hair, a two-toned platinum-auburn combination–platinum bangs and auburn pageboy–seems more tousled than messy. For all her hard living, there's something soft about her, a "please-don't-hit-me" demeanor, yet I'm still afraid, afraid she'll think I'm completely stupid. Sometimes, when she slurs her words, I can't understand her, and I have to ask her to repeat. She's impatient when I don't get it the first time.

Do you EVER think about Robin?

I think about my sister every single day. Robin would be 13 now, not a baby any more. No one has heard about her in years.

Stan, Robin's dad, has totally disappeared, it seems. My current stepfather Larry, like Stan, is a fantastic guy, good to Mom, nuts about her, and she barely pays any attention to him. The way he gazes at her, hangs on her every word–why does

Mom take up with such nice guys and then treat them like shit?

I ordered a big steak, medium rare, and onion rings.

Auntie, who was paying, nodded her approval.

I don't know why she cared.

After we ate, the group sang "Happy Birthday," I blew out 18 candles, and we picked at cake and ice cream. Then I opened my presents—mostly money, but Cee gave me a paperback of Lenny Bruce's *How to Talk Dirty and Influence People.*

"Your mom knew him," Cee whispered in my ear.

Mom already told me last summer about stripping in some of the same clubs where Bruce and his wife Honey performed and had given me a copy of the same book, but I thanked Cee anyway. She kissed me on the cheek, just missing my lips—she smelled like cigarettes, booze, and rancid suntan lotion.

Gross. I tried not to show my disgust.

For all my nervousness, nothing much happened. Cee got a little loud and raucous, and Auntie scowled, but no arguments or fights.

The party lasted about three hours. After saying their goodbyes and congratulations, the guests started drifting away, until only Mo, Dee, Auntie, and I were left. Auntie asked me back at the apartment, for a birthday drink. Now that I was 18, perhaps she thought it was cool for me to sling back a shot.

I tried to excuse myself.

"It won't kill you to come over for a half hour," Dee said. "Give us a proper goodbye."

"Act like you love us," Mo said.

A︎UNTIE LIVES ON HOLLYWOOD BOULEVARD, where a doorman greets you at the entrance; if you don't live there, he calls up the person you're visiting, just to make sure you're expected.

Carlos was on duty. He speaks with a heavy accent and likes to tell silly old jokes. He recognized Auntie and waved us toward the elevator. As we passed by, he said, "Hey, Jeneefer, should you eat friet cheecken with your feengers?"

I knew the punch line, but he loved telling what he thinks are new jokes. "No, Carlos, it's impolite."

"The feengers shoult be eaten alone. Ees gud, no?"

"Very funny."

"I told him that joke yesterday," Auntie whispered in my ear.

The four of us crowded into the elevator and ascended to the 11th floor, where Auntie lives in a corner apartment with floor to ceiling windows in the living and dining room. Before entering, we had to take our shoes off; Auntie handed us footies.

The view from her living room window is unbelievable, the Capitol Building a block away. At night the skyline looks spectacular, what with all the bright lights, including the permanent spotlight that circles the Hollywood night sky. The living-dining room combination is large, L-shaped, the bottom of the L, with the closing of an accordion screen, doubling as a second bedroom, where a sofa converts to a double bed. It's a groovy apartment, except for the white shag carpeting throughout, a bitch to keep clean. For all her airs, Auntie doesn't employ a cleaning lady. She's forever vacuuming dead flies from the floor window sill, and picking them out of the carpet edging the sill.

Her furniture is also white, even the dining room set and China cabinet; when company is not present, she throws covers over the sofa and stuffed chairs.

I prefer a practical design: floors and furniture easy to keep clean, second-hand stuff that doesn't matter.

Auntie enjoys being a rich person, always showing off her possessions. She's the only person I know who sleeps on pink satin sheets and wears a Harlequin eyeshade to bed; I find the sheets a bit too slippery–mostly, I end up on the floor–and the eyeshade too showy, especially for bed time. Who's she trying to impress?

This is luxury, and Auntie made sure we all knew it. Mo, Dee, and I totally out of place, Mo with her homespun, Iowa shirtdress look; Dee with his felt hat, gray Glen-plaid suit, and white shirt with blue tie; and I in my bellbottoms.

Where Mo is short and squat, Auntie is statuesque, if not exactly slender. She wore one of her signature red ribbon dresses, accented with gold and silver jewelry. As she moved about, she crinkled. Auntie's the only person in the world–that I know of–who still wears Harlequin glasses, dark rhinestone-studded frames with swirls like ocean waves.

She mixed some drinks, 7-Up for Dee Dee, sober since the 1930's, and Whiskey Sours for the rest of us, then sat in a straight-back chair and lit up a Parliament, using a sterling silver lighter with her initials "HL" engraved on both sides. To the rest of the world, Hazel Lewis–to me, just Auntie.

Mo bristled.

She has always hated smoking, cooking up a standing bribe of $100.00 for all the grandchildren not to start smoking before 21: so far, no takers.

Auntie ignored Mo's body language and offered a toast: "To 18, and many more."

We raised our glasses in rare familial solidarity.

I hung around for about an hour, sipping at my Whiskey Sour. I yearned for a rum and Coke, but that kind of slurpy drink isn't on Auntie's approved list. She's a purist when it comes to booze: drinks either have to be taken straight up or, if mixed, taste like something out of the medicine cabinet.

Then, the call of the street: I rose and stretched like a cat.

Everyone else sprung up.

"I have to go." I hugged my grandparents.

"You're an adult now," Mo said, in a low, serious voice. "You have new responsibilities."

I nodded.

Yeah. Like Rudy's party tonight.

"I don't want to hear of any nonsense."

"Yes, Mo."

"I'll keep close tabs on her," Auntie said, stubbing out her fifth cigarette in a crystal-cut ashtray.

"We're counting on you," Dee said.

Yeah, right.

One thing I have learned in the past few months about Auntie: she's basically self-centered and doesn't want to deal with anyone else's thing.

"Have a safe trip," I said.

"I'd feel better if you came home," Mo said.

"Enough, Olive," Dee said.

Auntie offered to drive me back to the dorm, but I couldn't stand another minute, cramped in her car, listening to her cracks about my clothes and friends.

"I'll take the bus."

I hitched a ride back to the Dorm.

I'm free!

28

Dread

January 1969

(Denver, Colorado)

*T*HUNK!

The wheels drop down and lock for landing; as we descend, Denver, twinkling and crisp, comes closer.

When we touch down, the knot in my stomach lessens, dread replacing it.

A few hours to Mo.

29

Mo: Bitter

January 1969

(Sioux City)

It is dark and bitter cold when Harley and Jennifer step off the plane, the hairs in my nose freezing as I inhale–a fitting welcome for that little snip.

I can't believe my eyes.

Jennifer looks so thin and pale. Harley said she wasn't eating right–and that god-awful hair, a floozy dyed black, all hanging down and straight! At least it looks washed, not oily and stringy like Harley described when he first saw her. I can only imagine...

I watch as they saunter over–Jennifer shuffling and kicking at the pavement.

"You look awful," I say.

"You don't look none so good yourself," she says, staring down at the ground–can't even look me in the eye.

"You ought to be ashamed of yourself."

"Stop it, Olive. We'll discuss this later."

Harley kisses me on the cheek and pulls both of us close together. "Let's go home."

30

Icy Chill

January 1969

(Sioux City)

There must be some kind of way outta here.
—"All Along the Watchtower,"
`Jimi Hendrix and Bob Dylan

WHAT A DRAG—it's not only literally cold here, but the icy chill coming from Mo is frightening; I definitely want to blow this joint as soon as possible.

Yesterday, when we stepped off the plane, I thought she was going to hit me. Instead, she said, "You look awful."

Like *she* looked so great herself.

"You ought to be ashamed of yourself," she said.

Dee Dee told her to ice it.

"How could you do this to us?" She burst into tears.

Like I personally set out to hurt her.

Back at the house, I fell into bed and slid into a dream, reliving my birthday party at Rudy's—once I ditched my relatives.

The night I met Rick, heartbreaker and prick.

Pre-Stoney.

31

The Birthday Party
October 1968

(Hollywood)

*F*INALLY! My real birthday party.

When Eleanor and I arrived at Rudy's, Pam was already there with her new old man, a tall–about 6'5"–dude from India, with wide shoulders and huge brown muscles.

"This is Draino," Pam, barely five-foot, said, tucked under his arm.

"I dreenk anything, hence the name." He crushed Pam against him.

"He drops anything."

The party in full swing, Mel, Derrick, and some chick with them were stoned out of their heads. She looked about 14–no way should she have been at a party like this.

Eleanor and Derrick were on the outs.

There were some new people here, too, my eye on a dark-haired dude across the room.

Rudy greeted me like I was his best friend in the world. "For the birthday girl, I have a special present." He handed me a tab of multi-colored acid. "Rainbow. Supposed to be the best on the street."

I slipped the Rainbow into my pocket. For later. I wanted to check out the dude across the room, who had caught my eye.

"We get together tonight?" Rudy slid his arm around my shoulder.

"Maybe later." I slipped away. "Thanks for the present." I found Pam, on the sofa, her top off, kissing Draino.

"Pam," I said, tapping on her bare shoulder.

"Honey, can't you see I'm busy?"

"I need to talk with you."

Pam sighed, disengaged from Draino, and threw on her top. "What's up?"

"Rudy wants to ball me."

"Cool!"

"Not cool." I nodded toward the dude across the room. "I want to meet *him*."

"You don't know what you're missing. You've been anointed."

"That's okay. How do I get out of it?"

"Look. The thing about Rudy, he doesn't push–doesn't have to. He's got women lined up. He'll get over it, maybe try again sometime, but not tonight. Go to Prince Charming over there."

I pulled the tab out of my pocket. "He gave me this."

"Whoa, girl, that's some super shit. You lucky bitch."

"Maybe I should give it back."

"That's another thing about Rudy–he's gives you something, it's for keeps. Now, I've got a date with a super-stud. Split."

I drew a deep breath and moved across the room.

Prince Charming smiled and introduced himself as Rick.

I was drawn to this guy, his dusky complexion, brown eyes, and perfect teeth. He didn't strike me as a true hippie–he was dressed too well and his hair was too short–but he was so gorgeous, and he was interested in *me*. He was already tripping, his pupils fully dilated, two black coals.

He could be the one.

I dropped my Rainbow.

We stayed up all night, talking and tripping–

A birthday sendoff, the best acid I've ever had.

Rainbow colors, dimensions, music that paints the sky with its broad strokes, fluid walls, incredible glittering trails flowing from our fingers and mouths, even our feet...

Maybe someday I can describe an acid trip without stumbling over my own words.

Rick and I slow danced, swaying to the music, even fast hard rock, he growing hard.

I was excited, too, but–

"I want you," he whispered.

"Let's just stay this way."

He didn't push, though I sensed impatient animal instinct, something sexually dangerous about him, like a panther, held back by a thin tether. That if I offered all myself, he'd rip into my body and consume my flesh, leaving behind nothing but a few bones.

We made out, French kissing and feeling each other up– each kiss reaching deep into my throat and down to my loins–

Each kiss a different color of the rainbow; a different note on the musical scale; each flick multi-textured: flutter, rock, hot lava, feather, pillow, sand paper, fire and ice.

He undid his belt and unzipped his jeans–no underwear. He thrust hard against my jeans, a shudder rumbling through him, me, the room, all of Hollywood, like a quake. He jerked upward and groaned. When he stopped, a warm wetness on my jeans. "Oh, baby."

Too stoned to worry about the stain on my crotch.

Rick grew slack; we sprawled on the floor, he, apparently satisfied and calm, I relieved I hadn't balled him.

We fell asleep.

32

Crash

January 18, 1969

(Sioux City)

A United Airlines 727 aircraft, flight #266 from Los Angeles to Denver and Milwaukee, crashed into Santa Monica Bay shortly after a night takeoff in poor weather. The crew reported an engine number one fire warning, shut down the engine, and initiated an air turn back before crashing into the water at high speed and an unusual attitude. Electrical failure was suspected.

All six crew members and 32 passengers were killed.

I'M GLAD I NEVER BALLED RICK—what a jerk. We barely got off the ground before crashing into the pits of hell. What a knockout guy, though.

If only he had a different personality...

I want to go out tonight, meet Isabelle and Susie, but Mo says no.

Damn. I'm not used to all these restrictions—Mo treats me like I'm back in high school.

"You live in my house, you live by my rules," she says.

Like I have a choice in the matter. I was dragged back here against my will. Who says I *want* to live here, in this old fogey house?

She won't say *why* I can't see my friends, just that I'm not allowed, not until they're approved.

Whatever that means.

So I lock myself in my room and play Beatle records as loud as I can stand it and start a letter to Jeff.

I'M NOT SURE WHY, but I keep dreaming about Rick, about making love to him, feeling him inside me. Although I hadn't known him long, I was nearly ready to give myself completely to him.

But he was *such* an ass.

One thing about Rick, though: he was at least honest about who he was–it was late October, during lunch at Cecil's Stand that he dropped *the* bombshell.

33

Just A Nice Girl
October 1968

(Hollywood)

"JENNIFER, I think you're a really cool girl, but—"

"But, what?" I asked.

"How do I say this? I could fall in love with you, but I have this thing about fucking—"

"I was ready to make love with you last night."

"Yeah, I kinda figured that out, but you should know how it is."

Okay, here it comes, "You're a nice girl, let's be friends, blah, blah, blah."

"I need it a lot. I like lots of girls. I *have* lots of girls around. I think you're looking for one guy. I mean, if you know how it is, we *can* be together, but I can't make any promises."

"You want to fuck other women."

"You make it sound so harsh."

"You-want-to-fuck-other-women."

"Well, it's how I am."

"Sloppy seconds." I got up from my stool.

He pulled me back. "You're my favorite, if that means anything."

"I don't want to join your harem."

"It's the sixties, Jennifer. Fucking doesn't mean a thing

anymore..."

"But making love does."

I wrenched away from him, and ran back to the Dorm.

It hurt like hell, and we went our separate ways; Rick, at least, offered me a choice.

Stoney, on the other hand, just plain deceived me–

Seduced me under false pretenses.

34

Flashbacks
January 1969

(Sioux City)

DEE DEE HAD A TALK with Mo; I'm allowed to go out with my friends after all.

So last night Susie and I hit the Loop, where we met her boyfriend Jim and Dan, a friend of Jim's. I wasn't up for a blind date, but I was so bored I could've screamed. Dan's straight as a board. We rode the Loop. Talk about deserted; the man wasn't even out, harassing innocent hippies. I have seen only one cop car since I've been home. L.A. may be super uptight, but I miss it and would love to go back.

I don't really like boozing, but it's something to do. No funny business, though. I'm through with all that. Besides, I'm falling hard for Jeff, and no one else matters.

I'VE BEEN HOME FOR THREE DAYS; Mo's been ragging on me ever since. My hair's too long, I wear too much eye makeup, my clothes are too hippie. I look awful and sick from all those drugs, I act like a slut. I *am* a slut, a down and dirty drugged-up slut. I shack up with filthy hippies–I have hurt Mo and Dee Dee; they will surely die of broken hearts.

Then there's Cynthia, my *ex*-best friend. Her mother refuses to allow Cynthia to see me. Not that it matters–I wouldn't hang out with her anyway, not after what she did to me, giving Mo that letter, which was supposed to be private, between us, not for old fogey eyes.

What a boring, hick town; I hate it! There's absolutely nothing to do, I'm *so* bored, so desperate I play Bingo at St. Boniface. Stoney would die, laughing his ass off, me an ex-acid freak screaming "Bingo!" in a church hall.

When I hear numbers called, I have flashbacks; I see bright, vibrant colors: B-13, a neon orange; G-74 green, a red trail; I-27 blue, a green trail.

Psychedelic Bingo.

A headache, like a migraine...the room spins and strange paisley shapes float across my Bingo card. Streaks of light, like a Strobe flash...all the colors in the room intensifying and glimmering, headache lifting, flashback transporting me back to when I was six...Robin and I, in an alley, look down an incline.

*

We roll stones down the hill.

Skid. Skid. Skid. Skid. Skid. Skid...

Something bumps my back. I turn my head: a silver bumper and an orange fender, pushing, pushing, pushing...

Help!

Robin screams.

My baby sister!

I'm on my back, looking up, underbelly rolling by. A wheel rolls over me, pressing my rib cage against my heart, crushing my breath.

Am I dead?

Suspended. A second—or a lifetime? No flow through veins, just aura, glow...warmth. No pain.

Do I go or stay?

Stay! Go! Stay! Go! Go! Go! GO, GO, GO, GO, GO, GO-GO-OOOOOOO-GOOOOOOOOOOOOOOO–

Mommy!

I'll never see Mommy again.

NO!
The tire rolls off, blood moves again, breath returns.
STOP! *Daddy Stan's voice.*
The truck slows, still drifting...
Pounding on the truck.
Stop it, Goddamn it! My little girls are under your truck!
Robin's your baby!
I'm your princess!
My ponytail catches under the back tire.
A crowd gathers.
Daddy shouts something at the driver.
Don't move, Princess!
Good, good, the baby's out, *a stranger says.* And she's fine.
Robin screams.
The crowd claps.
A girl in a lilac dress, white bunched up socks, and black patent leather shoes with buckles, peers under the truck.
Whatcha doin' under there? You gonna die?
I'm gonna die! I'm gonna die!
Please don't let me die!
I don't wanna die!
Mama? Mama? MAMA!

*

IN A FLASH, I understood: no one, even a child, is exempt from the possibility of dying–the choice to stay or go is rarely ours. The filament of being vibrating, Death nearby, scythe ready–

What would Death have been like?

Freaky. I'm more convinced than ever not to drop acid, ever again. If I hadn't known I was flash backing, I might have freaked out completely. Still, I'm scared when I feel out of control.

I called Peter's grandmother today.

He won't be back until the middle of February, and I'll be long gone by then.

Phew!

I still feel kind of creepy about that Dear John letter.

35

Dear Peter
August 2004

(Sloan, Iowa)

DEAR JOHN

*Cool
along the jungle trail
alert to lurking danger
manhood gentlefierce and poised
for any crisis on the path.*

*Animated
in a makeshift bar
exuberating joy
expanding through the
evening camaraderie.*

*Reverent
before ground made sacred
by spilled blood
by tried valor
and steel-forged meaning.*

> *Stunned now*
> *angry*
> *helpless*
> *bits of torn paper beside*
> *empty red mailbag.*
>
> –Jackson H. Day, An Khe, 1969

On the way home from the airport, Lyle, Colleen, Jerry, and I stop off at the WinnaVegas casino, a yearly ritual that officially opens our two-week Sioux City vacation, a pause before beginning my journey to Cherokee and then Skopje, Macedonia.

There is something soothing and rhythmic about dumping money into a slot machine, even though I'll eventually lose my $20.00.

I hit a small jackpot on a nickel machine. "I am Neptune, and I grant you great fortune," warbles a naked sea-man swimming with a pack of dolphins positioned over his vital parts.

Playing slots is something I do in Iowa; it's soothing and comfortable. I rarely win anything over $50.00—mostly I lose.

An unlikely person haunts me: Peter Raskin, a Marine from Sioux City serving in Vietnam who, in a 1968 letter, asked me to marry him.

I accepted.

I didn't love *him*–I, a flighty 17 year old who failed to consider consequences, loved the idea of being married. No sooner had I mailed my acceptance, I regretted it and spent the rest of the summer and fall plotting ways to undo it. But I had boxed myself in.

Soon a small box with an engagement and wedding ring from Sears arrived in the mail. I considered going through the wedding anyway: as atonement for my sin.

I can't do it! I have to tell him!

But every time I sat down to write the Dear John letter, my

blood ran cold. I had heard horror stories about soldiers stepping on land mines after receiving breakup letters.

Peter made arrangements for me to fly out to Hawaii during his R&R in December so that we could marry.

I wanted to wait two years.

He wanted to marry by Christmas.

No, I wasn't ready.

"I-want-to-get-married-by-Christmas."

"Two years!"

"NOW!"

"LATER!"

So we quarreled, back and forth, via the U.S. Mail.

Writing a Dear John: unthinkable. Even if I couldn't support the war, how could I do such a despicable act to a man fighting for our country? Yet how could I continue leading him on?

Just before moving in with Stoney, I had no choice: I dashed off the letter.

I don't recall exactly how I broke the news, but if my letters to Jeff offer any clue, it was probably an artless piece of prose, to-the-point blunt.

Peter's response was tepid, not at all what I had expected, which scared me even more.

"It's okay," he wrote.

"Should I send the rings to your grandmother?"

"Keep them," he answered.

I was going to send the rings back anyway, but when I left for Sioux City, I abandoned them at my mother's. I never saw them, or Peter, again.

This isn't a cautionary tale; Peter did not throw himself on a mine or step into the line of fire. He made it through the war and eventually married a woman from Michigan. As far as I know, he's still alive.

Not too long ago, I searched the internet for some Dear

John poems written by soldiers who served in Vietnam; most of the poems seemed trite and predictable, but Jackson Day's "Dear John" felt genuine and plausible, the emotion raw, yet somehow reassuring in that the speaker didn't kill himself.

I needed reassurance more than I needed art.

I showed the poem to my husband Jerry.

In one of life's impossible coincidences, it turns out that (unknown to me) Rev. Day had been Jerry's college roommate. Real life is funny like that, but don't try this in fiction.

If anyone asks if I regret any one thing in my life, accepting Peter's proposal would be it, one act I would undo in a blink. Other than that, I'm at peace with my past, even Stoney.

The slot machine siren goes off, along with flashing lights and a slot character's unwavering voice:

I am Peter, and I grant you complete absolution.

36

Inaugural
January 20, 1969

(Iowa)

RICHARD NIXON just gave his inaugural address; I didn't even bother to watch. I didn't like him back in 1960, and I don't like him now. I wish Bobby Kennedy hadn't been assassinated–he would be president now, instead of this creepy man.

I wonder what it's like in Pennsylvania? I heard that the towns run close together, but I can't imagine what that's like. I don't like small towns–everyone knows everyone else's business. I feel sorry for the people who live in them, and people like Jeff and me who are stuck in them. I'll just have to go there and find out what it's like.

If only Jeff would write or call...

MOM CALLS AT MIDNIGHT, totally juiced; I swear, she's really gone downhill since Cee's death. I can't imagine losing a close friend like that–I feel sorry for her.

I talk to her for a few minutes, but she wants Dee Dee, not me.

A relief, given how unstable she can be when she's drunk and upset.

37

A Suicide

November 1968

(Hollywood)

MOM CALLED ME AT NINE.

Something was wrong; she rarely called before midnight.

Pam was massaging a mixed potion of Lady Clairol Jet Black and Mahogany into my hair.

Mom was hysterical; I could barely understand her. For once, she didn't sound drunk, just distraught.

Larry came on the line. "Honey," he said, "Cee killed herself. She was found dead this morning."

"Oh, my God."

"Your mom just found out about an hour ago."

I didn't know what to say. I never liked Cee a whole lot; she was a bit crude, but not *this*.

"When's the funeral?"

"No funeral. Cee's family is downplaying it."

"Anything I can do?"

"Not much, honey."

"Let me talk to Mom."

"She's too upset–she just poured herself a glass of bourbon."

I hate when Mom drinks all the time, but, in her place, I would have done the same thing. "Give her a hug, and tell her I love her."

"I will, sweetheart."

After I hung up, my stomach started to churn, and I had to sit down.

"Jennifer!" Pam said. "I gotta rinse your hair before it cooks."

Yeah, I can see it now…black with purple highlights.

Larry's a good guy, treats Mom like royalty, even when she's mean to him. Daddy Stan, Robin's father, was the same way; she picks nice guys and then treats them like shit. Larry will help her through this, and she'll reward him by heaping a load of crap on him.

Mother loved Cee more than she loved *any* man.

38

Jobs

January 1969

(Sioux City)

MO'S BEEN BUGGING ME about finding a job.

Is she kidding? I'm not hanging around here long enough to find a regular job. I'll have to work someday, but the time isn't right yet.

Maybe I'll hitch to East Berlin, Pennsylvania, and find a job there.

I agree to work some banquets—only because it's temporary work, and I needn't get in that hang-up of having to quit again. My job record is shot to hell as it is. This banquet work is tiring, putting up with picky hungry people, unhappy with their food. Can't they just not worry about it? It's just one meal, for God's sake. I could never do this kind of work for the rest of my life.

I didn't handle myself too well at the bank—I hated the job with a passion. Even so, I should have quit properly, given my two weeks' notice, instead of just not showing up. I should have looked for a job in a head shop like The Crystal Ship, something groovy and fun, not boring, like checking credit histories.

A Credit Checker at Bank of America, Establishment extraordinaire.

For about the first month, the bank job was kind of fun—

Then Maggie left.

It was my job to call credit agencies, employers, mortgage companies, past lenders, and personal references and check the credit of applicants who wanted to borrow money for Toyotas and Fords. I was good at my job, quickly boiling down an applicant's credit history to its bare essentials. I had been notified that I'd be getting a pay raise, though only a few cents per hour.

Last August–seems like forever ago. I hated that job, sitting on my butt all day and calling all those credit bureaus and references. I hated making phone calls to strangers, but, on my first day, Maggie said, "It's gotta be done and done fast," so I went into a zombie state and just did it. Early on, I discovered that it was best to use a pencil when dialing–saved your fingers from getting sore. Also went faster.

The job was okay when Maggie was still there, but a month after finishing up with my training, she left to marry some 30-year-old dude with six-year-old twin girls.

I don't get it; she didn't really want to marry him, but she, very attractive, statuesque and blonde with a sunny personality, was desperate to find a man. She kept obsessing about dying an old maid. An old maid? She was only 22–lots of time to find her dream man. But too late: they got married the weekend after she left the bank.

She admitted up front that she didn't love the man.

"I like him, though," she said.

But if the chemistry isn't there, it'll never be there. I can't imagine spending the rest of my life living with a man who makes me feel dead inside. But she gave up a promotion to marry him; management was going to move her up to Collections after Gert, who stayed on until they found Steph, her replacement, handed in her resignation. For the next month, I endured Gert screeching all day into the phone at deadbeat borrowers.

Now I endure Mr. Redmond barking orders at Mo, Aunt

Doris, and me all evening as we schlep hot plates to diners. He's kind of mean, treating Mo like some stupid old woman. Mo may be a lot of things–irritating and bossy, mostly–but stupid she's not.

I'm glad this job's temporary–I just wish I knew what I want to do with my life. Get married and have kids. Maybe that's enough. Maybe the bank job wasn't all that bad, after all.

Carol, my co-worker, was cool.

She worked the Insurance Desk, figuring out ways to finagle homeowner's and car insurance for borrowers with iffy credit. She was good at her job, all efficiency and courtesy. But once five o'clock rolled around, she sloughed off the job and became Carol the wild woman–not wild like loose. Just fun wild. She rode a big Harley to and from work, but she was tiny and delicate, with porcelain features, milky skin, and perfectly aquiline nose. Just 23 and married, she had long red hair and large brown eyes. She was the mother of two boys, three and five, both with the same red hair.

"I like having fun," she said. "I dig my job, but when the day is done, I leave it behind."

I don't know how she separated the two–I found it hard to think like those bankers without wanting to puke.

Carol and I often went shopping on our lunch hour. She loved trying on sexy mini-dresses–and she looked good in them–but she rarely bought anything.

"We're saving for a house," she once said.

"I don't think I'll ever buy a house."

"When you have kids, you obsess about the future." She sighed. "You'll see."

I don't quite see it. I want to have kids someday, but I don't want to live a regular life.

"Dude gave me this," Mo says, shoving a magazine in my face. "Read this."

An ad in *Science News*, advertising a new kind of computer:

"The new Hewlett-Packard 9100A personal computer is ready, willing, and able...to relieve you of waiting to get on the big computer." It costs $4,900 and is designed to sit on top of a desk top, weighing 40 pounds and equipped with magnetic cards.

Uncle Dude, Mom's oldest brother, is always tinkering with one gadget or another.

"You should get into computers," Mo says. "Data processing's the future. That's where the money'll be."

Yeah, right: women, all women, sitting at their keypunch machines, will grind out punch cards all day, while men make all the important decisions.

My job at the bank stunk, but it was a piece of cake compared to what the keypunchers at the credit bureaus had to do. When I called them up and dictated all customer information, they had to get it right the first time; otherwise, they had to start a new punch card and retype the information from scratch. If they made too many mistakes, they got fired, because time is money. Though keypunchers are paid well, the pressure would get to me—they can have their big salaries. Callers have to speak clearly, spell out names and addresses carefully and slowly, "A as in apple, B as in boy...," etc. I'd hate to listen to that crap all day, day after day. The fast keypunchers get all pissy if you do each letter like that; by the time I quit, I was beginning to figure out who liked it slow and easy and who wanted it fast.

Keypunchers are *not* fun women to be around—they can have their jobs.

Mo has no idea what "getting into computers" *really* means.

I'M GOING TO SPLIT in exactly one week—where, I don't know, but I'm definitely going somewhere, anywhere but here. I haven't heard from Jeff yet. Maybe I scared him, and he doesn't want me coming to Pennsylvania. I sent him my awful school pic from freshman year—Beatle haircut and white blouse—Mo and Dee Dee hadn't yet bought my navy blazer with school insignia. Probably grossed him out. Maybe he's mad at me for coming onto him. Maybe he just wants to be friends, and I blew it for getting all gushy and lovey-dovey.

Haven't heard from Pam, either.

I've got enough money to get to Pennsylvania, but I would have to hitch back, and the more I think about it, the less I dig that idea. It's one thing to hitch with a guy, but alone...that's crazy. You never know who's behind the wheel–maybe a psychopath, like The Boston Strangler.

CYNTHIA AND I are on speaking terms, sort of. I don't feel the same about her anymore, not since she snitched and showed Mo that letter. Also, her mom is so annoying and naggy–she hates my guts! Thinks Cyn is still five years old. But we still hang out, sometimes.

This afternoon, Cynthia and I hitched downtown; it was three degrees, so we got a ride right away, but it's taboo here for girls to hitch alone, the looks we got. Gotta be careful; hitching's illegal here. Strange.

In Hollywood, I had problems hitchhiking only once, that time with someone I knew.

39

Running with Wolves

November 1968

(Hollywood)

Mr. Chauncey, one of my bosses at the bank, stopped to pick me up.

"Hop in," he mumbled, opening the passenger door. He was soft-spoken, about 60, thin and narrow-faced, bug-eyed, silver-hair styled in a strange pompadour, sort of like Liberace's, only bigger and fussier. He always wore a light gray suit, white shirt, and red tie; without the pompadour, he'd look like a cross between Ichabod Crane and Mr. Milquetoast. At the bank, he blended in like a chameleon; I barely paid any attention as he bustled about, doing what a middle-level bank manager does: shuffling papers and running back and forth to different offices.

I hitchhiked all the time and hardly ever experienced any trouble. Still, I was always a little nervous when I got into cars with strangers, so I felt relief when someone I knew gave me a ride.

Big mistake.

As soon as I shut the passenger door, Chauncey was all over me, rubbing the inside of my leg, practically had his hand inside my underwear.

"Stop it!"

"I want you. Let's go somewhere."

I slapped his hand away; he grabbed my chest. "Let me out of here!"

"You little slut." He sped up. "You're spreading those gams for every no-good piece of scum on the street. Why shouldn't I get some?"

My heart pounded...

If he does something to me, who will the police believe?

Not me.

"You asshole!" I shoved the steering wheel.

The car swerved–he struggled to keep the car from slamming into another car in the next lane.

"If you don't stop this car right now, I'll scream my head off!"

He sighed as if I've just dropped an anvil on him; he pulled over to the curb.

I jumped out of the car and fled to the bus stop. On the way to work, I resolved to march right into the bank manager's office and file a complaint, but by the time I got there, I wasn't so sure. Instead, I went to Carol and Steph, Maggie's replacement, and told them what happened.

"Well," Carol said, "You should think twice about hitchhiking."

"Wait a minute," said Steph. "Maybe Jennifer should be more careful, but no man has a right to force himself on a woman."

"If you run with wolves, expect to get attacked by wolves. It's that simple."

I felt sick on my stomach; I thought Carol was my friend, but now I wasn't so sure.

We all agreed that telling management wouldn't do any good–Chauncey was a longstanding employee with a steady, if not stellar, record; I was just an unreliable teenager who cut work and did drugs.

"I believe you, Jennifer," said Steph. "But we live in a

man's world. It'll change—a lot of women are pissed off at business-as-usual—but not for a long time. Maybe not even in our lifetime." She patted me on the back and went back to her desk.

Carol shook her head. "I didn't make this world, but I do my best to survive in it. I don't have time for those women's lib causes." She paused. "I'm not judging you—I'm just telling you like it is."

I nodded—no point arguing with her.

I shook all over at the thought of Chauncey slinking over to my desk and continuing his advances, but he didn't. In fact, he steered clear of my area, obviously so—fine with me, because if he *ever* touched me again, I would have screamed bloody murder, no matter if they believed me or not.

Funny. I never had a real problem with guys on the street scene. Yeah, some try stuff and use women who let them, but I've never had a street guy force himself on me, even Rick, who always stopped when I asked him to.

Maybe I've just been lucky...

40

Purgatory or Hell?

January 1969

(Sioux City)

I JUST HEARD about the United Airlines crash last Saturday, the plane to Denver crashing into Santa Monica Bay. Thirty-eight people killed, no survivors.

The day I wanted to leave.

I'm going to puke. Maybe I should have been on that plane. My life stinks: I've lost my freedom and, apparently, Jeff's friendship.

AFTER ALL THESE YEARS of attending Catholic schools, I have finally figured out what Purgatory means: I'm *living* it right now. My pathetic life is stuck in an endless loop: get up; eat breakfast; fight with Mo and Dee Dee; listen to them talk about their boring friends; run around greasy banquet halls, delivering plates of bad food to grouchy diners and getting paid next to nothing; go out to boring places with my Sioux City friends; get into more fights with my cranky grandparents; hide out in my room, play records, and write in my journal...

I have no regular job, hardly any friends, no boyfriend, and two old people on my back.

This isn't Purgatory–it's Hell on earth.

41

A Letter from Jeff
February 1969

(Sioux City)

*F*INALLY! I heard from Jeff; he says he's been writing me all along. I happened to be home alone when the mail came, and, *voilà!* a large envelope covered with psychedelic drawings, a peace sign, flowers, and a slogan: "My Country Tis of Thee, Sweet Land of Tyranny, in Subtle Forms." Inside, he let me know that he had written me a *very* important letter on the 20th.

Says he's turning into a nervous wreck waiting for my answer.

What answer?

I never received any letter from him dated January 20.

I couldn't even finish his letter, I was *so* mad.

I confronted Mo and Dee Dee, and we got into this *huge* fight. They've been stealing my letters, and censoring my phone calls. Maybe that's why I haven't heard from Pam and Eleanor, either. They denied taking any letters and intercepting my phone calls, but I know better. Those old coots are a two-person Gestapo! I hate them! How could they do this to me? Mo thinks I'm the biggest whore in town.

"Why would you want to shack up with all those guys?" she asks. "You'll have all the time in the world for that necessary evil once you're married."

Those two Nazi guards are watching over me; they want to

mold me into a dental hygienist and darling little housewife.

I called my dear, sweet mother to see if I could come back to L.A.–she told me to go to hell. Bitch. It's all well and good for her to drink until she's stupid and screw around like a jackal. What a hypocrite. Why can't these people stop hassling me? I want to do my thing, without everyone imposing their morals on me. But it looks like L.A. is out of the question; my mother thinks I'm a nut, and Auntie hates my guts. I went to my room and threw things around, just to make my point.

Mo and Dee are making me see this psychiatrist. I hate her, too; she's on their side, and I have no intentions of telling her *anything* personal. She'll just blab back to them. They're wasting their money. Now they want me to go to college. What a joke. It's waste of time and money; I don't need Auntie's college fund–she should find a kid who wants it. I hated high school, and I doubt if I'd like college much better.

I'm still clean off acid. The flashbacks keep coming back, but now I get a warning: a splitting headache. I hope the flashbacks and headaches eventually go away. I read somewhere that acid doesn't leave your body for at least two years. I still do whites and grass, but not very often. Bennies are hard to get here, though Isabelle turned me onto some fantastic Acapulco Gold a few days ago. But I'm getting tired of drugs. Weed makes me sleepy and stupid and hungry.

I babysat Aunt Colleen's kids the other night; I need all the money I can get so I can blow this town. After Colleen and Lyle got home, Mo called, worried about how I would get home; it's only a block away. It's a good thing she never saw me wandering the streets of L.A.

LAST NIGHT, I went to the Loft with Susie and her boyfriend, but Dan stood me up, story of my life. No big deal. I didn't like him much anyway–he was a bit of a creep. Besides, I don't like juicing with strange guys; they buy you a few Colt 45's, and they think they can ball you. Know what? We had a good time without him. Why can't guys just be friends with girls sometimes? I like having male friends, but I don't like the sexual games.

Like with Tom, who I met at Foster's Freeze, just after Stoney split for New York; he invited me over to see his pad. I told him my sob story, about being all alone. Tom offered me a place to stay, but that's not what I wanted–I already had a place to crash. I wanted someone who'd listen, a friend. But, then it was too late to hitch back to Ivar Street, so Tom said I could stay over–permanently, if I wanted. That meant only one thing, and I wasn't interested.

"I have the clap," I said.

That seems to cool a lot of guys off.

"I'll risk it," he said. "I'm really horny."

God, what a character. When I made it clear I wasn't going to ball him, he cooled off. He was actually pretty nice about it, and I stayed the night. Tom's a cute guy, but we had known each other for only two days and had nothing in common. He liked classical music, like *Madame Butterfly*, and I like The Doors.

Even Stoney and I didn't make love until after we'd been living together for about a week.

A COUPLE OF NIGHTS AGO, after reading an article about the Amish, I had a dream that Jeff lived in an Amish community–makes me think about Pennsylvania and what it might be like. What *does* happen in East Berlin, Pennsylvania, anyway? Makes me think of the Berlin Wall, and how life behind it is regulated–much like my life now.

Jeff's writing a 1,000 page book about a 28-year old guy on a super ego trip who's still a virgin. Cool. I haven't written anything since high school, just three awful novels, two about the Beatles and other rock and roll singers. The third novel is so-so, about a beautiful, smart 17-year-old girl who gets involved in an international spy incident with a German man, based on my high school pen pal Hans.

Jeff mentioned *Miami and the Siege of Chicago*, by Norman Mailer. I was kind of out of it during the election, with L.A., Stoney, and all that acid, but it sounds like a book worth reading. I like the way Jeff describes Mailer's style: "He chops up pages out of the dictionary into bite-size chunks and pours them onto a table and comes up with a work of genius." I've never heard a book described like that; this Mailer must be one heavy dude.

I haven't read anything important lately; my head's too screwed up. Just a short story in Aunt Colleen's *True Story*, a tear jerker about a woman who runs an ad in her local newspaper: "Wanted–Live-in Lover."

Mo interrupts my reading, something about a pile of dirty dishes to be done.

"Fuck you!" I scream downstairs, and throw some more stuff around.

Nag, nag, nag.

After I settle down, I finish reading Jeff's letter. He can't get me off his mind and wants me to come out to Pennsylvania.

How heavy is that?

He signed off: "Your loving Big Brother and fretting Also-Ran."

Stoney was never so poetic.

I don't need to hitchhike to the East Coast. I have more than enough money to take Greyhound. But Mo and Dee Dee say if I go, don't bother coming back–ever. As far as they're concerned, they'll write me off, forget they ever had a granddaughter named Jennifer. That's really unfair, making me choose between freedom and them. Maybe they would eventually come around, but I seriously doubt it–they are *so* rigid.

Maybe Jeff's right: we should create our own country and the hell with the U.S. and its Establishment values. Secede from the union and get rid of all the narks, parents, employers, and any uncool people.

I once met a guy who had the perfect plan for taking over

the country and populating it with freaks; he would take a quart of pure liquid LSD, and go from city to city, dumping a tablespoon in each reservoir. Eventually, everyone in every major city would be tripping and grooving; it would be easy, then, to conquer the country, place freaks in positions of power, and exile all the uptight people to one place, like North Dakota. Maybe it would be easier take over a small state; Jeff suggests Iowa might be a good place to hijack.

No way! I want to split so fast, leaving the black Iowa dirt from my shoes behind.

I MIGHT CONSIDER living with Jeff out of wedlock. Shacking up, as Mo calls it. Why not? If Jeff and I love each other, it only seems natural that we would want to spend our lives together. We wouldn't be committed legally, but emotionally we would take our decision very seriously.

As Dylan says, the times are a-changin'.

Evidently, Sioux City hasn't heard the news yet.

I'M BUMMED. Mom wrote and bawled me out. What gives *her* the right? She's nothing but a juice-freak, married four or five times, abandoning two out of her four kids. I'll never forgive her for what she did to Robin and me.

Why the fuck should I listen to anything she has to say?

Mo and I got into a big hairy fight again–as usual. She thinks she can stop me from leaving, but Dee Dee gave me permission, although not his approval–that's another matter. Mo can be such a bitch. When Tricia called–she got married last summer–to get my address, Mo wouldn't give it to her.

When Tricia asked why, Mo said, "Because I just don't want you writing her."

That kind of shit is for the birds. Tricia isn't even a hippie, just an ordinary girl who wanted to write to an old high school pal. If she had her way, Mo would chase away all my friends, and lock me up in a tower, and watch me wither of loneliness. I *am* lonely, which is why letters from Jeff are so important.

I HEARD FROM PAM. Jimmie, Eleanor's old man and major drug dealer, was busted and is still in jail. A lot of the other dealers have split, which is why, I think, Stoney left L.A. It frightens me–although I never dealt–well, maybe a little, but no more.

Just before I left the scene, a girl just breaking into dealing asked me to list the different types of acid, and what was good, what wasn't. I rattled off the names I knew: Purple Haze, Blue Moons, White Lightning, Orange and Strawberry Barrels, Blue Cheer, STP (super acid), Rainbow, and Sunshine. How do I know what's good or bad? Someone would give me a tab, and I'd pop it. How else do you determine quality of street acid? And this girl's younger than me.

When Dee Dee was in L.A., I pointed out a street woman to him. "Trash Can Tilly," named so because she spends her days rooting through the garbage cans around town, looking for food and junk. She's harmless enough, maybe a little nutty, but everyone likes her.

Dee Dee freaked out; he said, "You're going to end up like that, if you're not careful."

I hope not.

A lot of characters hang out at Wallich's Music City, like "Wild Man Fischer" and Caesar, permanent fixtures on the strip.

42

Merry-Go-Round
October 1968

(Hollywood)

As Stoney, Jeff, and I prowled the strip, we ran into Wild Man Fischer, clenching a tape recorder, one of those portable Juliettes, blasting a song from his new album *An Evening with Wild Man Fischer*.

He shoved it under my nose and shouted, "Hear my song?"

> *C'mon let's merry go,/ merry go, merry go round!/ Boop boop boop!*
> —"Merry-Go-Round," Wild Man Fischer

"Yes, Wild Man, we hear it."

"You like my song?"

"It's a cool song."

"You wanna buy it? Only ten cents."

"Not today, Wild Man. Thanks, anyway."

A pest, but harmless—probably a rich pest. He fit his name; he was manic, always wound up tight, fast like a fly or hummingbird. He even looked manic: eyes practically popping out of his head, his hair, black and frizzy, stuck out at all angles. He wore a loud yellow shirt with blobs of red, orange, and green, and flip flops, though, sometimes, only one, even when it was cold. Plus, he was constantly running around the strip with that tape recorder. I've heard that he'd spent some time in a mental hospital.

"I'll play it again," he said, pushing the rewind button.

"That's okay." We inched away.

I didn't want to hurt his feelings, but he had a way of getting under your skin. And then he'd be off to the next group of freaks. They were all out tonight, unusual for a week night: Julius Caesar, drag queens, streetwalkers–a circus. We verbally sparred with Caesar, an old dude, his Roman soldier costume stolen from 20th Century Fox. He harassed tourists, the middle-aged straights who arrived on the strip decked out in Hawaiian shirts, Bermuda shorts, straw hats, and sunglasses, big clunky cameras around their necks, loud voices: "Hey, Herman, look at the dirty hippies." Everyone was a dirty hippie because the straights couldn't distinguish among groups that populate the strip.

Caesar yelled out his standard slogans: "LBJ is a necrophiliac; he digs dead dudes" and "All the way with LBJ; Lady Bird Johnson is a nymphomaniac."

What a freak; his slogans angered many of the gawkers, who turned red.

Some even yelled back, "America: Love it or Leave it."

Caesar paid no attention to the counter-yellers–like he was in a trance.

What a nark.

43

Mo: Incorrigible
February 1969

(Sioux City)

JENNIFER'S INCORRIGIBLE; she needs counseling, but refuses to listen to the psychologist we've found for her. She goes to a few sessions, then announces, "There's nothing wrong with me! I hate shrinks!"

She threatens to leave, go to Pennsylvania to meet this Jeff character. I'm so sick about it. Doesn't she realize he just wants to use her? We can't tell her anything, she knows everything. We let it be known that she's not allowed to leave.

"I'm 18, I can do whatever I please!"

She screams and yells at Harley, calls him a liar–says he lured her here under false pretenses, and we're old fogies. "I hate you, both of you!"

Ungrateful brat. Doesn't she realize what we went through to get her away from her mother, to adopt her?

And this is the thanks we get?

44

Turn On
February 1969

(Sioux City)

AMERICA'S POPULATION is over 200 million. How does the government know which new baby to name the 200-millionth citizen? Does some government grunt go around to all the hospitals and give each newborn a number?

Subtract one citizen: a Sioux City boy was killed in Vietnam a few days ago. Douglas Hoffman. I didn't know him, but I still feel sad. It's not fair to send a young guy, barely out of high school, into an unjust war; I worry about Peter and hope he makes it through his tour.

I do know this: Iowa will soon lose another citizen. I was going to leave today, but Jeff doesn't have a job yet; I can't just bop in on his family–for one thing, I suspect his parents don't even know I'm coming. I still want to split, more than anything in the world–I'm all packed and ready to go–but I can't seem to get Jeff's phone number through information.

Bad scene. Money's short: after I pay bus fare, I've got exactly nine dollars. Maybe I'll earn some extra money first; I can work more banquets. I can't leave here with nothing. When I earn some extra money, it'll be cool. Then in Pennsylvania, I'll get an apartment and a job–we'll be supporting ourselves. Anything to get away from Sioux City.

A snippy letter from Auntie–she says I need my psychiatrist. If people don't act the way she thinks they should act, she just figures they're nuts. Her idea of solving a problem:

(1) Try not to notice that a problem is coming.

(2) After realizing the problem is here, ignore it– maybe it will go away.

(3) If ignoring fails, get all uptight and take out on everyone else.

(4) Ignore problem completely–lie to self and everyone else.

I LOVE THAT NEW ABC SHOW *Turn-On*. It's something like *Laugh-in*. One of the gags: "When I found out that my son had been popping pills, I went out and got drunk!" It spoofs organized religion, advocates the Pill and pre-marital sex, and loathes racial prejudice. A news commentator here believes that a show like this should not be aired before 9:00 p.m.

Why not? Kiddies wouldn't even get the gags; really, what kid under 13 understands "Sock it to me" as sexual innuendo?

Who says that kids are so poisoned by that stuff?

45

Mo: Why So Angry?

February 1969

(Sioux City)

As we wash and dry dishes together, I ask Jennifer why she's so angry.

After all, we've tried our best with her, even with the double generation gap. We might be old, but we read the newspaper and keep up with current events. We try to understand why this generation likes that awful rock and roll music, and why boys wear their hair long and wear funny-looking jeans with those wide flared pant legs.

The world moves too fast: fast cars, fast jets, fast music, fads that change every day. We know what's going on in the world, what with the Vietnam War and protests. I don't like that our boys are dying in a jungle halfway across the world, but I still believe we should support President Nixon as best we can, though I don't want *my* grandsons over there...

Still, it doesn't do young people any good being angry all the time.

"I'll make a list," Jennifer says.

The list arrives, carefully written out. Most of her complaints I already know: we never gave her enough freedom, we're too square, we lied to her about coming back to Sioux City, we stole her letters and screened her phone calls—the kind of grievances I expected to hear. But one triple-starred item puzzles me:

"You left Robin behind."

Her baby sister, Mary Lou's youngest girl. I'm floored when she tells me how much she resents not growing up with Robin–she doesn't understand why we couldn't bring her back to Sioux City instead of sending her to Arkansas. I thought Jennifer had gotten over all that long ago. Kids are supposed to go on with their lives, not harbor regrets about situations they can do nothing about.

I try explaining why we decided the way we did, but it's no use.

She turns away.

I can't make Jennifer see how difficult this decision was for me–but how can I expect her to forgive me when I haven't forgiven myself?

46

The Annotated Angry List
February 1969

(Iowa)

MO ASKS ME WHY I'm so angry all the time.

Isn't it obvious?

Her chronic interference in my life, for one.

"I'll get back to you," I tell her.

I wrote up my complaints, my angry list addressed directly to Mo, but I'm including Dee Dee because he does what Mo tells him to do. Number three pertains directly to him:

(1)*You never gave me enough freedom.

(2)*You're too square.

(3)**You lied to me about coming back to
Sioux City, saying it was only for
a few weeks and then reneging.

(4)**You stole my letters and alienated my
friends.

(5)***You left Robin behind.

Mo AND DEE allowed Stan Kraft to ship my sister off to her Arkansas relatives–not asking what *I* wanted. Just before we left Los Angeles for Sioux City, they yanked Robin away from me, and I'll never forgive them for it–

*

Mo, Dee Dee, Daddy Stan, and Mommy sit around the gray Formica kitchen table, suitcases piled around the living room.

Mommy and Daddy are getting a divorce.

Robin climbs around and over a pile of suitcases, laughing and giggling.

Mommy cries.

You know it's for the best, Mary Lou, Daddy says. God knows we tried to make this thing work.

The girls will be well-cared for, Mo says. That's what matters.

To Mommy: Maybe if you get help–

I don't have a problem!

You know, honey, it's the drinking that tore us apart. I wanted so much for us to be a family–

Just shut the fuck up!

Mommy said a bad word in front of Mo and Dee Dee!

I'm getting the hell out of here! Mommy grabs a suitcase and stumbles out of the apartment, slamming the door.

Robin bawls and reaches for the door. MAMA!

I'm scared. Mama's gone, Daddy's sad, Mo and Dee Dee are mad.

I pick Robin up, kiss her forehead, rock her back and forth.

At least we're together!

Daddy shakes his head. I still love her, but the drinking, the other men–

Daddy looks at us. The other problem just got to be too much for me. I'm tired.

Well, that's that, then, Dee Dee says, getting up and rubbing his hands together. He puts his hand on Daddy's shoulder. You did your best, Stan. Thanks.

Mo hugs him. Take care of Robin.

Take care of Robin?

Robin's going with us, isn't she, Dee Dee?

He looks away—they all do.

She is! I just know she is!

I squeeze Robin close to me.

I'm sorry, honey, Daddy finally says. She's going to Arkansas.

Robin riding on my hip, I stand by the door.

Then I'm going to Arkansas, too.

Mo puts her arm around me. You have to go to Sioux City with us.

She takes Robin away from me.

I want my baby sister!

Tears sting my cheeks.

Robin cries louder. Jeffer! Jeffer!

You can visit her, Dee Dee says.

We'll drive down to Arkansas next year, Mo says. I promise.

I'll write, Princess.

You can't take my baby sister away!

Mo hands Robin, kicking and screaming, to Daddy Stan.

We'd better go. Daddy grabs a suitcase.

Robin grows stiff in his arms.

The movers'll get the rest.

They leave me behind, Robin screaming, JJJeeeefffferrrr! JJJeeeeffffferrr! JJJeeeefffferrrr! JJJeeeeeefffffferrrr! JJJeeeefffffeeeeerrr! JJJJeeeeeeeeeffffffeeeeeerrrrrrrrrr!—all the way down the hall and into the street, her screams eventually fading to...

Nothing.

*

WE NEVER DID GO to Arkansas.

Somehow, the time was never right.

Occasionally, Robin's aunt wrote and sent pictures of Robin, a blonde girl who looked a lot like the Semple clan, but her letters urged us to stay away–

"In the best interests of the child."

"I DIDN'T REALIZE," Mo says after reading my angry list.

"You never asked."

"It didn't occur to us–you were so young, Jennifer..."

"Robin belonged to us..."

"I'm sor–"

"*You* threw her away."

47

Mo: Regrets

February 1969

(Iowa)

$\mathcal{D}$EE DEE AND I DROVE out to California to check up on you and Robin.

Eleven years ago. We found appalling conditions, but that's another story. We petitioned the Los Angeles court for temporary custody; Stan wanted us to take you to Sioux City, at least until your mother straightened out her life, but, of course, he had no say, and she refused to budge.

Your dad couldn't be found; we had to fight our own little Missus in the courts, air all our dirty laundry in public. It broke my heart. A mother should never have to fight her children, but what choice did we have? We did what we had to do, though we were too old to be raising young children.

You remember waiting until Christmas night to open your presents? You bawled when Mary Lou locked herself in her apartment all day and refused to let you and Robin in. No way to treat children, especially on Christmas. Pitiful.

Dee Dee and I decided for sure to take you back with us. We figured your Aunt Colleen and Uncle George would help out with you, but I wasn't sure about Robin...I didn't feel up to raising a baby, but I've always done what I had to do.

Then we had a family conference with Stan. He offered an alternative: his mother and sister back in Arkansas wanted to raise the baby.

How could we refuse? I didn't think you'd throw fits and bawl all day after Stan took the baby away. Still, I figured you'd get over it, and I assumed we'd see Robin regularly.

We thought it was for the best. Dee Dee and me were in our late 50's, what were we going to do with a two-year-old? We were tired, honey–in a few years, we'd be applying for Social Security, and we wouldn't make a whole lot of income, don't you know?

You've got to understand how it was then. We just wanted some time together to do things, maybe travel some–though, as it turned out, your Dee doesn't like to travel anyway, but that's beside the point.

We felt Stan's mother and sister in Hot Springs would be good guardians to Robin, they promised to raise the baby as a devout Catholic. The aunt said Robin would be the daughter she never had. I admit, it was an odd situation. In my wildest dreams, I never imagined it'd turn out the way it did; there would be plenty of opportunities for visiting back and forth, right? When you were 11, we even planned to take you on a trip down to Arkansas for a visit, but the aunt wrote and said, "Don't come." She said it'd be rough on the child, you know, figuring out her people. I suppose it's not good to confuse kids about family matters. Still, I've never understood why she wouldn't allow you to see your little sister, but I had to respect her wishes.

Don't think this was an easy decision for us. We talked about it for days on end. If it's any consolation, we almost took her, but when Stan told us about his sister, well, it changed everything. Said she was divorced and couldn't have kids and really wanted Robin. It seemed selfish to deprive a woman of motherhood. All women want children, don't they?

We knew it'd be hard on you for a while, but you'd get over it. I mean, you never really got to know Robin, did you? Still, if I'd only known...

To this day, I regret not taking that baby with us. Dee Dee wanted her with us in the worst way, so don't be angry with him. I made the final decision. I don't harbor many regrets in my life, but this is one I'll carry to my grave.

But it's all water under the bridge, isn't it?

AFTER STAN TOOK ROBIN AWAY, we tried to shield you from the court battle; I gave up the apartment, and we moved to Torrance to stay with relatives. Dee Dee was still working; he had to get back to the business, so he returned to Sioux City.

"I want to go to Sioux City," you said. "I want to be with Dee Dee. See snow."

"Soon. Be patient," I said.

We stayed in Torrance until March, when Mary Lou had a sudden change of heart; she up and signed the custody papers, just like that. Dee flew back, and we turned right around and drove back to Sioux City, before your mother had a chance to change her mind and drag us back into court. You never know with her.

I never looked back. I suppose we should have tried to get help for Mary Lou, but, by then, her problems were way beyond me. We'd spent years and years cleaning up her messes.

We were tired.

Now we had another chance with you to make things right. So what's happened? Your mother's sort of settled down–not perfect, mind you, but at a level we can live with. Besides, she's Larry's problem now.

Now it's *you* out of control, and we're right back at square one, dealing with another problem child.

Will it ever end?

48

This is War

February 1969

(Sioux City)

Who thought I'd eventually forget my baby sister?

Is she kidding?

I think about Robin every day of my life.

Now that bitch wants to keep me away my friends and Jeff.

I haven't heard from Jeff in over a week.

When I ask Dee Dee about it, he says, "Looks like your hippie friends have forgotten you already."

If Jeff's letters are still being confiscated by those two relics from the stone age, they'd better stop—otherwise, I'll never speak to them again.

THIS IS WAR!

Another local boy has been killed in Vietnam—Sp4 Carroll Paul O'Neill, 22 years old. I don't know him, either, but sooner or later, someone I know will die.

God, I hate this war.

49

Mo: "That Hippie"
February 1969

(Sioux City)

THAT HIPPIE FROM PENNSYLVANIA calls long distance, but, thank God, Jennifer's not home. I tell him to never call here again; we're getting help for Jennifer, and he needs to butt out.

He calls me and Harley "uptight Hoosiers," and we can't stop him from writing letters.

But he promises not to call again.

Maybe we can't stop him from writing, but we can put the kibosh on her receiving the letters. We make sure we get to the mail first–not hard since she lolls in bed half the day–and hold his letters back.

But one day, while we're at a funeral, she gets hold of a letter from him in that morning's mail. We find her in a rage, screaming obscenities and throwing bills, circulars, letters, newspapers, and magazines all over the place.

"You've no right to monitor my phone calls and steal my letters!"

"We don't want you having contact with that hippie," I say.

"It's not your decision!"

She shoves some pages under my nose.

"Jeff's told me about everything you've done. He keeps writing, hoping that one or two of his letters will get to me.

Well, this one did. And he wrote a note to you."

She reads aloud what that filthy hippie wrote to me. I can barely even repeat it, it's so dirty:

Dear Mrs. Semple:

In the event that you get this letter before Jennifer can see it, keep in mind that—I only promised not to call any more—I made no mention of letters. Also keep in mind that I am unscrupulous & underhanded and will probably go back on my word & call again if I get desperate enough.

Sincerely yours,
Jeff Brown

P.S.–Please at least wish Jennifer A Happy Valentine's Day for me.

I CAN'T BELIEVE THE LANGUAGE of today's generation. Why Harley would no more write such sass to my father as jump off a ledge. What in the world is wrong with young people today?

"You are such a bitch!" Jennifer screams.

"Don't talk to your mother like that," Harley says.

He doesn't get mad often, but when the red creeps around his collar...woe be unto you....

"She's not my mother, my real mother lives in California! And she wouldn't read my mail and keep me away from my friends."

"Maybe you should go back to your mother," I say.

"I'm going to Pennsylvania and live with Jeff."

"Oh, no you're not," Harley says, clenching his fists.

I'm afraid he's going to hit her, but Jennifer stomps off to her room upstairs, where she bangs around and throws things.

"I want all my letters back!" she screams from her room.

After we all settle down to a dull roar, Harley gives her one letter back. "That's all I have."

I suspect he threw some of them away, but she seems satisfied for now.

She snatches the letter from him. "And I want to call Jeff. In private."

We allow her a five-minute call, after which she seems much calmer, almost cheerful.

That night, she comes into my bedroom and asks to sleep with me, and we snuggle together, just like when she was seven. Maybe this is the corner we need to turn–

Perhaps everything will be okay now.

50

Threats

February 1969

(Sioux City)

*E*IGHT OF OUR FINEST state legislators are probing the use of LSD and filthy language among our young people to see if it's "Communist inspired."

Are they *kidding*? Don't the commies have better things to do than worry about the morals of American teenagers?

BIG FIGHT! My room is such a mess because I keep throwing my things around, I get *so* mad. I calm down enough to get them agree to allow me to call Jeff.

"Okay, but this is *it*," Mo said. "Five minutes and no more."

It's just easier to nod in agreement, but if she thinks, for one minute, that I'm going to cut all contact with Jeff, she has another thing coming.

During the call, Mo hovers over me. How can I ever have an intelligent conversation with my boyfriend? But he does give me his phone number, now etched permanently into my brain.

Jeff worried that I'd get to York with no way to get in touch with him; there's about 200 Browns in the phone book, so maybe it was a good thing I waited until I knew the number. Last week, he thought I had split already and sat up all night waiting for me to call. Bummer. By now, he probably thinks

I'm a neurotic chick with no sense of humor. I couldn't say a whole lot with the censor in the background–not even that I loved him.

Jeff has called me twice, but both times Mo was sitting on top of the phone and told him to get lost–that my shrink says no more letters or phone calls from anyone. My shrink? Who gave *her* permission to meddle in my life? I can't believe it! And Mo then babbled something about my not learning my lesson after 12 years of Catholic training. How dare she?

And that shrink is history, too.

"I don't want some chick that a shrink created as a cross-section American female," Jeff said, "I liked you the way you were…"

I don't like what I'm becoming.

AFTER WE TALK, I write Jeff a letter, to say what I couldn't with the eavesdroppers around–that I've quit acid, probably for good. Drugs are so expensive–money that could be better spent getting to Pennsylvania.

No doubt that Jeff will put down eventually.

"I've got some compulsion to do something really important," he said over the phone. "And I can't support a chick on principle."

He has cut his hair and shaved his beard, so he can find a job, for us. It's more important he earn enough money for us to be together, than to hang onto his hair and beard. At least hair grows back. Still, I know what a sacrifice that must've been; I'd be quite lost without my hair, it's grown so long, but if he asked me, I would cut it off in a minute. His mom wants him to get a job *now*, but it was hard for him because of his hair. No one wants to hire a "dirty hippie with long hair," even if the job itself requires a strong back and a small mind.

Evidently, Mo has already poisoned Jeff's mom against me. Bad scene having his mom hate me before she has even met me. But I like her already because she bore Jeff. Too bad she lives in an uptight society that decides what her morals should be. Jeff refers to us as misfits, but I don't see us that way. Prejudiced people want us to believe we are less than human.

Hippies are like the Negroes—we're harassed, discriminated against, given absolutely *no* credit for any kind of intelligence.

Mo and Dee Dee have threatened to stick me in Cherokee, and I'm scared shitless. There's no way I'll go to the loony bin—I'm *not* crazy. I've got to get out of Iowa; I'm leaving Monday or Tuesday; I'd leave today, but the Establishment determines when I get paid, and that's on Monday. The extra bread will give me a $30-$40 cushion. I'm scared, but I'll play it cool and not confront Mo about leaving town because it'll just cause more trouble.

I called the bus depot today, to get the ticket price to York, Pennsylvania, and the time of departure. Cost: $43.00—I have just enough money. The bus leaves every day at 9:15 a.m. and involves three connections: Des Moines, Chicago, and Pittsburgh. Tomorrow morning I'll split, but I want to sleep on it.

For sure by the 19th or 20th.

51

Donnybrook

February 18, 1969

(Downtown Sioux City)

Dee Dee slinks behind a department store column.

Conspicuous in his oversized raincoat and hat with feather in brim, bumbling around like some hick private dick:

Inspector Clouseau.

Does he really believe I can't see him? I pretend not to see him. I slip inside the depot and buy my ticket to York, Pennsylvania. Which leaves me about $4.00–but, with Jeff's help, I'll get by. The bus isn't scheduled to leave Sioux City for another 90 minutes. I try shaking him, trick him into thinking I'm not splitting yet.

As I turn to leave the station, Dee Dee blocks my way. "Absolutely *not!*" Dee Dee grabs my arms.

"Let go!"

He grips so tight I can't move without pushing him to the floor.

"Let go of me, old man." I try to break free without hurting him.

"You're not going anywhere."

"You just try and stop me." Still trying to break his grip.

He squeezes more. Vise grip.

"Leave me alone!"

Damn! That asshole has *no* right to hold me against my will. I should just push that old man to the floor, turn tail out of Sioux City, not stopping until I cross the state line into Nebraska or even Illinois.

Instead, "Let's see what the police have to say."

Nothing to fear, right? I'm of age, after all, and I've done nothing wrong.

After I tell the police about quitting LSD, weed, and Bennies, they'll let me go.

Yes?

Dee Dee releases me.

I flee to the police station, a short distance from the bus depot, Dee Dee at my heels.

52

Dee Dee: Informant
February 18, 1969

(Sioux City)

AFTER THREE DAYS OF SCREAMING and carrying on, Jennifer suddenly became quiet, almost serene. Olive felt only relief at the rare peace and quiet, but I knew something was wrong.

So today I followed the little sneak downtown; she wandered into shops and looked around and then went to the Greyhound Station, where she bought a bus ticket to Pennsylvania.

I intercepted her—we got into a huge donnybrook, right in the bus depot, in front of at least 30 people. I admit, I lost my cool, and I think I may have hit her, but it was an accident. I was just trying to keep her from leaving.

I was desperate.

Somehow, we ended up across the street in the police station, talking to Opal Casey, the police matron—Jennifer yelling at everyone...

I informed on my granddaughter and signed a form stating I believe her to be fit for involuntary commitment to the Cherokee Mental Health Institution...

...Second thoughts.

Begged that my name be crossed out as informant...

Mixed feelings...

Yes, the whole procedure could have been handled better...
Though Cherokee's probably for the best–

At least for now.

53

Circling

February 18, 1969

(Sioux City)

*T*ODAY, A TOTAL DISASTER.

All because I decided it was time to get the fuck out of Sioux City *now*–nothing here for me anymore.

I got into a huge fight with Mo this morning about some dirty dishes I left in the sink last night. Big deal–I was going to do them this morning, but I wasn't about to do them after that old bitch yanked me out of bed and called me a dirty, lazy hippie whore.

Who needs this abuse?

"I'm getting the fuck out of here," I said, struggling into my jeans, sweater, and shoes. I grabbed a travel bag and threw in my diary from high school, all my letters from Jeff and Pam, and a change of clothes. What else did I need? In Pennsylvania, I could get a job and buy all the clothes I needed–I just wanted out of here, big time.

Now.

I slammed the front door behind me and headed for the downtown bus depot to buy a one-way ticket to York.

Dee followed me, and we got into this huge fight, right in the bus station.

"Let's see what the police have to say," I said.

As we stepped into the police station, a short walking

distance from the bus depot, I knew immediately I had made a *huge* mistake.

That police matron wouldn't even listen to me; instead, she had me locked me in some tiny room while Dee Dee told a bunch of lies.

They told me only one thing:

Tomorrow, I'm scheduled at the courthouse for some hearing to determine my sanity.

I wish I could reverse the clock.

54

A Possible Scenario

February 18, 1969

(Sioux City Police Station)

A DISTRAUGHT TEENAGER, Jennifer L. Semple, stormed into the police station, alleging that Harley D. Semple, her grandfather, has been attempting to restrain her against her will.

For her own safety, the girl was moved to a locked interrogation room.

Opal Casey, police matron, interviewed the grandfather and filled out "Mental Illness, Inebriety or Epilepsy," an informant's report:

> HARLEY SEMPLE
>
> Jennifer needs help, I'm afraid. I don't know what to do.
>
> OPAL CASEY
>
> You could commit her to Cherokee for observation.
>
> HARLEY SEMPLE
>
> Seems rather drastic, but what choice do I have? She's so angry, and the drugs...she scares me.

OPAL CASEY

(Sighing as she scribbles in his name on the information form.) These kids today... *(Shakes her head.)* Don't know what's good for them, what with all these strange drugs and immoral ways. What *is* the world coming to, anyway?

HARLEY SEMPLE

(Scratching his forehead.) I don't know, but if she gets wind of this, she'll despise me...

OPAL CASEY

You're doing the right thing.

HARLEY SEMPLE

I don't know if I can do this. *(Pauses.)* Who'll pay the hospital bill, anyway?

OPAL CASEY

(Taps her pen.) I'm afraid you'll be financially responsible, Mr. Semple.

HARLEY SEMPLE

(Wringing his hands.) I don't know. We can't afford hospital bills; my wife and I are on Social Security and barely making it now. This would kill us financially.

OPAL CASEY

(Takes in a deep breath and sighs.) I can't tell you what to do here. It's your decision.

HARLEY SEMPLE

(Shakes his head.) I can't do it. Scratch my name

out. Sign as informant...Please, *PLEASE*?

OPAL CASEY

(She sets down her pen and steeples her hands.) I don't know the girl. I see she needs help, but, to what extent, I can't say for sure. It's really your word against hers.

HARLEY SEMPLE

(Burying his face in his hands.) I beg you. Oh, God, I'd rather die than betray her. *(Raises his head. Pauses, as if he's formulating a thought.)* It's not the money, really. If I thought committing Jennifer would help, I'd do it in a blink and worry about the money later. But she doesn't trust me as it is; this would kill anything between us.

OPAL CASEY

(Silence. She sighs and picks up her pen again. She taps it against the paper a few times. Then she scratches out "Harley Semple," and scribbles in her own name.) This is between us, Mr. Semple.

HARLEY SEMPLE

(Brushes his hair back with his hand. Softly:) Thank you. *(Buries his face in his hands and visibly shivers.)*

With one scratch of Mrs. Casey's pen, Woodbury County and Iowa assumed financial and legal custody of the girl.

II

Verdict

February 19, 1969

55

Mo: Relieved

(Sioux City)

I DON'T KNOW what went on yesterday between Harley and Jennifer at the bus depot and police station. I thought life was settling down to normal–Jennifer had been cheerful–maybe cheerful isn't quite the right word, but peaceful. For the past few days, she hadn't yelled or screamed at us, and she'd done her chores without complaint.

I thought maybe easing up about the letters and phone calls had settled her down, but then Harley called from the police station. Jennifer went crazy at the bus depot, so the police matron was filling out some paperwork to commit the girl to Cherokee.

Then today's hearing to determine her mental status...

–Incorrigible. Crazy as a bat, I fear.

I must admit, I'm glad the county, not us, has committed her to Cherokee. But I'm relieved she's there. Like it or not, she'll get the counseling she desperately needs, and she'll have to stay in Iowa for the time being. She's exactly where she needs to be–I've no regrets about her being sent there. If she's angry with us, then so be it.

Now I can sleep at night without worrying about finding her dead in a gutter, a needle in her arm.

JUST BEFORE THE COMPETENCY HEARING, I asked Jennifer,

"Whatever happened to the moral girl we sent to California last summer?" Then, again, I gave her that filthy letter she wrote to Cynthia. "Is this *really* what you have become?"

She had no answer.

What has this world come to when you send a sweet, deeply religious girl to California, and she comes back a dirty long-haired hippie, addicted to drugs, with no morals left?

Special Insert

Informant Report

on

Jennifer L. Semple

Regarding

Involuntary Commitment

at

Cherokee Mental Health Institute

INFORMATION [Informant Report]
Mental Illness, Inebriety or Epilepsy

To the honorable Commissioners of Hospitalization, _Woodbury_ County, Iowa:

    Information Date: _Feb. 19th_, 19_69_

    Hearing Date: _Feb. 19th_, 19_69_

    Hour: _11 am_

    NAME: _Jennifer L. Semple_

    Legal Settlement: _Woodbury_

    Address: _XXXX W-3rd St._

    Age: _18_

    Resident of: _Woodbury_ County

    Since: _Lifetime_, 19___.

    Employer: _None_

    Father: ~~Robert~~ _Harley Semple_

    Address: _XXXX W-3rd St._

    Phone: _252-XXXX_

    Mother: _Olive Semple_

    Address: _XXXX W-3rd St._ Phone _252-XXXX_

    Request Commitment to: _M.H.I. [Mental Health Institute]_

    Transportation by: _Sheriff_

Your Informant respectfully represents that the above named person now in said County is afflicted with

    _X_ Mental Illness

    __ Inebriety

    __ Epilepsy

And a fit subject for custody and treatment in the Mental Health Institute at _Cherokee_ as he/she therefore asks that the necessary steps be taken to investigate his/her condition as the law provides in such cases.

                                              Opal Casey, **Informant**

STATE OF IOWA, _Woodbury_ County

I, the undersigned, do solemnly swear that the matters and things alleged in the above information to which my name is affixed, are true as stated, each and all, as I verily believe.

~~Harley Semple~~ Opal Casey, Informant

Subscribed and sworn to before me by:

~~Harley Semple~~ Opal Casey,

the affiant, this _19th_ day of _Feb_ , 19 _69_

WITNESS my hand and official seal the date last named.

[signed] *Maurice Flanagan*, Clerk,
By [Left blank], Deputy Clerk.

[End Informant Report]

Note About this Report

A photo of the preceding Informant Report has been posted at

http://memoirmadnessphotos.blogspot.com/2012/10/chapter-55-informant-report-for.html

To protect the current residents of Jennifer L. Semple's childhood home, her personal address and phone number have been removed from this document.

56

Dee Dee:

Double Generation Gap

(Sioux City)

I'M NOT SURE how we ended up this way.

Jennifer's mad as a hornet at Olive and me.

Cherokee wasn't in my plan–incidents simply spun out of control. *Jennifer* went out of control, becoming belligerent and incorrigible.

Thank God I didn't have to sign those commitment forms.

I was sure she'd come around and get some help and forget about this Pennsylvania hippie and settle down here, maybe go to Briar Cliff or Morningside. But when she found out Olive was intercepting her mail and hanging up on that hippie, Jennifer blew up and screamed at her grandmother, calling her some profane names, not behaving like the highly moral girl we raised, the same girl who just a few months ago would not even go out the back door in her robe to pick up a newspaper.

But then this is the girl who lived with a dirty hippie and did unspeakable acts with him...

I can't even think about it.

Olive may have overreacted by insisting I hide the boy's letters from her, but she only had the girl's well-being at heart–doesn't give Jennifer the right to abuse us, the only people who took her in when no one else wanted her.

I can't do anything about the double generation gap; we're

old and come from a slower time, before television and jet planes, practically before automobiles. Growing up, we had none of this caterwauling rock and roll—we were too busy doing farm chores—and nobody I knew took drugs, just lazy bums.

People from good, hardworking families didn't have time for such nonsense.

W E'RE TOO OLD FOR THIS. It was hard enough dealing with Mary Lou and all her men and alcohol problems—and she still doesn't have her life straightened out.

Now Jennifer.

Where have we gone wrong?

It's enough to drive a sane man crazy.

III

Driven

57

Driven to Forget and Escape
February–April 1969

(Cherokee, Iowa)

*D*RIVEN:

To the institution.

I remember this part in black and white.

The police car threading up a hill, wheels crunching the ice.

Bare deciduous trees, black evergreens, a grayscape of snow, dead grass, frozen earth. A dreary castle at the apex, spires, turrets, a place where a dungeon might exist, not a place I wanted to be.

Having to pee and wondering if I would make it.

The car stopped just short of a stone portico. The woman unlocked and opened the door, motioned me out. "Come along, you."

The sheriff, the escort, and I climbed some steps. The woman pushed me through the door.

I disappeared inside Cherokee.

DRIVEN:

To forget. I don't remember much about those first few hours in Cherokee: an intake report, a brief physical, a mug shot. Maybe even a bathroom break.

Just the terror, the anger, and the thumping of my heart, all in *bas-relief*, the physical details distorted behind crackled glass.

DRIVEN:

To escape.

For two months, I plotted, begged, cajoled, and lobbied for my release. I wanted only to flee the institution, Iowa, my grandparents.

58

State of Denial

February 1969-April 2002

*D*RIVEN FOR 33 YEARS:

To keep secret.

For years, only a few people knew about my experiences in Cherokee and only in broad brush strokes. It was something to be forgotten, tucked away, and denied on job applications:

Question: *Have you ever been committed to a mental institution? If so, explain.*

Answer: *I'm not crazy!*

More than anything else, the prying question stands out; it felt intrusive then, it feels judgmental now.

I just wanted to forget, put Cherokee behind me.

But I couldn't.

59

Ignited

April 2002

(York, Pennsylvania)

IGNITED.

Writer's block and a spark: driven to question.

As I stared at a blank screen and keyboard, my foot bumped against a chest.

My letters to Jeff, his to me.

A gentle nudging, then an incessant nagging. I tried ignoring the impulse to read, those reminders of a past that no longer existed, not even as a puff of fog–

I don't want to become like some older people who dwell in the past, who talk incessantly about the "good old days"–

I couldn't remember too many good old days. Yet the letters tugged, chanting like sirens, "Read, read, read us."

So I opened the chest, selected a letter, and read.

HOLDEN CAULFIELD.

I folded the letter, postmarked February 14, 1969, and slipped it back into the envelope.

I married Holden Caulfield.

Drawn on the front, just below the canceled 6-cent stamp, a G.I. firing a rifle, his bloody target a shirtless barefoot Viet Cong in the defensive position. The caption below the address:

WE *CAN* WIN IN VIETNAM: PROVIDED WE KILL EVERY MAN, WOMAN, CHILD, PIG, SHEEP, BIRD, DOG, BUFFALO, AND GOAT.

Jeff. A long distance courtship, a child, a marriage, a divorce, another husband–in that precise order. A slew of letters, intense, hot, yet oddly ambiguous love dispatches, saved for over 33 years, last read, God knows when.

Years ago, my brother-in-law Keith built and finished a small cherry chest for me as a Christmas present; I gathered together all the letters Jeff and I had exchanged between December 1968 and May 1969, arranged them in order according to postmark, put them into the chest, then forgot them. When we divorced in 1980, I asked Jeff if he wanted my letters to him back–I didn't offer him his letters to me.

"Naw," he said. "Throw 'em away."

Why would you want to keep souvenirs of a failed marriage?

But I couldn't bring myself to toss them. They represented history, a painful and, at times, ugly history, but it was an important personal history, chronicling in detail a landmark in my life. I hadn't thought about those letters in years. They simply existed, tucked away underneath my work table, waiting to open a fissure.

DRIVEN TO READ.

It took three full nights to read the 90+ letters. I read them covertly after Jerry went to bed–a guilty secret. What would I find in those dispatches from the past?

My own letters, a disappointment: I had remembered them as being great art, the inner workings of a young girl-woman who had taken on the Establishment and won. Instead, young Jennifer recounted, sometimes endlessly, the minutiae of life in a mental institution. She often obsessed about her relationship with Jeff, the tone of her letters often immature, manipulative, and rambling, some implying future self-destruction should Jeff decide to ditch her. Still, I perceived some insights, epiphanies, self-discoveries, and a vague sense of searching for meaning out of a horrifying experience.

Jeff's letters hinted of a vividly curious mind that it hardly seemed possible that he would even consider me as a future mate. Yet he loved me as only an exuberant 18-year-old boy can; in a March 8, 1969, letter, he wrote:

> *I can get out your picture, and imagine (if I try real hard) you're here: your voice, your matter-of-fact way of speaking (always as if you're explaining something somewhat important—as much, or more, to yourself than anyone else—with a casual formality of tone, and abundance of asides ["and you see," and "it's like this"] and very expressive hand movements), your smile (much too sunny and radiant for a street chick. You're a hopeless idealist!), your old hat, brown outfits with yellow handbags and shoes, very light freckles, skin too white to ever allow you to be a native Californian, and long, brown hair, sometimes dyed black, that, I enviously recall, could blot out your whole face when you combed it.*

What girl wouldn't melt at such a description?

Throughout our brief, but intense, correspondence, his letters, for the most part, retain the optimistic exuberance of a young man who saw a formidable challenge ahead, but who knew that the outcome would be positive.

I was jealous of his letters, even after all those years.

And, yet, despite the superficiality of my own letters, I realized that I just had to read between the lines and reach deep into my memory for the fear, anger, sadness, guilt, and ecstasy I felt back in 1969.

Perhaps I would write a book.

First, I needed my hospital records.

I took a deep breath and emailed Cherokee.

60

Convergence

May 2004

(York)

CONVERGENCE of two milestones: my husband Jerry hears from Fulbright: we'll be spending the upcoming academic year in Skopje, Macedonia. Then my son Eric calls and announces that his wife is pregnant.

A girl, to be named Rhia Alden Brown, due in November.

While we are away.

I don't want to go overseas; I want to be here for her birth, to hold her minutes, even seconds, after she's born. To assure our bond.

A thud in my stomach.

How could this happen? How could my daughter-in-law get pregnant *now*? When Jerry applied for the Fulbright, we had no idea that a grandchild would be born while we were away. But, then, children don't center their plans around ours, nor should they.

I consider asking my husband to pass on the Fulbright this year, but he has already taken a sabbatical. Also, this Fulbright is important.

Jerry suggests a compromise: we'll return to the states in mid-January, during his break, to see and bond with the baby.

I agree.

We negotiate yet another deal: I will not have to teach in Skopje—the free time will be mine to write a book.

About Cherokee.

Later this week, I'll photocopy the letters and my hospital records and place the originals in a safe deposit box. In August, when we're in Sioux City, I'll go to the courthouse and get copies of my commitment papers, which I hope will explain, at least in part, the why—though lugging copies of my past across the ocean will feel off kilter, out of place. This book should be written here in York or in Sioux City. I'm not even sure this book is possible—maybe my memory is too fried—but I have to try, and maybe the letters will help.

I *will* write about Cherokee as I await, in a foreign land, the birth of a grandchild Jeff Brown and I share.

Our romance probably should have never evolved into a full-blown relationship and our eventual marriage, yet as I anticipate the coming of Rhia, our connection and path back then feels exactly right.

Leaving Cherokee behind, once and for all, my metaphorical journey, via Skopje, Macedonia, through those months between December 1968 and May 1969, will, perhaps, help heal old wounds.

To revisit 18-year-old Jennifer and try to understand her.

No matter, I *will* enjoy a year of catharsis.

61

Urgency

August 29, 2004

(To Sioux City)

"I WANT TO GO TO CHEROKEE tomorrow," I announce to everyone in the car.

Silence.

"I want to take pictures."

My husband Jerry and I have just lost $50.00 on the Argosy River Boat casino. As usual, Aunt Colleen and Uncle Lyle have come out ahead—at least that's what Lyle says. I almost never win, which is why I reserve playing the slots for vacations. By nature, I'm not a gambler, but by nurture I am; along with other vices, gambling seems to be a family trait.

A week ago, I visited the Woodbury County courthouse for copies of my commitment papers. Together with my hospital records, which I've had since May 2002, these court papers explain a lot; I'm now ready to face the next demon.

"Last time, you wouldn't even get out of the car," Jerry says.

"May we borrow your car?" I ask Colleen.

"Well, okay," she says. It's a halting, unsure permission.

Last week, when I told her about getting copies of my court records, she asked why.

"I need to know," I said.

"Well, I'm not sure I'd want to dredge up that old stuff."

Part of me doesn't want to, either.

"You weren't in Cherokee very long," Lyle said.

True.

THOUGH MY INCARCERATION felt like a lifetime.

In a sense, it *was* a lifetime, a lifetime spent questioning and second guessing my own sanity.

Even now, I obsess about the way time moves, how it zips by when you're happy and having fun and crawls through difficult and boring events.

Cherokee *seemed* like two years–perhaps because I didn't know when I was going to be released–

And when I finally got a copy of my hospital records, I was shocked to see that my time there had been less than two months.

Perhaps flawed perceptions explain why memoirists often get their time lines so wrong.

Then there was my LSD time, super slow and rapturous, the inverse of regular time: elastic minutes stretching to hours, hours to days, days to months.

Perception warp.

Ecstasy. Religious experience.

Perhaps explaining why so many ex-acid heads eventually turned to Jesus–The Rapture–as evidenced by the 1960's popularity of Reverend Blessitt's "His Place" on Sunset Boulevard.

For years after my last acid trip, I struggled with my resolve to quit.

So difficult to quit...although I knew I could *never* again touch acid.

Back and forth...acid, no acid, acid, no acid, teetering between heightened sensory perception and risking blown synapses.

As I worked through altered-perception addiction, I

insisted that we—Jeff and I—could mimic the psychedelic experience with black lights, music, sex, and, perhaps, a bit of weed, but, as much as I might have wished it so, that wasn't exactly true.

Acid *had* magnified my psychedelic experience a hundred times over and no amount of pseudo-tripping could ever replicate LSD's effects.

No denying it: my Christmas Eve trip with Stoney had been the best ever.

"I just wish acid weren't so dangerous," I often told myself.

Before my commitment, I had already quit for good, but my craving for the mind-altering and life-changing LSD, a multi-year struggle.

Slowly, though, my desire disappeared.

OLD COUNTERCULTURE JOKE about the perception of time:

> *Two hippies, high on pot, are sitting in the Golden Gate Park in San Francisco. A jet aircraft goes zooming overhead and is gone; whereupon one hippie turns to the other and says, "Man, I thought he'd never leave."*

"I VAGUELY REMEMBER you being in Cherokee," Colleen says, jarring me from my daydream. "But I didn't give it much thought. I was busy raising kids, and it was all I could do just to keep up."

She's not being insensitive, just honest. If she were to write her memoir of that time, I, and the changing times, would likely be blips.

"I *will* get out of the car," I say to Jerry. "I *have* to."

"I'll drive you there," he says.

62

To Cherokee

August 30, 2004

*T*HIS WARM SUMMER DAY, I am driven.

Again.

This time, a voluntary commitment: to confront an involuntary past.

Destination: Cherokee, Iowa, northeast of Sioux City, to revisit the Mental Health Institute.

Metaphorically, this trip has taken 35 years and thousands of detours and dead ends.

Today's trip takes about 75 minutes of traversing country roads in Colleen's white station wagon, a magnetic "Why USA–America's Real Estate Alternative" sign stuck on the panel.

From Sioux City, we ride almost 60 miles, first east through Bronson and Lawton and then north, via Washta and Quimby, until we finally turn onto East Main Street in Cherokee.

We have arrived.

I'm glad my husband is with me.

I would not want to make this trip alone.

I'm not that driven.

IV

Cherokee

Sometimes when you walk under a tree, it can be just as annoying to have a leaf fall on you as a fly to land on you.
 —*Jennifer L. Semple, recorded in her hospital records*

A battery of psychological tests reveals that the patient manifests some "mild acting out tendencies which is consistent with past behavior. It is probable that the inclination to conflict with social convention will persist but genuine antisocial behavior is contraindicated."
 —*Evaluation of Jennifer L. Semple,*
 by R. Lowenberg

Without the USPS, this story would have ended in Hollywood.
 —*Jennifer Semple Siegel (August 2004)*

63

February 19-28, 1969

(Cherokee, Iowa)

WEDNESDAY, FEBRUARY 19

On admission, the patient was alert, anxious, depressed and appeared immature with a poor self-image. On the ward, she was noted to be quiet and cooperative in the ward routine. She was slightly depressed but showed no sign of anxiety at the time of the interview. She expressed extreme hostility toward her guardians who are her grandparents. She admits to experimentation of drugs. Consciousness was clear; she was well-oriented, and there was no disturbance in memory. She showed fairly good ability to counting and arithmetical calculations. Abstraction ability was good. Her insight and judgment are not impaired. Her conflict, as noted in the diagnostic staff note, appeared to be external rather than intrapsychic.

–Dr. Mariano A. Favis, Jr., "Initial Summary: Mental Examination"

O H-MY-GOD.

I can't believe they did this to me. When I tried to leaving for Pennsylvania, Dee Dee and I got into a huge argument–

what a scene.

All this crap after he said I could leave. He lied to me.

Suddenly, I'm in court for a bogus hearing; they declare me crazy; hours later, after being locked in an empty, windowless room without food, water, or bathroom facilities—I had to pee *so* bad, and did they care?—some sheriff dude drives me (still no bathroom, I almost peed myself), stuck in the back of a caged cop car, to Cherokee; and here I am—in the funny farm. What chance did I have?

Even my lawyer was against me, the old fart.

I can't go anywhere. I'm in what call an admission ward, a fancy name for locked ward, where they bring my meals to me. They said I have to earn my freedom. Shit. I thought I was in America, the land of the free. Only if you join the Establishment and play by their rules. In a few days, I'll get an escort card, which means I can go places only if I'm escorted by a staff person.

Every time someone talks to me, I start to cry. Can't they see I don't belong here, that this is all a huge mistake? I hate all the questioning they have put me through—I'm so tired of it all. I'll be in here forever, locked up, never to be seen again. I'll grow old in here, no husband, no children—no life.

Damn Mo and Dee Dee; I'll *never* see them, ever again, at least not voluntarily; they have put me through more misery in one month than I have experienced in my *entire* life. I have lost *all* respect for them, nothing but lies, lies, and more lies. Broken promises, sneaky and underhanded conduct. No wonder I'm paranoid.

One minute the nurses say I won't be in here very long, and the next, they yap about having to earn ground privileges. All my outgoing mail will be monitored, which means I have to be careful what I write to Jeff and my friends. I don't know about incoming mail. I would think not—I'm not in jail, am I?

Or am I?

But at least I'll receive all my letters, read by my keepers or not, privacy notwithstanding. I never received Jeff's last letter—he said he sent it on Valentine's Day—so I assume Mo and Dee Dee still have it and have probably read it.

At least I talked to Jeff yesterday—I told him about the court hearing, so maybe he'll figure it out and not worry. The minute I have a free moment without some stranger hovering over me, I'll write Jeff and tell him I'm okay. I don't want him to panic or give up on me because I'm crazy, though I'm scared I'll never get out of here.

Damn scared.

Thursday, February 20

I FEEL BETTER TODAY; I try to keep busy, and that helps. I can't change the fact I'm here, so I might as well play the system. I'll get out that much sooner. I even went to a dance tonight—not as cool as L.A. happenings, but better than nothing. There are lots of people here, but many of them aren't insane, just struggling with emotional problems they want to solve, most staying a month to six weeks. I want to make friends here, if only to keep from being isolated and bored. I kind of like rapping with the ward clerks and nurses, though some of them act like they feel terribly sorry for you, which I don't like. But most of them deal with us as human beings. That's really groovy.

Today, they took my mug shot in the x-ray room. I had quite a frown. I thought they'd cut my hair and make me wear a jail jumpsuit, though I did have to undergo a physical—inside and out, except for the pelvic exam, which will be done later—something to look forward to.

Nothing like a stranger sniffing up your pussy.

So far, Jeff's been so patient, but for how long? He might decide out I'm not worth the trouble, especially after dealing with Mo and Dee Dee.

Friday, February 21

I'M NOW A PROUD OWNER of a ground card, which means I can go *anywhere* on the hospital grounds with another patient without being accompanied by a nurse. I'm moving up rapidly. God, it sure feels good to get out and get some fresh air.

Mo and Dee Dee still haven't sent my clothes. I've been wearing institutional wardrobe, clothes older than God. At least I did wear a dress to the hearing, so I don't have to wear a mumu for the social events.

I keep myself busy and continue attending all and any social events, although I don't have an earth shattering time–it passes the time faster.

If only they'd let me sleep in; they get us up with the chickens, 6:00 a.m. We sit around until 7:00, then breakfast, wait for lunch. I've been reading and playing cards with the other patients, mostly poker, hearts, and gin rummy. This morning, the hospital offered exercise sessions, which I need badly–Mo and Dee have driven me to compulsive eating. Daytime TV stinks. If they'd let us sleep longer, the days wouldn't seem so long. On Monday, I'm supposed to start Occupational Training, O.T. for short, a fancy name for Arts and Crafts and Basket-weaving. I was told I might be able to get a job on the outside while I'm here, but the Chaplain said to wait about two weeks before bringing that up with my doctors.

I hope to hear from Jeff soon.

Saturday, February 22

MO AND DEE have accused me of stashing acid and pot around the house. How ridiculous is that? I don't have a big time connection in Sioux City, and, besides, I wouldn't take that risk. I have decided–emphatically–that I'm swearing off drugs. I've seen nothing but heartache: flipped out people, bad trips, and paranoia. Drugs run the dope head's life, making him a slave, just like Mo and Dee are slaves to their old ideas. I feel sorry for them. Stoney, too, because I think LSD and the heroin will kill him.

I realize that Stoney doesn't really want to love–he wants to die.

Acid is a bore; I've done about 120 hours of tripping on the same thing: colors, patterns, sounds, and I don't notice any of the so-called insights. I quit just in time–I'm not quite so paranoid, I no longer have the feeling I'm being watched all the time, not even in here.

I've been living in a world of two extremes, trading one for the other: Mo and Dee's narrow-minded world of false morality and the upside down world of drug abuse.

I'm not surprised at Mo's lies; she keeps her word only when it suits her. But if the truth stands in the way of something she wants, all bets are off.

But Dee Dee surprises me; he has always been a man of his word. I adored him; he was my model, and I wanted to be as intelligent and informed as he seemed to be. He kept his cool in any emergency. When I was on drugs, I didn't want him to know about it, but when he found out my secret, I didn't deny it. I thought I could trust him. So what does he do? He breaks his word, lies, and then expects me to beg for forgiveness. So he declares me unfit for society and sticks me in here.

What a joke. The court appointed me a lawyer for my hearing, and they didn't even give me a chance to consult him alone. He might as well have been on the other side. When I tried telling my story, they interrupted me. One man kept saying, "Don't you realize what LSD can do to you?"

Damn, I know, I *know*. What was he trying to prove?

Okay, I was on drugs. But now I'm off–obviously, they don't believe me. I've made mistakes, but I love life, and I want to explore my future.

If I ever get out of here.

Sunday, February 23

Wolfie flipped out at recreation tonight. I was dancing with him—he seemed okay—but then he squeezed me around my waist and pushed me against the wall. I thought he was going to smother me to death. I told him to stop, but it was like he was in a trance—he just stared at me with those strange beady eyes, like he was going to drill into me. As three orderlies peeled him off me, he screamed and writhed like a snake, and they had to drag him across the floor and tie him to a Gurney.

Scary.

I later found out he's in the men's locked ward for doing something horrible. What, I don't know. The other patients don't seem to know the specifics, and the staff isn't saying.

Why would they allow people like that to mix with the rest of us?

I haven't heard from Jeff yet; he'll probably get my first letter from here by tomorrow, but it seems like forever since I've been in the shrink house. I couldn't bear it if he turned his back on me now. I just want to get out!

I'm being so self-centered—at least I don't have to worry about the draft. Jeff has that worry hanging over him.

What if he gets drafted before I get out of here? I would absolutely *die*.

Maybe if I talk to my social worker, he'll see how I am and recommend my getting out as soon as possible.

I wrote Pam last night; I hope she isn't mad at me.

Dee Dee got his hands on her last letter; she called him an uptight Hoosier. Boy, was he steamed. He called her a 14-karat tramp.

If she's a tramp, then so am I.

I hate when he judges my friends according to Establishment standards.

After four days, *still* no clothes. You'd think Mo and Dee would at least send them by mail, but I suppose they're still going through my stuff, reading my letters and diary, finding all the dirt they can dig up and use against me.

Monday, February 24

I talked to my social worker today, a Mr. Benson–he's a bit of a twit.

I asked him if I had to go back to my grandparents.

"Well, that's up to your doctor, but we won't *make* you do anything," he said.

"Look," I said. "I don't want to go back to them, and you'd just be wasting your time if I'm forced into staying with them–I'll just run away, and this time, I'll succeed."

He had no answer.

I won't allow *anyone* to push me around. At one time, even last year, people could just lead me around, and I would follow placidly.

No more!

Mo and Dee are on a huge ego trip, the way they impose their values on other people.

They act like they're God.

I'm anxious to start O.T.–I have a picture in mind I want to paint: dusk on the ocean just after the sun has set; it's not quite dark yet–there's a corona of color, mostly orange, some of it reaching into the scattered clouds and lighting them up. The sea is restless and dark–I will mix a dot of Prussian blue into Ultramarine for that effect, with a muted orange for the sea foam, which reflects the color from the sky. There are a few rocks about. On one of the rocks, a person–maybe it's me–silhouetted, will be observing the spectacle before her. Then again, I might paint a dock with the observer sitting at the edge, dangling her bare legs into the waves.

I'm reading *Gone With the Wind* for the umpteenth time. I love Scarlett O'Hara–she knows what she wants, and she gets it. She doesn't allow her prissy mother or that busybody Mammy get into her way. Too bad she realizes her love for Rhett too late, but I suspect she'll go after him just like she did with Ashley. Melanie is too sweet and naïve, can't figure out what Scarlett's up to. Melly's just too trusting! Why she loves Scarlett like a sister, I'll never know.

Like Scarlett, I'll fight with every inch of my being.

Flash: I wonder what will happen to people like Stoney 50 years from now?

I think he'll be dead.

WEDNESDAY, FEBRUARY 26

I'VE BEEN MOVED to South Ward 4–I'm improving! My outgoing and incoming mail no longer gets read before I send or receive it. I've also made some friends on Ward 2–Carrie, Penny, and Anna. Penny will probably be moving back up here soon.

I don't know why Penny's here in the first place–she's been here over a year–and she keeps flip-flopping between Wards 2 and 4–maybe it's because she's mouthy and sassy and takes no lip from the staff. I call her Perky Penny. She's small, and has a cute round face and short black hair styled in a flip, which makes her look a little like The Flying Nun. But she has a loud, gravelly voice, swears like a sailor, and smokes Kools, one after another. Only 17, she has a five-year-old kid by her married boyfriend, who's raising the kid with his wife. How screwed up is that? Penny and this man ran off to Puerto Rico when she was 11, he 24, and that's when she got knocked up. I can't even imagine what kind of sexual appeal an adult male would see in a kid–he must be some kind of weirdo. But she seems so together, has never done drugs, just alcohol, and not very much, at least from what she says.

"Why are you here?" I asked her.

"I've got nowhere else to go," she said, and left it at that. Her parents live in Sioux City, in Morningside. Maybe they think she's incorrigible too, so they stuck her here–evidently, that's what happens to incorrigible kids who don't behave according to Establishment rules.

Later, Penny told me how mad her mother got when she returned from Puerto Rico, pregnant. Wanted to disown her. Excuse me, but shouldn't her mother's anger be directed at the father, *a grown man*? Penny's just a kid; how could she be held responsible for having sex? Probably didn't even know what it was.

But, then, Mo wasn't too sympathetic when I told her about that older boy who did things to me when I was nine, even when I didn't want to and *told* him I didn't want to.

She said I should have known better.

I didn't know shit.

Mo and Dee Dee came today, but I refused to see them. I thought for sure I'd be demoted to the locked ward after that little scene.

They could have saved themselves 60 miles by calling first, but they tried forcing their way onto the ward, Mo screaming, "We're going to your doctor and tell him you're forbidden to receive that hippie's letters!"

I was so upset, afraid they could–legally–have that much power over my destiny. But Dr. Favis, my primary doctor, said that (1) I have don't have to see them, and (2) they have no say over my mail–I'll receive every letter sent to me.

Evidently, they got their hands on the letter from Jeff when he asked me to come to York and live with him. "He's nothing but a tamed ape!" Dee Dee yelled as the guards escorted them out of the ward. In the future, I'm going to hide my stuff better and be more careful what I write.

Those two have closed their minds to any possibilities except what they have already decided for me.

They could have at least brought my clothes.

THEY FINALLY GAVE ME the dreaded pelvic exam today, cold and sticky and gross. They even give them to the old ladies here–like they would be knocked up or have the clap. Wouldn't it be funny if they find out I have the clap?

We saw *How to Save a Marriage and Ruin a Life*, starring Dean Martin; it was funnier than hell. Not the greatest movie, but the recreation, while not earth shattering, helps pass the time. On Monday night, we heard a Barber Shop quartet, and last night "An Evening with Lawrence Welk."

Total crap, but better than sitting around, feeling sorry for myself.

Still waiting to hear from Jeff.

THURSDAY, FEBRUARY 27

I'VE BEEN DECLARED LEGALLY SANE.

I wonder why it took so long?

I'll likely be leaving here in two weeks–maybe less. Groovy. But I told Dr. Favis–emphatically–I would *not*, under any circumstances, go back to Mo and Dee Dee's, even if it means jail. God, I could stand jail more than those tyrants.

A promise: if I do end up back with the tyrants, I *will* leave. I'll *never* give up fighting for my independence.

"A girl like you doesn't belong here," Dr. Favis said. He said that Mo and Dee didn't even stay to talk to him yesterday, which he found a bit odd, given they had driven 60 miles, no doubt to see him and to let it be known that Jeff's letters upset me.

Dr. Favis explained how I, mistakenly assuming that 18 was the magic number, ended up here against my will: a person isn't emancipated in this hick state until 21, *unless* they get married. An 18-year-old female can get married without parental permission, but a guy has to be 21. So in order to be free at 18 in this state, one must have the approval of the clergy, and a man has to have permission to get married, but not to get drafted, sent to Vietnam, and ordered to kill Viet Cong.

These laws are so friggin' stupid.

So that's why Dee Dee insisted I come back "to get my head on straight"; he knew the law would be on his side, and there wouldn't be a damned thing I could do about it. When I do get out of here, I'll have to sneak out of Iowa, just to be considered a free person. What a dirty, rotten, underhanded trick, and I fell for it!

Dr. Favis is *so* cool, and for an Establishment person, he's sympathetic and kind, a beautiful person.

I'm glad Dr. Kirkus isn't my doctor—he hates me and doesn't hide the fact. He thinks they should lock me up here and throw away the key. Even his patients don't like him all that much; they say he treats them like nincompoops. He always looks sloppy; his wispy hair, what there is of it, sticks out every which way from the static electricity. His flushed, ruddy complexion, which would make a normal person look healthy, gives him a boiled pig appearance. His belly, round as a taut melon, sits upon two skinny legs, his pants (always brown polyester) held up by a belt, tucked under his belly. He has no butt, so his pants droop; behind his back, we call him Dr. Droopy Drawers.

"Do you respect me?" I asked Jeff in today's letter.

I'm afraid of the answer.

Friday, February 28

They ran a bunch of tests on me today: intelligence, aptitude, and personality tests. I had to build some crazy designs with blocks—I'm not very good with spatial relationships, but I did my best. Mrs. Lowenberg asked me to draw a house and a tree (separately) and gave me five whole minutes. Man, I'm an artist, not a scribbler. I came up with a very stereotypical house—and the tree? It didn't have any leaves—no time to put them on, and I said so, but Lowenberg said not to worry. She said I was very intelligent, but I don't believe it. I think they say that to everyone, at least to their faces.

I can only imagine what my records must *really* reveal about me. But Dr. Favis assures me that I'm normal as anyone else and don't belong here.

TODAY I met a girl on 5; she's also 18, and her parents had her committed here because they don't like the guy she's engaged to. He has long hair and is Mexican, so they spread all kinds of slanderous stuff about him.

Less than two weeks left in here. Dr. Favis says he'll try to get my last paycheck to me—I had worked some banquets back in Sioux City, and Mo and Dee have my last check. I'm splitting the minute they release me.

If they find me sane, then Mo and Dee can't stick me back here, right?

They had better give up their reign of tyranny—they are *so* wrong if they think for one minute I will *ever* stop loving Jeff.

64

Main Street

August 30, 2004

(Cherokee)

WHERE *HAD* WE ALL GONE so wrong?

A burning question, still having no good answers.

A specter dividing me and my family, even to this day.

Still, some life events too razor-sharp to ignore—Cherokee, *the* watershed event, shaping my adult life.

Today's landscape: a brilliant late summer day, sparkling blue sky and lush greenery, 75-80 degrees, unlike those frosty, foggy winter and drenched early spring months of 1969, which saw record flooding.

In Summer 1990, during Jerry's NEH Institute in Ames, we had taken this same trip, but I had been unable to get out of the car. We simply looped around the grounds and past the main building, Jerry coming to a sliding stop.

I couldn't even snap photos, although I had my camera ready.

I wasn't yet ready to confront this part of my past.

"Get me out of here," I said.

Now, though, we make a day of it, skirting the institution by stopping in the town proper—a sort of deep breath before facing my ghostly demons.

We eat at Little Panda, a Chinese restaurant tucked on W.

Maple St.–not great food, but certainly adequate. Satiated, we stroll through town, on E. Main St.; the day feels like ours. The main street has gone through a renaissance: an art gallery, antique shop, consignment shop, and bookstore, juxtaposed with a locksmith/hardware store and bike shop.

I don't remember much about Cherokee in 1969–my ground card did not extend to the town itself. The few times I went, I must have been accompanied by a chaperone, or on my way to the depot, to catch the Greyhound to Sioux City for a trial visit. A scene from *Girl, Interrupted* offers a sense of *déjà vu* as Susanna Kaysen and other patients are led into an ice cream parlor by their chaperones. But I can't say for sure if I was ever afforded an excursion into town, escorted by mental health employees.

I don't feel anything about Cherokee the town, simply a digression before motoring over to the hill.

We stroll down Main Street, admiring the thriving shops along the way. We visit Trash & Treasures, apparently specializing in local art, and chat with the owner, who says he will expand his gallery to include antiques. A few scattered items–an old typewriter, ephemera, table, some bottles–are mixed with the local artist paintings, sculptures, pottery, and hand-blown bottles. He sells other local bric-a-brac; I buy a tee-shirt bearing an engraving of the mental health hospital complex. I'm not sure why I need a tee-shirt with a picture of my former prison, but it now seems appropriate; back in 1969, I might have burned it.

My story tumbles out–I tell this stranger about my incarceration at Cherokee, that I'm writing a memoir.

The man doesn't seem shocked at all–how many other former patients have returned to exorcize the past?

"Some patients got out and settled down here in Cherokee, got jobs, raised families," he says.

I can't imagine settling down in this place, where I'd see and feel, day after day, my former prison hovering over me like a dark thunder cloud.

Were these former patients' lives so awful before that they could not possibly return to their hometowns? Are they still tied to the institution, perhaps sensing they may need to return some day for reinforcement therapy? Or are they simply stuck, unable to move forward to new lives?

Stuck, perhaps, in a Cherokee inversion, a Twilight Zone town, in middle America, where the hospital hovers over the daily lives of Cherokee residents?

My map of Cherokee, "...made possible through those efforts of...progressive business and community leaders," does not name the mental hospital, only offering the outline of the grounds. If one were to come to town and not have the address, one would not easily find the institution without having to ask for directions.

Even now, a sort of local shame at having to endure the hospital on the hill, west of downtown, overlooking the town, only a vague outline with no name on the map sponsored by its progressive citizens.

65

The Miami Incident
(Miami, Florida)

SATURDAY, MARCH 1, 1969

I'M NOT TALKING ABOUT REVOLUTION, I'm not talking about guns and riots, I'm talking about love.

An intoxicated Jim Morrison struts the stage.

Love one another. Love your brother, hug him. Man, I'd like to see a little nakedness around here....

You didn't come here for music, did you? You came for something more, didn't you?...

WHAT IS IT? You want to see my cock, don't you?

...YEAHHHH!

Morrison waves his shirt in front of his crotch in bullfighter tradition.

See it? Did you see it?

66

Rock God

Mid-December 1968

(Hollywood)

*O*H-MY-GOD! *Jim Morrison's across the street from Wallich's Music City.*

I can't believe it!

He's a God, I swear, an absolutely beautiful God, the most perfect human being I've ever laid eyes on. I have never seen such gorgeous, long hair; his dark curls cascade to his shoulders like a model's. He's tall, almost as tall as Stoney, and lanky.

He wears a black and white striped shirt, black leather pants, a leather belt with a huge silver buckle, and black boots.

Hair blowing slightly in the wind.

The bulge in his groin tells the whole story.

I want to run over to him, grab his arm, and profess my everlasting love, worship at his feet, but, of course, I'm much too lowly of a creature.

I'd be nothing to him.

Stoney leans toward God, but I pull him back.

"You can't," I say.

"Why not?"

"Because-because..."—I can't really think of a good reason why he shouldn't—"It wouldn't be right!" finally spills out.

He's mine!

Stoney laughs, but, for once, he listens and hangs back.

Like two morons, we gawk at Morrison, our mouths gaping.

Overgrown teenyboppers.

Time stops, and God Morrison holds court on Sunset and Vine, doing nothing but leaning against a building, smoking a cigarette, the world stopping to pay homage to the greatest rock star of the twentieth century: freaks and straights alike.

Even traffic seems to halt.

I love Stoney, but I'd throw it all away for just one night with the God of Rock...

Like he's read my mind, Stoney says, "I'm not queer, but, for Him, *I'd make an exception."*

67

Reality

March 1, 1969

(Cherokee)

SATURDAY, MARCH 1

Jim Morrison's image dissipates—I call to him, but he laughs and waves me away.

A God needs a Goddess...Goddess...Goddess...

Bizarre flashback.

I wouldn't have the nerve to expose myself to 12,000 people.

I'm not liking that girl who drooled like a slut, so besotted by Morrison—

That I might have gone off with him and—

Actually, he's kind of pathetic.

You know what?

Jimbo didn't have to expose himself in front of that audience—

They would have loved him anyway.

I *FINALLY* RECEIVE A LETTER from Jeff.

"Whose idea was it to have Jennifer Lee Semple committed to a mental institution?" he asked. "Your grandmother told my mother it was your idea. From your letter, I received the impression it was the other way around."

Is she kidding??? As if it was my idea to come here–that's the kind of crap Mo has been feeding Jeff and his mother. I can't believe that Mo had the nerve to call Mrs. Brown and dump a load of shit on her.

"While I sweated and groaned," he said, "your grandmother filled my mom in all those kinda facts and/or suspicions concerning you and me that would probably be crossed out by the censors if I went into detail."

She not only snitched on me, but also defamed Jeff, spewing all his secrets, plus things that never even happened.

"Jeff's letters disturb Jennifer," Mo told Mrs. Brown.

WHAT?

Mo and Dee's *interference* upsets me. They're trying to kill the only good thing that has *ever* happened to me. I *hate* them! If they succeed in scaring Jeff away, I'll hate them forever!

Mo ordered Jeff to stop writing me.

"My old lady is scared your grandmother will ring in the heat," Jeff said. "And my parents asked me to stop writing for a while."

Now Jeff's confused and doesn't know what to do.

If he stops writing, I'll absolutely die. How could I bear another minute in this madhouse, if I can't get any letters from him?

"I forced a concession," Jeff said. "That I be allowed one letter, to let you know *why* I'm not writing–provided I *do* decide to quit writing for a while. Maybe I ought to play your grandmother's game for a while...When I knew you, you weren't, what I would consider, a candidate for a mental hospital–maybe you've changed!!?"

No way. He's got to know that.

"Anyway, it's not forever," he said. "You sound like the old Jennifer, and that's who I fell in love with...Don't worry...everything is going to work out."

By the end of his letter, Jeff has decided he can write once a week.

Bummer. Only one letter a week.

I answer Jeff immediately, begging him to keep writing, to reconsider the once-a-week rule.

I just hope he doesn't forget me and stop writing altogether.

68

What If?

August 30, 2004

(Going to Cherokee)

*I see something of God in each hour of the twenty-four,
    and each moment then,*
*In the face of men and women I see God, and in my own
    face in the glass,*
*I find letters from God dropt in the street, and Every-one
    is sign'd by God's name,*
*And I leave them where they are, for I know that
    wheresoe'er I go*
Others will punctually come for ever and ever.
    –Walt Whitman, *Leaves of Grass*, Part 48

*

The letter that never arrives: What could better suggest the pathos of communication gone awry?...But what is the meaning of the letter...whose writer does not know it is lost and whose recipient does not know it was ever sent?
    –John Durham Peters,
        *Speaking into the Air: A History of
        the Idea of Communication.*

*

STILL POKING AROUND in Trash & Treasures, I flip through a box of old letters from the 1940's; they appear to be from a man to his wife, a one-sided view of a personal history.

Could these lovers still be alive? If so, do they realize that their secrets are up for sale to the first stranger willing to fork over $25.00?

The possibility of my and Jeff's letters being sold to the highest bidder gives me a chill, but isn't memoir writing also an exhibition of a personal history?

What about the conventions of snail-mail correspondence? Letters stolen or lost could have changed entire lives.

What if, in 1969, we had cheap cell phone access? Instant Messages? Email? Blogs?

Although my grandparents complained about the fast pace of 1969 life, private long-distance communication was still limited and expensive. Television was just coming into its own as an important conduit for the Information Age, but the flow was still one way and its control limited to the rich and powerful. The fledgling internet, limited to government use, was unknown to most. Ordinary people still depended on the United States Postal Service, a system that, essentially, hadn't changed much since 1847, the issue year of the first national postage stamp.

Without the USPS, this story would have ended in Hollywood. As it was, mail service was slow, at least by electronic standards: our letters traveled two or three days across the country, an ongoing dialogue or argument punctuated by days, even weeks of waiting for responses, answers to life-changing questions hanging suspended in midair.

At least one important letter from Jeff was confiscated, temporarily interrupting an important link between us. No doubt: without Jeff, I would have never traveled to York, Pennsylvania; those yellowing letters link directly to my current life.

Their bulk and physicality affords them a permanence and substance that doesn't exist for electronic messages.

Writing a letter takes considerable effort: finding just the right paper, pen, and envelope; planning what to write and how to write it; placing the pen to paper; sealing and stamping the envelope; and waiting for the mail carrier, finding a mailbox, or taking a trip to the post office.

Quality of paper and envelope, color of ink, type of stamps selected and how they are placed, drawings on the back (and sometimes front) of envelopes, scents (a mixture of post office official and perfume added by the sender) reveal important personality traits.

I learned a lot about Jeff from his considered statements; neat handwriting; well-executed, colorful drawings; and his love for different kinds of stationery.

He must have figured out my impulsiveness through my slapdash handwriting, sloppy drawings, and stream-of-consciousness sentence fragments.

Even now, receiving a letter marks a special occasion.

Is it any surprise that postcards, letters, and other ephemera are now hot collectibles?

69

March 2-5, 1969

(Cherokee)

SATURDAY, MARCH 1, 1969

DEE DEE HAS BEEN WRITING sweet, syrupy letters–says he's concerned about me.

Dr. Favis has a definition for concern: guilt complex. He said that if he were really concerned, he would work *with* me, not *against* me.

SUNDAY, MARCH 2

I'M SCARED TO DEATH of Wolfie; he's a sex fiend. Ever since he cornered me, I've been keeping my distance. But, at the socials, he chases me, even when I beg the chaperones to keep him away. Once, he even asked me to go out and play in the snow at 8:00 a.m. (?). Of course, I refused, but I'm afraid he'll get loose and do something awful. The other patients call him the Big Bad Wolf. He resides in North 3, which is the guys' locked ward. God, I don't know why they allow people like that to mix with the rest of us.

ON WEDNESDAY, I have to go to a staff meeting. A committee of doctors, nurses, and social workers are going to observe. If I'm as normal as Dr. Favis says I am, why am I going through all this hassle? This place is getting to me–I'm tired of all the weird tests. I think about running away, but from what I hear, if you do, they hunt you down like a wild animal until they find you. Then they drag you back and stick you in isolation for a week or more. God knows how much time they add to your sentence.

I wait and wonder if I'll *ever* get out.

I'm worried about Carrie, a 15-year-old girl I have befriended. She shuffles between Ward 2 (wacko unit) and Ward 4, depending on her behavior. She's on 4 now, but I'm afraid she's headed back to 2 very soon.

She babbles about wanting to stick a dead rat up her vagina, and when I ask why, she says, "Just for something to do."

Should I say something to the staff? I dunno. I wouldn't want anyone narking me out about some dumb comment I made during a bull session. We all say crazy stuff just to be bull shitting, but, somehow, I suspect Carrie really means to harm herself. I'll wait and see, and hope her doctor is keeping close tabs on her.

Carrie goes to Heelan but is out of school because of being here. Besides, she's too fucked up for school, which fucks kids up anyway. She landed in here because she carved "Father Falon" all up and down her arms; she showed me the scars, and, sure enough, his name is still faintly visible. "I love him," she says when I ask why she did it. Father Falon teaches at Heelan, and, I must admit, when I was there, I had a crush on him, too. But it wouldn't have occurred to me to carve his name on my arms. I have never heard of such strange stuff.

Behind her back, I call her Carrie the Cutter. Mean, I know, but she pissed me off when she suggested, as we were bathing, that we have a Lesbian relationship.

I politely declined, and she let it go at that.

In the bath area, three tubs, no curtains, so everyone can see each other naked. Makes me uneasy—I like my privacy too much. But Carrie seems to like company when she bathes.

Never again; from now on, I'll take my baths late at night, when I'm alone and away from all prying eyes.

Carrie appears slightly retarded; her mouth droops open a little, she hunches slightly, and she has yellow teeth, pointy buck teeth with a wide space between them, but I don't think she is actually mentally lacking. She's too wily and dreams up all these complicated plots for escaping this joint, complete with accomplices and getaway cars. All talk, I'm sure. Still, it takes brains to think up these schemes.

She loves shocking and burning herself on the coils of those huge electric cigarette lighters stuck on the walls. The shocks are just static electricity, but they hurt, and most of us try to avoid them, but Carrie loves hearing the zaps snap against her index fingertip. She goes from lighter to lighter, finding the one offering the biggest thrill.

These lighters are ominous oblong bronze boxes that hum like those strange electrical contraptions in old horror movies. Rube Goldberg apparatuses, some inventor taking a simple object and complicating it. It's funny to watch someone light a cigarette; it looks like they're kissing the box. The state is afraid we'll burn the place down if we're allowed matches or lighters, but I've figured out a way to create a flame by sticking a piece of loosely rolled paper to the coil—not that I'd ever show Carrie how to do it.

This is *my* secret.

I have no desire to set a fire, but it's always good, in a pinch, to know these things.

With due respect to Carrie, this place needs a humidifier like bad; every time you touch metal—the box lighters, water taps, TV, stove in the communal room—ZAP! Crackle! Pop! When I comb my hair, it crackles and sticks out. Feels funny, like I'm going to take wing, via my hair, which takes longer to get dirty, and my skin is so dry it cracks. Lip balm is my best friend. You'd think the state could pop for some humidifiers, instead of sticking innocent teenagers in here to fry themselves.

The tunnels here, probably built for Iowa winters, link all the buildings. The one to Donohoe, a gloomy gray, has never been painted, but it's great for singing. Last night, on the way to the social, Penny, Carrie, and I sang "They're Coming to Take Us Away, HA, HA!" at the top of our lungs. The attendants didn't like that too much. But you've got to cut loose around here, or you *will* go mad.

The guys around here are persistent–not just Wolfie–and I have tried to be polite in discouraging them. But I've discovered that you have to use THE BIG BRUSH OFF–big trouble if you don't. The truth is, I really have to watch out for myself because the staff has other things to do, like administering tests.

I experienced a flashback today that lasted three hours–most annoying because I was trying to read. I don't tell Dr. Favis about most of my flashes; he might prescribe Thorazine, and I'd rather work through my problem without drugs.

I asked Jeff if I could call him collect. I just want to hear his voice.

Monday, March 3

Miss Semple, a slightly overweight 18 year old female, was co-operative, pleasant, rather cheerful, and somewhat adolescent in manner. She wore poorly applied eye make-up which gave her a slightly unusual appearance. She responded quickly and with fairly good efficiency, Some manifest anxiety was noted in her tendency to repeat questions before answering. She showed some looseness, e.g., on the Fly-Tree similarity item she said, "Sometimes when you walk under a tree, it can be just as annoying to have a leaf fall on you as a fly to land on you."

–Evaluation of Jennifer L. Semple, Cherokee Mental Health Institute

TODAY I had a very interesting discussion with Dr. Kirkus. What a dude! He says the only reason I love Jeff is because he's my ticket out of Iowa. I tried telling him I was in here *because* of my relationship with Jeff.

He just shook his head, and said, "I don't understand you."

I don't understand him either.

I said that I disliked school–never use "hate" in a shrink house–except for Spanish and Art, and, sometimes, English.

He asked, "Why?"

"Because most of my teachers were complete idiots–they didn't know how to teach shit."

He gave me a bunch of bull that if I wanted to learn, I would learn despite how my teachers taught.

The world is filled with straight people who would cram Establishment crap down your throat.

Another syrupy letter from Dee Dee–straight to the circular file. A few days ago, I wrote to Jeff's parents; they should receive the letter tomorrow or Wednesday. I figure if everyone was writing them and telling them their side of the story, then I need to get my two-cents in. Maybe if they hear what I have to say, they won't dislike me so much–hope it doesn't upset them.

It was so hard getting up at 6:00 a.m. today; actually it was 7:30 when I woke up to a pair of eyes staring down at me. I let out a weak, "Oh..."

"Yeah," the nurse said. "I'll 'oh' you. Get up!"

I've got to be more careful; I'll be put on report if I oversleep anymore.

I miss breakfast when I get up so late, but who cares? The food here is *awful*. For supper, they served green powdered eggs. That stuff not only looked bad, it even smelled funny, and my gut hurt afterwards.

I had inkblot tests today. I hope I *never* have to go through *that* again. It's hard to see pictures in a stupid inkblot; all I could see was mirror-image African bush twins carrying baskets on their heads. I wonder what that says about me?

And the rooms they give these tests in! Too small, over-heated, and no windows. I thought I'd pass out.

Dr. Favis said I'd be out of here in two weeks, and that was a week ago. I hope he's right. This place isn't really so bad, but I just don't belong–I can't think of one thing that's bothering me, except Mo and Dee Dee, but that's no reason to stay.

Even without Jeff, this place *still* wouldn't be my bag.

DR. FAVIS ASKED ME if I had any regrets about the last few months. I said, "Getting involved with Stoney." I'll never quite forgive myself for that. But I can't make excuses, either. Just to say I made one huge mistake.

Another regret: accepting Peter's proposal without much thought and then having to write that Dear John.

Funny. When you do things you know are wrong, you seem to ignore your conscience until you've already done them, and then it's too late.

"You can't undo the mistakes you have already made," Dr. Favis says. "Just vow to do better now and in the future."

I'm just lucky I didn't end up with Stoney's baby.

BAD VIBES about Pam. I don't know what's going on with that girl, but I have a feeling her head isn't where it ought to be. She's supposed to be in some nurses' training program–flunked it the first time. I hope she passes it this time, before she gets in trouble with her parents.

TUESDAY, MARCH 4

DEE DEE AND UNCLE DUDE showed up today. I refused to see Dee Dee, but I did agree to see Dude–I have nothing against him, except that he's probably on *their* side.

We had an interesting rap session.

Dude insists Dee Dee had *nothing* to do with the interception of my mail–God, what lies! Dude gave me all this bull about reconciling with Dee Dee–that he and Mo could die tomorrow and I would regret our rift–and this situation is slowly killing them (blah, blah, blah!). So I handed Dude a pencil and piece of paper and told him to take notes while I dictated terms under which I would speak to Dee Dee.

First, he will have to return *all* the letters that have been intercepted, or no deal.

Two, Dee Dee had better not use any of Jeff's letters against him, or I will take legal action against him for intercepting my mail in the first place.

Three, I will not see Mo under *any* circumstances. She'd just get hysterical; she bugs me anyway. She has always underestimated me.

Four, I want my diary and the book that I was writing returned to me.

Five, I want his word that he will sit down with me and talk like a human being–save the threats and legal actions for Mo, because I'd rather stay here than to listen to that bull. If Dee Dee is really sincere, he'll agree to my terms. If not, we're right back where we started. I don't want to remain on bad terms, but if Mo and Dee won't give me some breathing room, I'll have no choice but write them off.

I loved Dee Dee, I *trusted* him. Now, I'm so angry at him. I don't exactly hate him, but I can't say that I love him, either.

Can we *ever* fix this?

WEDNESDAY, MARCH 5
(Cherokee)

STAFF MEETING TODAY. About 30 or so doctors and nurses sit in on this gala affair. More like the gallows. I'm not sure why they have these meetings–I feel like a bug stuck on a pin, struggling for life.

When Carrie had her staff meeting a few months ago, she

ran out in the middle of it, and ended up on locked ward for two months.

Dr. Kirkus will be here–that dude scares the shit out of me.

And he's *late*. This session is supposed to start at 9:45 a.m., Kirkus rolls in at 10:10.

I swear, he does it just to make me sweat.

A nurse I don't know calls me into a room designated "Group Therapy I," where I face an audience of unfamiliar and familiar faces, all watching, waiting to see if I trip up.

Maintain, Jennifer, maintain.

I assume a pose of certainty, but I feel dizzy and lopsided. I take my place up front, in a chair, positioned exactly in the middle. I smile at the audience as if I were going on a picnic instead of a grilling.

Dr. Brooks introduces himself and begins his questioning.

I answer truthfully, and to my surprise, quite calmly. Everything about my past six months: job, drugs, sex, boyfriends, family fights, all laid out on the table. None of it looks ugly anymore because it's past, I can't change it, and I'm ready to move forward. I'm well prepared for this battery, which surprises me–I thought I'd be tripping all over my tongue, but I'm not.

I like Dr. Brooks–he asks questions in a way that encourages.

I don't feel like hiding anymore.

Dr. Favis, today an observer, peeks around another doctor, smiling–I've never seen him yet when he wasn't smiling. He nods his encouragement to me, I nod back.

Dr. Brooks announces that the floor is open for questions from other doctors, and I just know whose hand will pop up.

I'm right.

Dr. Kirkus, smirk on his face, slowly raises his hand. It seems as if everyone else in the room has vanished, and it's Dr. Kirkus and me facing off in a duel. He stares me down; I stare back. He smiles sweetly, a sarcastic "I gotcha!" smile.

"What states would you have to pass through to get to Pennsylvania?" he asks.

The very same question asked at my bogus hearing! A snap!

I nearly blurt out, "That's a dumb question," but I hold my tongue.

I gather my thoughts. "You would go straight west to east," I say "You would start out in Iowa, from Cherokee or Sioux City, cross the Iowa border into Illinois, pass through Illinois into Indiana, from Indiana to Ohio, and, finally, into Pennsylvania, where you would travel about 225 miles southeast to York."

I have memorized the route to Pennsylvania.

As the meeting breaks up, I know I have won—I have proven my sanity, once again. I'm all smiles when, a few minutes later, Mr. Benson, my social worker, confirms I have won my case—I'll be released in two weeks—though I haven't quite won because I will need to stay in a foster home for a few months and work for a while to earn some bread.

We'll see.

I applied for a town pass for Saturday. Cherokee's nothing but a hick town, but it's an escape from the nuthouse.

I'll grab whatever I can.

70

To West Cedar Loop
August 30, 2004

(Cherokee)

I'M REMINDED of small town culture when a police officer enters Trash & Treasures and informs the owner that no one saw a perp exiting his gallery earlier that day with stolen goods.

A fear pinches me.

Jerry and I, strangers in town, could be prime suspects. After the officer leaves, I make sure the proprietor understands that I don't approve of stealing–does that implicit denial, in itself, place me at the top of the suspect list, and, perhaps, another stay at the hospital?

After we settle our bill with the gallery owner, we visit Main St. Antiques, more of a flea market that also carries collectibles and tchotchkes, like those booths found in antique malls near exit and entrance ramps on America's highways. A "Cherokee, Iowa," car plate, like the one I bought last week in Sioux City, hangs on the wall. I ask the proprietor if she knows when the plate was manufactured, but she doesn't.

"My husband might, though," she says. But her husband isn't here and not due any time soon, so origin will remain a mystery for now.

Her nearly-pristine plate isn't for sale, she says without my having asked, just for display. My plate has issues–rust, dents, and dings, but, somehow, that seems fitting.

I don't feel too comfortable in this shop–perhaps word has spread about the phantom thief blowing through town; the owner seems uneasy. Still, my eye catches a glass cardinal, and I buy it for my eight-year-old granddaughter. I pay my $6.99 and leave.

I haven't told this woman why I'm in Cherokee.

Jerry spies a newspaper box, stops to buy today's *Chronicle Times*, and tucks it into his brief case.

Continuing on E. Main Street, we find ourselves in front of The Bookseller, the kind of small bookshop being swallowed up by the powerful chains. I'm a bit skittish about bookstores these days, having visited several about my recent short story collection and been rebuffed. Also, I have forgotten my promotional materials and copies of the book.

But Jerry prods me to enter.

"You might find some books on the institution," he says.

The owner offers that a 100th anniversary booklet was published in late 2001 by the Cherokee Mental Health Institute Centennial Committee, but she has no copies in stock, and it's out of print.

"Sorry to disappoint."

The owner seems so friendly that I tell her my history with the hospital.

"I wish I could help you," she says with what seems like genuine sympathy. "Try the hospital. They might have a copy or two around."

The hospital.

Our next stop.

Jerry mentions my book. I give her my business card and tell her a bit about the collection–she seems interested in promoting local authors, including those who grew up in Sioux City and fled Iowa 35 years ago.

We buy, at half price, Ralph Ellison's *Invisible Man* for Jerry's overseas collection–soon, we'll leave the U.S. for Skopje, Macedonia, where Jerry will teach, which is why this trip to Cherokee is so important. I need to carry much of my information with me, and I can't obtain this kind of personal research through the internet.

We ride west on Main Street, and turn right onto North 11th Street, then left onto West Cedar Street. We continue up a hill to the M.H.I. property, where a large blue sign with white letters announces the institution.

At the property line, West Cedar Street changes to West Cedar Loop, address 1251, a change from 1969, when the address was 1200 West Cedar Street, Cherokee, IA, 51012–only the street number differentiating between sane and crazy–perhaps explaining the change to Loop for the hospital.

My heart skips as the car inches toward the main buildings–

Would the shadow of 9/11 bar visitors from wandering the grounds at will?

Will a burly cop pull up behind us and chase us away, or worse yet, growl, "I know you! You're Jennifer L. Semple, and you *must* finish out your sentence here!"

I exaggerate, but the visceral often trumps logic.

The art gallery owner had assured us that the grounds are open to the public, just like in 1969, and that locals often picnic and ride their bicycles here on weekends.

I can't imagine such frivolity; I spent two months devising schemes for my escape from these grounds, and now picnickers use them for recreation.

The disconnect astounds me.

As we look around the grounds and trails, Jerry pulls into a dirt parking lot, next to an official state car. We sit for a minute or two, while I fiddle with the digital camera, a first generation

Sony Mavica. Sliding in a floppy disk, I contemplate my next move, not quite as fearful as during that past revisit.

I draw in deep breath, slip the camera strap around my neck, and exit.

71

March 6-7, 1969

(Cherokee)

THURSDAY, MARCH 6

WOLFIE SHOWED UP in the canteen today, escorted; I was sitting at a table, minding my own business, when he lunged at me. I jumped out the chair and pulled away from him. He chases all the women, tries to corner them, I found out.

A pervert.

The staff says he's harmless, but I don't believe it for one second.

He's a maniac who should be kept away from us and locked up.

FRIDAY, MARCH 7

I *FINALLY GOT MY CLOTHES*. It's great being in my old funky bell bottoms. Mo and Dee Dee sent me some other things, too, like my notebook, where I was writing my book. I found a letter from Jeff there. Mo must have missed it. What a relief–that letter told plenty, and I'm glad Mo and Dee didn't see it. They *did* get my diary, but my last entry was Christmas Eve, so there was nothing outrageous about Jeff.

I doubt if Dee Dee is going to comply with my terms. If he doesn't, he might as well forget he has a granddaughter. If he returns my letters from Jeff and Pam, then we'll begin peace negotiations—this time, on an adult level.

My town pass was denied—for what reason, I don't know. They never said.

Bummer.

I think Dr. Favis wanted to see my reaction, a test.

I'm not all that broken up about it. It would have been nice to get out of this place for a few hours, but I'll be getting out for good soon enough, anyway.

Patience.

A plane was hijacked to Cuba yesterday, just like that one last fall, October or November. Not too sure, though—I was pretty out of it. A terrifying thought, crooks being able to take control of a plane so easily.

Another reason to hate flying.

I OVERSLEPT TODAY and missed O.T., first period. I was put on report. Darn it all! Haven't they figured out that some people in this world are *not* morning people?

There should be three shifts for patients, just like for the staff.

In O.T., I have completed five paintings—I've been working quite feverishly. My favorite is an interpretation of Melanie Wilkes from *Gone With the Wind*.

A few days ago, I finished reading *Gone With the Wind*—fifth time. For just one day, I'd like to go back to the Civil War, with Jeff as the notorious, unscrupulous Rhett Butler. That's a stretch, perhaps—I can't quite imagine Jeff as a scoundrel, though he'd stand up to any obstacle.

I'd be the beautiful, strong-willed Scarlett O'Hara.

He may disagree, but he isn't at all like the weak-willed Ashley Wilkes, who cares too much what his neighbors would say. Jeff quietly does his thing, and if no one likes it, too bad.

I have never seen the movie—Mo said they made it back in the late 1930's with Clark Gable and Vivien Leigh (Who? Never heard of her) as Scarlett—so I don't know what the movie version of Melly looks like.

I went by Margaret Mitchell's description of her and came up with a thin, pale girl with large wistful brown eyes, and wispy brown hair blowing around. It's funny that I would choose Melanie to paint instead of Scarlett. It's just that, in my mind, I can *see* Melanie, but Scarlett eludes me.

QUESTIONS:

Does Pam still plan on going to Pennsylvania to see Jeff?

Does she know about anything that has happened in the past month and a half?

I'm afraid she, in her own casual way, will show up at Jeff's, and really blow things out of proportion, like riling up Jeff's parents. Don't get me wrong: I *like* Pam—she's a great chick (and I wish she'd write), but her head is somewhere in the fifth dimension—and she's a bit cavalier about sex.

Rudy, Draino, and Levi—these are just the guys I know about, though she bragged about others, back when we were still in the dorm...

72

Admission
November 1968

(Hollywood)

"I did it once with a Spade dude," Pam said, out of the blue. She, in pink underpants and matching bra, sat crossed-legged on the bed. "A Black Panther."

The Black part didn't bother me so much, but the Panther part scared me shitless. I've heard they're possessive and rough with their chicks. Pam was really messing with some scary guys.

"Where's he now?"

"Dead. Police shootout last April."

I let out a sigh of relief.

"It's true what they say about Black men."

"Which is?"

Pam rolled her eyes. "You're so naïve."

"What?"

"You know, their dongs..."

"What about their dongs?"

"Size, honey."

Oh, man! I'd never heard anything one way or another about the size of Negro men's–things.

"Big, bigger, biggest."

I blushed.

Shock flashed across her face. "Oh, no, don't tell me you're a..."

"Virgin."

73

March 7-14, 1969

(Cherokee)

Friday, March 7

Before Stoney.

I *was* a virgin.

But, now, what if Pam decides she has a thing for Jeff? A girl doesn't plan a 3,000 mile trip to ball a guy who's just a friend, right?

Maybe I'm being a bit melodramatic.

After all, in the past month or so, she's been hanging out seriously with Levi, so why would she want to move in on Jeff?

Damn. How do I protect my interests when I'm stuck in this poky, cow town shrink house?

Saturday, March 8

I wonder if Jeff's a virgin?

I never asked before today's letter to him; it really doesn't matter. Guys have to sow their wild oats some time, and I doubt very much if they get their experience in the marriage bed.

Rumors really fly here. Just because I have been nice to one guy here, my name has been linked to him. God, Ray's divorced with four kids; even *I'm* smart enough not to get mixed up romantically with someone like that. He just needs someone to rap with.

Earlier today, I went for a walk with a 16-year-old boy; he's a sweet person, but extremely shy. He has a slight crush on me, but I doubt if he'd ever do anything about it. He's much too young; I just wanted to befriend him and bring him out of his shell–now I've been linked with him.

It doesn't do any good to deny these rumors; to say that I belong to someone else gets me nowhere–no one believes me.

Mr. Benson says I'll have to stay in Iowa for at least two months after I'm released. God, a lifetime. I want to split *now*. I told Jeff that maybe it'll be okay–that way, he'll have time to get organized and settled with a job and pad.

Maybe he could come here? Yeah, right. Mo and Dee would have him arrested so fast, his feet would barely hit the ground. I also suspect he would never move away from Pennsylvania and his family, not even for me. But I don't care–I'm willing to go to Pennsylvania, and never see Iowa, ever again.

My book is about 44 pages now; I'm also trying to write about my experiences in California, but it seems so faraway, and I'm having difficulty filling in the blanks. Weird. It wasn't all that long ago, and my memory is fading already. Maybe Jeff can help me rewrite my story, make it more colorful.

I hope he lets me read his novel. I want to find out when that 28-year-old male virgin on an ego trip loses his virginity.

I started a story about a super-genius chick (300 I.Q.) who must decide whether to lie about being a spy or tell the truth and blow up the world. I think that she will stick with the truth because she has no choice.

She must stay true to herself.

If Penny is a lost kid dumped into the institution and Carrie a bona-fide wacko, then Joyce is just plain scary. I don't hang out with her much; for one thing, she's too old, at least 35, married with two kids—a boy and a girl. Her husband put her here—against her will, but only because she tried to kill herself with downers, like Mom's best friend Cee—only they found Joyce in the nick of time.

Joyce definitely needs to be in here. She's what they call manic-depressive—happy one minute and unhappy the next.

It's true, too; she turns on and off like a Christmas tree. I feel sorry for her because she doesn't want to be in here, and she's totally pissed off at her husband for signing her in, but what choice did he have?

She's on shock therapy—it sounds gruesome, but it seems to work. Before the attendants take Joyce away for her treatments, she's sullen and morose, and, when she does talk, she counts and recounts ten ways of doing yourself in—I didn't know that one had so many options for slipping one's body into the sod:

> *One, pills; two, rope; three, gun; four, knife; five, drowning; six, car crash; seven, smothering; eight, jumping; nine, poison; ten, strangling...*

She repeats this litany, over and over, like a mantra.

But after treatment, she's exuberant and wants to soar like a bird; she raps like a speed freak cranked up on overdrive—it's obvious her brain is faster than her mouth; she sounds like a 33 1/3 record sped up to 78, and she doesn't finish sentences. Hell, she doesn't finish *words*, so understanding what she's trying to say is challenging, if not mostly impossible.

For about two or three days after her treatments, she's kind of fun being around—though I cringe at her detailed descriptions of getting jolted, I'm fascinated, too, so, after a few days, when I can finally get a word in between her non-stop chatter, I ask, "Tell me all about getting shocked."

"Well, it's kinda scary," she says. "But they tell me it's for my own good, so I go along. The first time, though, I fought the doctors tooth and nail, and they had to tie me down. Now I like how I feel afterwards, so it's a small price to pay."

In the shock room, they tie her down on a Gurney (which she hates, and I'd hate that too) and give her two injections, the first, some kind of insulin–why, she doesn't know (who knows why?) and, second, a downer to calm her nerves. Then they attach some electrodes to her temples (yikes!) and in the middle of her forehead and stick some device in her mouth so that she doesn't swallow her own tongue. And then they flip a switch.

"I've been told that they shoot 70-150 volts into me, depending on my mood," she says. "But once they shoot that juice into me, I black out for hours, though when I wake up, it's as if I'm another person, not this creepy, sad person. I'm ecstatic."

It seems so extreme–makes me wonder why they can't invent a pill that would do the same thing and not be so traumatic.

I can't believe that shooting electricity into a person's head could possibly be a good thing, at least in the long run.

Especially since the treatments only last about a week or so, and then Joyce is right back at the bottom.

Jesus. Whenever I feel sorry for myself, all I have to do is look at Joyce, and tell myself, "That could have been me."

She must feel very lonely.

Monday, March 10

You know you're in trouble when your boyfriend writes, "This is not going to be good news."

I've been here before. *You're a nice girl, but...*

"In a way, it's not news, because it's about an A-1 problem–and I'm undecided what to do about it."

Kill me now, put me out of my misery.

"Do you remember me telling you, right after you decided

Stoney was your guy, that I had to go back to Pennsylvania because I had to find my chick?"

Yeah, I remember, but I thought you were just trying to make me jealous.

"I wasn't assuming I'd find one in Pennsylvania. I knew who she was."

Now you tell me.

"It was Lizzie, more than anyone else, who brought me back home—I think I love her."

%3@#)&*!!!

"I've never balled her—she's a virgin."

A virgin, huh? Now it matters? Guys can be *so* two-faced about morality.

"I'm not the kind who gets all up-tight with a chick if she's not a virgin, but it's just a point."

Right.

"I think it's only right to tell you this; it wouldn't do us any good to have secrets between us. I don't know how much I love her. I still love you—but I still love her. I wrote her a letter today, and I couldn't even bring myself to tell her about you... and that's not good."

Where did this Lizzie bitch come from, anyway? A chick from Altoona (where the hell is *that?*), fresh from the loony bin, writes a letter out of the blue, and, all of a sudden, Jeff's in *love* with her?

Jesus.

Well, she sounds like one *crazy* chick; at least I never tried to kill myself, and, if she was in a mental institution, it was because she *needed* it.

Jeff met her *where?* At a *cough syrup* party?

How romantic.

"This isn't a Dear John," he says. "It's a problem."

It's a problem, all right—he's screwing with my head, and I don't like it.

"You and she are so very much alike—"

I don't think so; I didn't try to kill myself—twice, yet.

"She's just a little girl."

Please, spare me the melodrama.

Lizzie is a virgin because she doesn't know any better—she's in high school, for God's sake.

Once "the virgin" figures out how it works, she'll be screwing every guy in sight.

And when I tried calling collect—with Jeff's permission yet—he refused the call. It had *better* be because of his parents.

"Damn, I feel rotten."

How does he think *I* feel?

"...after all the promises I made, I sure turn to jelly quick."

Jelly, my ass: "Jerk" is more like it.

"I hope you have a tolerant nature."

We'll see.

A LOUSY DAY ALL AROUND: my old man is about to dump me, and CBS canceled *The Smothers Brothers Comedy Hour*.

Too controversial, they said.

Jerks. *Someone* has to tackle topics like the Vietnam war, flower power, and racism.

Those network censors are *so* out of it.

TUESDAY, MARCH 11

I MEET A NEW FRIEND today—it's kind of cold, a cruddy day, but I have to get out of that stuffy building and take a walk, get away from Carrie and her wild stories. Try not to think about Joyce and her suicide chant.

Clear my head, figure out this thing with Jeff and his sudden feelings for that Lizzie chick.

I *will* go mad if I don't go out and kick some snow banks.

A middle-aged guy, carrying some two by fours, is tromping through a snow bank when he drops the boards, stumbles over them, flips, and then falls flat on his rear.

I run over to help. "You okay?" I assume he's part of the maintenance staff.

"No, no, I mean, yes, I'm okay."

"Let me help you." I grab his hand and help him up.

"Thank you." Very formal.

"You're not hurt?"

He laughs and brushes himself off. "Nope." He sticks out his hand. "I'm D.J."

He looks about 35, a big man but not fat, with dusky, reddish skin and slicked shiny black hair, blue eyes, and thick lips. He wears a red knitted winter cap with ear flaps. No mittens or gloves.

I take his hand. "I'm Jennifer." D.J. has the biggest hands I have ever seen, broad like paddles, with long thick fingers. His handshake is tentative, respectful.

He wears no winter coat, but he's obviously layered in several shirts, the top one a gray flannel. A matching scarf wrapped around his neck. He's clad in brand new overalls and old rubber boots, the kind with those lattice metal buckles we all wore as kids. He looks a bit unsteady on his feet.

"You sure you're okay?"

"Yeah, I'm always tripping over my own feet. I got a little bit of palsy." Then he says, with a bit of a stutter. "I'm-m re-*tard*-ed."

"I see." I help him pick up his boards and walk with him to a maintenance shed, just to make sure he's really okay. We rap–mostly, *he* raps–all the way to the shed.

D.J.'s kinda cool, and he's only slightly retarded–if he hadn't told me, I would've just thought a little slow. He works on the grounds, but he's also a patient.

He's been here for 26 years, since he was 17!

Oh-my-god! I can't even imagine being here when I'm 43.

I'll be an old lady, one foot in the grave.

But D.J. seems happy. When I asked him, "Don't you want to split this joint?"

He shrugged. "Not really," he said. "I been here almost all my life. I got a job, my own room, and three meals a day."

"But what about your freedom?"

"To do what?"

"Well, you could get an apartment, a job on the outside, an old lady–"

He shook his head violently. "Naw, no, I don't think so. See, I don't add and subtract too good, and I can't read or write none too good either."

"You like it here?"

"I dunno. It's all right, I suppose. I don't know any different."

I hadn't considered the possibility that someone would actually *want* to stay.

Maybe that's what happen when you get stuck in the system and can't get out.

WEDNESDAY, MARCH 12

I'VE STARTED SMOKING AGAIN, like chain smoking–my nerves are shot; this Lizzie thing has really thrown me off balance, like she came out of nowhere.

I'm playing it cool, not push things too hard–see what happens.

But his March 8 letter barely mentions Lizzie. He sounds like the old Jeff again; I'm not sure what to think.

I'm not the type of chick with a melodramatic air about lost love; we *were* friends in Hollywood, and who says our relationship must be all or nothing? I told Jeff we could be just friends, but, to be honest, it would smart to see him in love with someone else, especially a 17-year-old high school cock teaser.

Pam called Jeff last week; he says she's already written me.

I never received the letter. Pam's got a house in Arizona and will be moving there soon and has invited Jeff and me to come out next summer. The Crystal Ship is also moving to Arizona. The earthquake last spring is making a lot of people paranoid. Pam's been hanging around with Levi and can't get a job.

She mentions "big plans" for Jeff.

That worries me big time; sounds like it worries Jeff, too.

The *biggest* news: Stoney's back in L.A. My heart did a little flip; I never expected him to return to L.A. But I can't go back to him now; I'd never be happy with a drug addict. It's just as well I made the break, even if I didn't mean to.

Still, some nights I find myself thinking about him and the far out times we *did* have...

I'm making a complete break from my whole family; it's the only way. I can't go through life like that, and I *won't*. When Dee Dee writes and tells me that they "love" me very much, I just want to scream. If love on a hook is all they have to offer, then I want no part of it. It's a sadistic, mean love.

God help me. If I ever turn on my own kids like that, I'd rather die. My kids will have enough love, but not the smothering kind. If they want to go out into this world, like I do, and learn from their experiences, well, once they're 18, I'll show them the door. I can give them that one thing: the world to explore.

I promise this to my future children.

One thing for sure: I will *not* shove organized religion down their throats.

I like Jeff's view: "Religion is pretty cool, in a way–it gives a person a sense of belonging–although I don't take the Bible literally; if you pay attention to the basic philosophy, that book is *heavy*. Christ must have been the greatest person who ever lived...it's a pity he's been misrepresented over the years. (Kill a Commie for Christ!)."

Cool!

I'M GOING TO SEND the Melanie painting to Jeff, but I have to wait until it dries. People here say it looks like me. The only thing, Melanie has brown eyes and I don't, but the painting could represent me–that innocent part that attracts Jeff.

My next painting will be a monochromatic–Prussian or midnight blue will be my base color. When I first got here, I was too freaked to paint, so I started to string some love beads–blah. I don't know how someone could string beads, day in and day out. I love to paint, especially when a painting is going well, but when I hit a snag, I just want to throw the oils, canvas, and brushes out the window.

Temperamental.

Jeff draws comic books; that is *so* cool–I wish I had that kind of talent–I have trouble sketching. He is gifted in so many ways.

He promised to send a picture of his whole family; he has three brothers and a sister and two dogs, one named Popeye– he has one brown eye and one blue. Must look very strange. They also have a guinea pig and four gerbils.

I hope his mother comes around to our side, but she's adamantly opposed to our living together. How can I convince her that I'm no monster out to ruin her son when my own family hates me?

YESTERDAY, PENNY, CARRIE, AND I sneaked into one of the interview rooms and held our own Group Therapy sessions; each of us did a pantomime of the doctors we dislike. I did Dr. Droopy Drawers, a bit difficult since he's bald and has a watermelon belly and balloony pants. A nurse walked in and asked what was going on.

"Group Therapy," Carrie said.

The nurse wasn't too happy and told us to conduct our sessions in the rec room.

We were just cutting up.

I've lost some weight–the food is loathsome. Rotten lunch of liver and onions. I *hate* liver–it seems to be standard institutional fare, though. The Dorm served liver at least three times a week, but they tried disguising it as various dishes, such as Swiss steak.

Who were they kidding? I can smell liver at least a mile away.

Jeff digs that I compared him to Rhett Butler because he has always liked Clark Gable. I don't remind him of Scarlett O'Hara at all–she's on too much of an ego trip, a first-class bitch–and I'm the kind of person who avoids trouble, even willing to give in to minor details, but I won't sacrifice freedom for security.

Thursday, March 13

I sat up half the night, writing letters, chain smoking, and watching TV. I wrote letters to Jeff and Pam, but nothing seemed to help.

I was so tired I overslept, and I missed O.T.–again. I hope I don't get put on report.

The rest of my novel came in the mail today, but I can't seem to weave things together. Writing about L.A. is difficult, even when it's fiction; it doesn't feel real to me any more– almost like a circus where all the humans are really animals in disguise.

I'm not getting Pam's letters–Jeff says she's been writing me. Maybe she's still using Aunt Colleen's address.

Might as well throw them in the gutter.

I asked Pam to send her letters in care of Jeff, and then he could stash them in with his letters to me. Maybe that will work.

I heard from Aunt Julie today. She wrote me a very nice letter, sympathizing with me about Mo and Dee Dee.

Maybe I don't have to write off my entire family, after all.

Mo and Dee are upset with Dr. Favis, because he told Dee Dee that they need to back off.

I hope to be out of here in a week or so.

I WORE MY NEW LILAC DRESS to the dance tonight—I bought it just before I was stuck in this place. It's rather low cut; this creep (not Wolfie—I won't let him get near me), kept trying to look down my chest. I pushed him away.

So many perverts in here!

FRIDAY, MARCH 14

I HEARD FROM PAM TODAY—she seems depressed. She realizes her head's in a bad place. I let her know that a lot of people care about her. I'll write her more often, help keep her spirits high. She deserves a lot more than guys like Levi or Stoney. I'm glad she's decided not to live with Levi because he's *not* good boyfriend material—he's okay for a friend, but he doesn't respect women.

Just after Stoney left, Levi and I had a long rap session about relationships; he said he wasn't about to settle down with anyone. He's more interested in how many chicks he can ball—he told me this himself—than in developing a lasting relationship with Pam.

Pam must feel very alone right now, scared that she's flipping. She hinted that she may be putting down; I hope so and that she will stick with it. We became very close at the Dorm—she even warned me not to live with Stoney because he was big trouble.

She's going to ask her sister about going someplace—I hope she doesn't mean the shrink house. She's not mentally ill, just mixed up.

I just don't want Pam to become like Joyce, who's sinking fast again; this morning, on the way to breakfast, I heard her chanting–in that tiny voice of hers–

> One, *pills;* two, *rope;* three, *gun;* four, *knife;* five, *drowning;* six, *car crash;* seven, *smothering;* eight, *jumping;* nine, *poison;* ten, *strangling...*

I tried talking to her, but she shook her head and waved me away.

She'll be heading to the shock room soon.

Pam doesn't need that, especially if she puts down now.

She'll be so surprised how fast her head will clear–mine did. I hated that foggy, unreal feeling when Pam and I were whooping it up so heavily. It's ironic; during all those months of use, I never realized what a prisoner I was to all those drugs. In a way, I'm freer now than I ever was, even though I'm physically locked up–no grandparents or cops on my heels. I can take a deep breath, think about my future, and not worry about paranoid episodes.

For now, safe.

Speaking of Stoney, Pam did say he asked about me, wondered what happened. I never thought about how my disappearing from his life might, in a way, affect *him*. I just assumed he'd just shrug it off and move on to another girl. Come to think of it, Pam didn't have a lot to offer about Stoney and his current activities, so maybe he *has* moved on...

...I can't think too hard about what Stoney's doing–

I have a *new* life now.

THE NEWS OUT OF VIETNAM looks pretty grim. *Time* magazine says that last month, the first week of Tet, over 450 of our soldiers were killed.

God. That's more than the size of my entire high school class.

I can't help but think about Peter and all my guy friends

still there.

When is all this slaughter going to stop?

I SKIPPED O.T. again today. It's not that important anyway, since I'll be released next week. Instead, I wrote to Pam and Jeff–much more important than dabbling in some dumb painting.

"I'd be lying if I said I'd jump for joy if you chose Lizzie," I wrote to Jeff. "But I'll live, and once I'd adjust, I'd be very happy for you."

You know what? It's true!

74

March 15-17, 1969

(Cherokee)

SATURDAY, MARCH 15

Dr. Favis made an appointment for me to see some lady for rehabilitation.

She told me that since I was in here courtesy of the state, I'm eligible for financial help, like if I wanted to go to Pennsylvania, they'd give me money to go, *but* because I'm under 21, my legal guardians would have to sign for permission. Right. That would go over big. Never in a million years. So I'm back where I started.

Joyce is bugging me in undefinable ways; she seems to hover all the time. Everywhere I look, there she is, a shadow. She doesn't *say* anything, she just *is*. Maybe it's me.

Carrie says that Joyce's last treatment didn't quite work the way it should have, and, it's true, she seems to be suspended in a state between just weird and suicidal. I just wish she'd hover somewhere else, like on locked ward.

It's really strange, but I have seen Joyce in both manic and depressive states, and it's almost like she's two different people. The depressed Joyce slumps and drags her feet along the carpet—which actually crackles from the static of her slippers. Her belly puffs out, making her look at least 30 pounds heavier. She wears polyester pants and striped tops, the kind old ladies wear. Her eyes are a dull gray, almost hazel. Her hair is straight and uncombed, and she wears no makeup. She looks about 50 and acts 80.

But when she's manic, she curls her hair, and it seems to cascade all around her shoulders. She applies makeup, lots of it, pancake powder, rouge, bright red lipstick (which went out about 1962), and thick eyeliner, mascara, and eye shadow. Her eyes are sapphire, an eye color I have never seen before. She sucks in her gut and slips into bright red, low-cut slinky satin tops—no bra—skin tight black leotard pants, and pink ballet slippers—she looks positively slender. Then she leaps all around the ward, like a ballet dancer—she seems to walk on air—singing old songs from the late 1950's, like Patsy Cline's "Crazy." She's not very good at it, but you can't help get caught up in her exuberance. She looks about 21 and acts 15.

I've never seen anything like that before.

But, today, she's neither, nor. She's kind of stuck in some strange foggy middle ground. You would think that would be called "normal," but it's not. Maybe normal doesn't actually exist in her bag of mood shifts.

Joyce seems to be more like a specter caught between finite life and the infinite hereafter.

To escape Joyce, I go to Donohoe to shoot baskets and then go for a walk and see D.J. again. I only ever see him when I'm outside, walking the grounds, never in the dining room or at any of the events.

When I ask him why he never goes to the social events, he says, "I'm too shy."

A LOT OF OTHER LITTLE THINGS are bugging me today: I'm still trying to figure out where Pam's head is at; her letter is still getting to me. She didn't say exactly what her problem is, but I suspect it's something serious. She should know by now that she can tell me anything. Pam's like a little sister to me.

Also, that 16-year-old boy is beginning to get on my

nerves—he follows me around everywhere. Like today. I just wanted to shoot some baskets at and listen to some music at Donohoe, and there he was, my shadow. I'd like to tell him to get lost, but I feel somehow responsible for him. Maybe I'll ask Dr. Favis what to do; I'd feel rotten if he flipped out because of me.

I feel sorry for him, but I can't dig him.

While I was at Donohoe and out for my walk, Joyce was put into isolation—when I left, I knew she was on the edge of something, but am I glad I didn't have to witness it. I don't know what happened during her last shock treatment, but Carrie heard that she freaked out when she woke up—evidently, she has these horrible, pounding migraines. Maybe they gave her too much juice, though I would think they could regulate that very carefully.

Why can't they find another way of treating someone like Joyce?

Maybe I'll take another short walk to clear my head and lungs—this place is nuts, literally.

ON MY SECOND WALK, I meet up with D.J. again; I swear he must live outside.

I tell him he should go to the dance tonight, but he just shakes his head violently. "Too many people."

I can't imagine isolating myself like that. Scary to think that I might be D.J.'s only friend.

"I went to a dance once, when I first got here," he says. "Some boys called me 're-TARD-do,' and boxed me into a corner."

Some guys are *so* immature, picking on someone like D.J., who's about as sweet as they come. "Didn't the attendants do anything?"

When Wolfie danced me into the corner, they were on him like a fly on shit.

"Naw, they just laughed."

Man, this place must've really sucked back then. "It's probably different now. You might have fun."

He shakes his head, so I let it drop.

"How did you get in here, anyway?"

"My mother told me I had to live here."

"Oh." How must he feel, being rejected by his own mother?

"My dad left when I was five. Said he didn't want to live with no retard. Mom tried her best, but when I turned 17, she got sick. I had to go to court."

"Yeah, I know all about that."

"You had to go to court?"

"Oh, yeah."

"Are you retarded, too?"

I laugh. "Just stupid."

His face brightens. "My mom visited me every week, but then she died."

"I'm sorry."

"It's okay. It was a long time ago. But she's still right here," he says, his hand over his heart.

"You have a good attitude, D.J."

"Do you get visitors?"

I picture Mo and Dee Dee driving to Cherokee, via icy back roads, only to be turned away. "A few. All my friends live far away."

"I don't get visitors no more," he says.

"Oh, D.J."

"But it's okay." He outstretches his arms and twirls around. "*This* is my family now."

I can't even imagine it.

AT THE DANCE TONIGHT, I met a guy who's in here for possession of uppers and weed. Can't remember his name, though. The court gave him a choice: jail or the locked ward in the shrink house. Of course he chose here; this may not be the Taj Mahal, but at least he's not among all those creepy felons, like murderers and rapists—well, maybe around rapists.

I asked him what it was like being cooped up with Wolfie.

"That's one spooky dude," he said.

I warned him to watch his back, but he said that Wolfie spends most of his time in isolation.

Isolation or not, he'd better watch Wolfie.

I doubt if any kind of bar or locked door could hold that psycho for long.

This new guy has never been in L.A., but he's been in Denver and Boston, got busted here in Iowa for holding a bottle of uppers and just under a kilo of weed. He wants me to tell all about the L.A. scene, but I doubt if he'll see the light of day for a very long time; his lawyer says he might end up here or jail for up to 20 years—maybe more if they think he's been dealing! Still, it's kind of cool knowing someone who knows the scene so well.

SUNDAY, MARCH 16

NO MAIL. It seems that every day I don't get mail is another eternity spent in Hell, in boredom. I sort of fold up on Sundays and wait for Monday.

I *hate* Sundays, but, for an Iowa winter day, it is rather nice outside—at least it's sunny—so I may go for a walk. I woke up late, as usual, missed breakfast; the nurses have pretty much given up molding me into a morning person. I guess they figure it doesn't matter, anyway. I went down to the canteen to buy cigarettes and to rap about nothing much to anyone who would listen. Headed for lunch: overcooked roast beef and gravy with sage dressing, mashed potatoes, and peach pie for dessert. Tried not to eat like a pig. Still coming down with something.

After lunch, I read *The Sioux City Journal*—that March 6 hijacking was done by a Black Panther wanting to escape to

Cuba—scary after that one a few months ago. I don't know what's going on in the world, with all these radicals hijacking airplanes. Someday, people are going to die if this crap isn't stopped. We live in a strange, crazy world, where people are willing to risk the lives of innocent people, and for what? A one-way trip to Cuba?

The current news is almost always bad, so I switched to the comics and society page—Tricia had a baby girl! Maybe that's what she wanted to tell me when she called and Mo wouldn't allow her to get in touch with me. I'll bet she wanted to send me a baby announcement! Damn that old witch! My old high school friends are all getting hitched—Susie or Isabelle might be next—or having kids.

Except Joanie. I haven't seen Joanie in ages—she's in college.

A brainy girl.

ON MY WALK, I look for D.J. He'll be out and about today for sure—it's so nice and sunny, even though the ground is snow-covered. But if you sniff hard enough, you can smell a hint of spring, though you can't let down your guard—not in Iowa, anyway.

Anything can happen in the next month.

Sure enough, I see him halfway down the hill, putting down some mulch around a fir tree, where he has cleared away the snow.

"Isn't it a bit early for gardening?" I ask.

"Naw, mulching don't do no harm."

"But won't you have to do it again after the snow melts?"

They're predicting record floods for April once this snow starts melting, and I would think that the mulch would run off with the water.

"Just a touch up."

No wonder they love D.J.—he works like a horse and keeps at it, no matter what. I don't understand it, this drive of his. I could understand if he were writing a novel, painting a masterpiece, or creating a symphony, but mulching?

"I love being out here," he says, as if reading my mind. "I live for the outdoors. If you listen carefully, the trees and the plants will talk to you."

"What do they say?"

"All kinds of things. They're like people: they love and hate, they complain about stuff, mostly the weather and sometimes humans, too. Most people don't pay no attention to them, and that hurts their feelings. Like us, they just want to be noticed."

He may not be book smart, but he's sure in tune with his surroundings.

I nod toward the fir tree. "What's it saying to you now?"

He laughs. "He's still kinda sleepy–sap's a bit slow, but he likes what I'm doing with the mulch. Makes him feel all warm inside."

"Why do you call it 'he'?"

D.J. shrugs. "He told me so. There're girl trees, too." D.J. pauses and spreads some more mulch. "He's had a hard year–almost didn't pull through winter, which is why I'm giving him extra special care. I always start with the sick trees first."

I'm touched by his kindness and sensitivity; when I think of all the Hollywood assholes passing through my life, someone like D.J. is a refreshing change. He wants nothing from me: not sex, not money, not material goods–just my friendship and understanding.

Jeff, too, looks at the world from a different angle. He, of course, doesn't have D.J.'s innocence, nor does D.J. have Jeff's brilliant mind, but they could almost be brothers.

I wish I could do something for D.J., but, from what I can see, he has everything he needs right here.

Monday, March 17

What a wild weekend.

Anna, a chick who was admitted shortly after me, and her boyfriend Benito, took off from the hospital on Saturday. I knew that they were planning an escape, but I didn't say anything to the staff. I figure it was their bag–they would have to suffer the consequences, whatever that might be. Also, even after Anna told me about their plan, her daring escape still surprised me; of all the people I have met in here, Anna seemed the most together and the least likely to pull off such a bold stunt. She's smart, a natural leader, always reading the great books, and always very carefully groomed, unlike the rest of us who slouch around like bums. She's not a pretty girl, at least in the traditional sense. She's tall and raw-boned, swarthy complexion, but almost sapphire eyes. She has short black hair, but with a hint of gray–although she's only 19–and it's styled in early Beatles mop top, pudding bowl. She exudes a mannish quality, both in the way she dresses in golf shirts and slacks that look like they're part of a man's dress suit, and her mannerisms, especially her strident gait, like a business man on the way to an important meeting.

Goes to show that appearances aren't always what they seem.

But, alas, Anna and Benito got caught on Sunday–they didn't even get to the state line–and dragged back by the police and thrown into locked ward (separate, of course). God, they'll be there *forever*. They might even go to jail.

Makes me think twice about running off into the night–no money, no extra clothes.

Carrie cut herself again and showed me the gash–it wasn't very deep, but I had to tell the staff because she's threatened to cut deeper next time. I think she wanted me to snitch; she digs the attention.

Well, she got it; they moved her back to the locked ward. I want to slowly disengage from Carrie—she depresses me with her strange stories of rats and snakes.

There's weird and then there's psycho. She's just too psycho for my taste.

Maybe I'll be out of here before she's moved back to Ward 4.

Mostly, I hang around with Penny; I'll never understand why she's in here. She's just a kid who got a tough break, and the system didn't know what to do, so they committed her. I'll never understand Iowa laws, and why the father of her baby wasn't thrown in the slammer after he took her and ran off to Puerto Rico—especially when she came back pregnant.

Yeah, it was the 11-year-old girl's fault.

And I was under the distinct impression that it's against the law to cross state lines with minors without parental consent. I certainly couldn't escape Iowa, and I'm not a minor.

Even after all the shit she has endured, Penny remains cheerful and optimistic about her life, although there's a wistfulness about her when she talks about her child, always showing his picture around. "He was taken away from me," she says from time to time. "They didn't even ask me what *I* wanted. They just gave him away. But when I go home, I get to visit him."

Pathetic.

The rumor mill: there's mescaline flying around here. I haven't seen it and don't want to. The most we have ever done in here was paint finger nail polish on our cigarettes for a mini high. I don't think that's illegal. Anyway, I expect to get out in about a week, and I don't want to be associated with anything that could get in the way of my being discharged—especially dope.

Also, I heard that Joyce will be released soon, though I don't know why; she's still in locked ward after that flip-out episode. God, I can't believe that they'd even *consider* discharging her yet, but her husband had signed her in, and now, from what Carrie says—how does she know all this stuff, anyway?—he can sign her out, even if the doctors recommend against it. Joyce told Carrie—they both seem to be in lock-up a lot these days—that he wants her out because the kids are running wild and need their mother.

Yeah, I can see how that'll work out, with Joyce freaking out or chanting her suicide list to the kiddies.

What a fucked-up world—Joyce free as a bird and I still locked up like a felon.

I still have my doubts about my discharge any time soon. They still haven't found me a place—I don't think they're looking too hard. For now, unless I'm willing to move back in with Mo and Dee, I have to stay here.

I'll stay here.

I CAN'T STAND WHEN VISITORS come to gawk at us; I don't mean people who come to visit specific patients, but those mucky-mucks who come to stare at us and take pictures, and shake their heads at the plight of the crazy people. They have no idea what it means to be locked up against your will, even in a place that's somewhat comfortable.

It's just the idea of being locked up, period.

Today, six of us went on a walk outside, and we ran into some politicians and ministers. We decided to give our sane visitors a show, show 'em how the crazy people live. We sang, "Roll Me Over, in the Clover" and "99 Bottles" at the top of our lungs.

I dropped into the snow and flailed around like someone having an epileptic fit or in some kind of religious rapture.

75

Intruders

August 30, 2004

(Cherokee)

WILL I BE ALLOWED to take pictures?

The only way to know without asking: just start snapping.

I feel like an intruder, and, in a sense, I am, and, yet, I *am* entitled to recapture some of my past through photographs.

I also respect the privacy of current patients. I remember only too well when sanctioned visitors mobbed the grounds to observe us, the crazy people:

> *On cue, we thrash around in the snow.*
> *Those gawkers want a good show?*
> *Then we'll give it to them, work ourselves into a frenzy—*
> *Like the Jesus freaks on the Sunset Strip.*

A chill runs through me. I'll just photograph the buildings and grounds, to make some sense of that time and jar loose some of those murky memories.

Memories of other patients who became intense, albeit temporary, allies...

In another place, another time, we might not even acknowledge each other, but, for now, we're united in protecting our merry band of looneys from the true scrutiny of the Establishment: ministers, doctors, teachers, politicians, police matrons—the very creeps responsible for sending us here...

We ratchet up our performance; we thrash around in snow drifts, broken snow angels kicking up powdery snow in all directions.

As the gawkers drift away, we still thrash around, but it feels real now, almost like the pure rapture experienced by Rev. Blessitt's Jesus freaks at His Place, the famous hippie church on Sunset Boulevard.

I saw with my own eyes the Reverend's converts working themselves into a frenzy.

76

His Place: A Toilet Service
October 1968

(Hollywood)

Jeff, Eleanor, Pam, and I were hanging out at Wallich's, though not much happening.

Eleanor met up with Jim, her new guy, and split.

Before Pam, Eleanor and I had been getting close, but now we seemed to be pulling away. Maybe it was because she was still in high school. True, she had all this freedom to come and go as she pleased and did drugs on weekends, but she still had to go to school and do her homework, so we didn't do as much together anymore.

When we were roommates, I had to be quiet on week nights.

I also found out that Eleanor wasn't supposed to do drugs on school nights, only on weekends; her dad came down hard on her when he discovered she was dropping acid on weekdays.

Rick, who stood me up the previous night, showed up.

My heart skipped a beat.

"Sorry about last night."

I tried to act nonchalant. "It's cool."

Rick eyed Jeff up and down and threw his arm around my waist.

"Hey," Pam said. "Let's go to His Place."

"What's that?" Jeff asked.

"It's this really cool church on the strip, filled with freaks," I said.

"I don't want to go to church," Rick said.

"It's not an ordinary church," I said. "You'll just have to see it to believe it."

"I heard someone spiked the Kool-Aid with acid one night," Pam said.

"Groovy! Getting high for Christ!" Jeff said.

"Over a hundred kids were stoned out of their gourds. Must've freaked out Rev. Blessitt."

"Gives Jesus freaks a whole new meaning," I said. "I can't even imagine being around 100 acid heads. In church, yet."

"Good thing the pigs didn't get wind of it," Rick said.

"Funny thing. The cops weren't even around that night. How lucky was that?" Pam said.

"I still don't wanna go," Rick said.

"Come on, it's really far out, and they serve food," I said, suddenly starved. I couldn't eat the gruel served at the dorm: Fish sticks and overcooked broccoli.

"Bagels and sandwiches, Kool-Aid—"we all snickered "—and coffee."

"I *am* hungry," Rick said.

WHEN WE ARRIVED at His Place, a toilet service had just begun. Rev. Blessitt read from the Bible, "Therefore, if any man be in Christ, he is a new creation; old things are passed away; behold, all things are become new" [2 Corinthians 5:17]. A few heads witnessed in the john as they tossed their dope into the toilet and sang,

> *Down, down, down, down,/ All my dope is gone./*
> *Down, down, down, down,/ All my dope is gone.*

I fished around in my pocket; I still had that Blue Cheer from Rudy's party two weeks ago–no way was I going to dump it down the toilet and watch it swirl away.

After the service ended, we dug in and ate bagels smothered with peanut butter and jelly.

We hung around for a bit.

I don't buy into the religious bit, but I can't help it: I like Rev. Blessitt. He believes in what he does, not just going through the motions, like some of those priests back home. The Reverend puts his ass on the line every day, and the Establishment kicks it daily, especially the religious Establishment.

What hypocrites.

You'd think they'd want to help Rev. Blessitt in his mission. But they can't see past the run-down church on the strip, the long hair, and the dope.

Still, there was something creepy about ex-heads taking up Jesus in place of acid.

The worst converts in the world, always shoving tracts and Bible verses in your face, the "Eithers/Ors," the black and whites–you're either for Christ or against him, no room for doubt.

If I wanted to be told what to believe, I'd still be going to Mass.

77

Shadows

August 30, 2004

(Cherokee)

We laugh our asses off, ecstatic we have sent those gawkers off to a sleepless night, filled with visions of our godless rapture, just like Rev. Blessitt's disciples...

I SHAKE OFF THE MEMORY of broken snow angels, other patients, my cohorts in harmless hijinks, and resume snapping several shots of the buildings and grounds.

I no longer remember what room or even floor I resided, only that the ward common area faced the front parking lot, and my room faced the back; I don't remember a window, but it didn't matter. I didn't stay in my room much, and my roommate, a depressed woman whose name I don't remember, did.

No one stops me from taking pictures—as I wander, the unfamiliar focuses into the familiar.

Donohoe! Yes, the patient social events took place here, starting after dinner and ending by 8:00 or 8:30 because most of the patients were medicated with archaic psychiatric drugs that also zonked them. Men and women were allowed to mix only during meals, social events, or on outdoor excursions. Donohoe, where I met Drew, a young man about my age, caught with a small amount of illegal drugs (but suspected of dealing), and where Wolfie, a psychopath, danced me into a corner. I never did find out what Wolfie had done, but I'm convinced he had done something horrendous–rape and murder, perhaps. Although we were never informed about the history of the other patients, we intermingled with them.

I never enjoyed the social events much, but they were all we had as entertainment; I needed to socialize, yearned for human interaction in a way that I had never before or since. If I were to be admitted now, I would probably be happy on my own–that is, if I had a computer, internet connection, and printer–and look upon the time as a writing opportunity–a twisted writer's residency, with psychological therapy as a minor nuisance. But, as a young patient, I was more interested in the opposite sex, popular music, clothes, and willing to grab whatever scraps I could, even cheesy dances sponsored by the mental institution.

After wandering the grounds, Jerry suggests we go inside the main building.

I'm not sure–something visceral holds me back; my gut tightens and panic sticks in my throat.

"They're not going to snatch you away," Jerry says. "The worst that'll happen is they'll toss you out."

We climb the steps beneath the portico and enter the building–a long, wide dreary corridor, yellow and old, with frosted glass doors on either side, greeting us. More memory surfaces–being led by Deputy George Grimesey of Woodbury County to an intake room.

The smell! A combination of ammonia, old dust, wax, and floor compound, and something medicinal, like a dentist's office or hospital room. To our left, a door leading to the receptionist. We enter, and I introduce myself to a young lady behind a glass barrier. I tell a short version of my story, as if a summary of my past could gain temporary entry into this place, but not enough of my story to land me here indefinitely. I still harbor phobias about being taken away against my will, although I trust my husband and the two powerful Supreme Court decisions protecting people from involuntary commitment.

I ask if I may wander a bit.

"You may go as far as the sundial," the receptionist says.

78

March 17-21, 1969

(Cherokee)

MONDAY, MARCH 17, 1969

We crank up our performance, thrashing around in snow drifts, fervent snow angels kicking up powdery snow in all directions.

After the gawkers have drifted away, we still thrash around, but now it feels real...

I'LL BET THOSE PILLARS of society will have something to talk about when they get home tonight.

ANDREW IS THE GUY who got busted for dope, Drew, for short. We've been rapping quite a bit–that is, when I can see him. It seems like the hospital is restricting our visits. I don't know why; we're only friends–maybe they think we're passing mescaline back and forth, but we're not.

Too much at stake for both of us.

They keep Drew on the locked ward, where he's being held until his upcoming trial. He's allowed two visits to the canteen per week, and he can attend the socials, but that's all. Wow! That could be Jeff or me. We're *so* lucky! I'm glad that Jeff never got involved in dealing.

I hate the U.S. Post Office; it's too slow. Jeff and I seem to be at cross-purposes and have to wait two or three days to get our questions answered. It's like we're totally out of sync with each other. There's got to be a better way!

Tuesday, March 18

Finally! I got to talk to Jeff; he's landed a real job! At a flour mill.

Things are finally looking up for us—now I just have to get out of here...

This place is really strange. I had the money to talk for 10 minutes, but the hospital said only five minutes, no compromise. I'm not sure why they were so inflexible—since it was *my* bread, not theirs, on the line—but, still, it was the best five minutes in the world, just to hear Jeff's voice, the happy vibes he emitted. He said to watch for his next letter, that it will cheer me up.

Jeff thinks Pam doesn't have a thing for him, but I wonder. She's been very mysterious lately, hinting around about all kinds of changes in her life, but never really revealing anything. He thinks she, for now, has too many hang-ups to love anyone.

Mo and Dee Dee have been dormant lately—are they up to something nasty?

Mo accused Jeff of threatening to knock her teeth down her throat. He's just not that way—he's gentle and sensitive; I doubt very much if he would ever do harm to a living creature, even Mo, who probably deserves it. I believe Jeff over Mo. I have caught both Mo and Dee in too many other lies.

I'm going to ask Dr. Favis what I can do for legal help; I'd better be prepared for the worst. I don't have the money for a lawyer, so I'm not sure how I can protect myself. I can only hope that Mo and Dee will come to their senses.

The flashbacks are getting worse; I feel so helpless when they just pop up. It's like having a nosy aunt coming to visit, and she's the last person in the world you'd want to stop by unannounced. A friend here knows someone who can give me some Thorazine, to help bring me down, but I don't want to mess with *any* kind of drug, legal or illegal–especially illegal. Too scary. If I get caught with a non-prescribed drug, I'll *never* get out of here–they might as well throw me into the rubber room with Carrie. I used to believe acid offered insights and opportunities for self-discovery, but that's just a myth. Maybe in controlled circumstances, a shrink close by and the right setting–even then, it's risky.

In his March 13 letter, Jeff complained of profound loneliness. I'm lonely, too, maybe not in the hot sexual way that Jeff describes, but I long to snuggle up against the warm body of the man I love, and hug and talk and giggle–make plans for the future. Pen and paper can only impart so much emotion. My letters are so dull and flat; I'm not sure how Jeff can draw any emotion from them, although he says he looks forward to reading them. Still, he's impatient about waiting two more months for my journey to Pennsylvania.

I'm doing the best I can. If I could slip out the door and know that it'd be okay, I'd split tomorrow.

WEDNESDAY, MARCH 19

I REALLY BLEW MY COOL today. Mo and Dee Dee came to see me; I told Dr. Favis: flat out no.

But as I rushed out of Mr. Benson's office, I ran smack into Mo.

"I want to talk to you," she said in that sarcastic way of hers.

"I don't want to talk to you!"

"I have your income tax form and W-2's!"

"Give them to Mr. Benson, but leave me alone!" Crying, I ran back to the ward.

Evidently, Mo and Dee showed Mr. Benson a letter that

Jeff had written to me and one to them.

I didn't even know he had written to them.

"I think your Jeff sounds like a pretty great guy," Mr. Benson said, "and not all that obscene." Benson got them to promise to leave me alone and that he'd make sure they stick to it.

I don't have much faith in anyone these days, though.

Mr. Benson says I have to stay in a foster home for at least two months, maybe even six months, before I can go to Pennsylvania; if I run off before I prove myself, they'll just drag me back and re-admit me.

"If you and Jeff are meant to be together, he'll wait for you," Benson said.

Good point.

But I wish they'd hurry up and find me a good foster home so that the clock could start ticking.

Mr. Benson's a trip; he's only 25, but acts much older. He's so calm, which pisses me off. He's never smoked grass. "That's not my bag," he said. "It's too dangerous."

What a rube.

I got upset today and yelled at him.

"Now, now, Jennifer, we're going to help you," he said. "Please get hold of yourself. I know this place is getting to you. You've been here too long, anyway. But please be patient."

They'd better hurry. I'm getting tired of that green carpet in the ward; I keep seeing patterns and flashing back. I'm climbing the walls.

I FILLED OUT the tax form and sent it in; I'm getting a $116.41 refund back from Uncle Sam! Add that to the $50.00 from the bank, plus the $50.00 I have here. If I had all my money right now, I *could* leave this place and never look back.

THE FLASHBACKS are getting worse–last night, I just gave up and went to bed early. Felt better this morning. I asked Dr.

Favis about the possibility of taking Thorazine, just to eliminate the LSD from my body.

"You don't need it–you're handling the flashbacks very well," he said. "Besides, you're the one who wanted to avoid all drugs."

We agreed that I could do this without psychiatric drugs.

I LET PENNY READ Jeff's last letter, and she allowed me to read a letter from her boyfriend Larry; he's in jail–I don't know for what, and she won't say. His letters are really dull, not lively and filled with emotion like Jeff's.

Tonight, Penny, Carrie, and I performed some informal skits on the ward. I mimed how four types of chicks smoke a cigarette: the biker chick, hippie chick, social butterfly chick, and ordinary chick. Everyone howled.

Jeff sent me a picture of himself–I love it. He looks *so* hippie and cute!

THURSDAY, MARCH 20

AT THE DANCE tonight, Drew and I rapped for a long time; he's leaving for jail tomorrow. He doesn't seem optimistic about his chances of getting out any time soon. He could be in for as much as 20 years. Bummer.

Drew is very attractive, tall with brown eyes and light brown hair. Personality-wise, he's very much like Jeff–a Virgo, even, a few days younger than Jeff. Also, I get vibes that Drew has a thing for me, but I've managed to keep our relationship on a friendship level.

If Jeff and I ever broke up, Drew might be a logical replacement, although replacements are never as good as the real thing. Besides, Drew's going to the slammer for a very long time.

No mail today; last night, it rained and then froze over–the mail trucks couldn't get through. It has been rumored that only six letters (for the entire hospital) were delivered.

The snow is still deep; a bunch of us went out and played in it, and I stepped into a snow bank and sank all the way to my hips. The weatherman has predicted serious flooding this spring, what with all this snow.

Friday, March 21

Jeff's letter, the one he told me to watch for, arrived today. Wow! What a natural high. He sounds so happy–everything is finally coming together for us: job, money, his mother's begrudging acceptance of us.

Pam told Jeff I don't want her writing him anymore.

Huh? Where'd she get that idea?

I love Pam. Of course, I want her to write to Jeff. I'll write her and explain that I never meant to imply that she was supposed to cut all contact from him.

I'm going on a trial visit to Aunt Julie's, just for the weekend, from Saturday morning to Monday evening. I'm not going to do anything wild, but it'll be *so* groovy being able to come and go as I please without signing in and out.

Mo told Jeff's mom that I balled drug dealers for dope. Is she kidding?

I'm not about to freak out because of her lies. I just hope Mrs. Brown doesn't think I'm a whore.

Evidently, Mrs. Brown thinks Mo is responsible for her own misery.

I've told Dr. Favis and Mr. Benson I want Mo to quit writing the Browns. In fact, I asked Jeff to forward any letters from her to me, and I'll turn them over to Mr. Benson, who can take legal action. I don't *want* to take legal action against my own grandparents, but, if I have to, I will.

They don't dig Dr. Favis; they get belligerent and uptight

around him.

Were they surprised when they found out he's on my side, not theirs? Is the world now against *them*?

Jeff wants me to come to Pennsylvania around the middle of April; if they allow me a visit there, I'll just not return. It will cause a ruckus, but who cares?

I'M WORRIED about Carrie; for the past three or four days, she's been complaining of horrible chest pains. She told the attendant she wanted to see a nurse, but the nurse refused–said she was faking. So Carrie asked to see the night doctor; he refused. Although Carrie's a bit batty, I still like her, and I don't think she's faking this. It's just been going on too long. I kept after the attendants and nurses, and still they refused. Two nights ago, Carrie's pain was so bad I was scared to go to bed– that if I left her alone, she'd be dead by morning. So, I blew up at the R.N. and told her to get the damn doctor in here. They took her to the infirmary.

I don't know what's wrong with Carrie–she looked better when I visited her today–but even if her illness is in her head, it's better to err on the side of being wrong than sorry.

It's scary being at the mercy of the system–they can decide life and death matters, and there's not a damn thing you can do about it, other than make lots of noise.

I WANT TO SAY GOODBYE to D.J. before leaving on trial visit. I find him sitting on a bench, his head in his hands, crying.

"What's wrong?" I put my arms around his shoulders.

"All the hospital trees and plants are scared for their cousins off the hill."

"But, why?"

"The coming floods. Gonna be bad this year, kill lots of plants and trees in town and along The Little Sioux River."

"I'm so sorry, D.J. Maybe they'll be okay."

"They're helpless; they can't run and hide like us. They're stuck."

I wish there was a way I could console him. Instead, I have to tell him I'm leaving for the weekend and that if everything goes right, I might be gone until the beginning of April.

"All my friends leave, sooner or later," he says, sniffling.

79

The Sundial

August 30, 2004

(Cherokee)

THE SUNDIAL! As a patient not yet granted a ground card, I knew the sundial was the demarcation, the DMZ, the place where outside life began and stopped.

"May I take a picture of it?"

"No," says the girl at the desk, emphatically.

Obedient even now, I put my camera away, to show good faith.

As we near the sundial, the past crashes upon me in way that memory, documents, and old letters cannot.

I have heard that smell is the first sense to awaken and the last to exit our bodies as we die.

I'm transported to a time of old smells, dark, musky buildings and burnt dust, dry crackling heat, an acrid cleanliness, wax, overcooked cafeteria food, perhaps old newspapers.

It is now February 19, 1969, and I'm being led, against my will, to a room, where I will be photographed and interviewed. I'm confused and upset, and livid with my grandparents and all of Iowa for bringing me here. I hate Iowa, and all its hick town, hayseed connotations intact, and I vow to never return should I ever escape.

Why am I here?

Who the fuck do they think they are?

I'll get even for this!

I'll never speak to my grandparents, ever again, for setting this debacle into motion. After I'm free, I'll run away from Iowa, and the entire state can sink into a large vacuum, for all I care.

The anger boils over into something I thought I had forgotten—I have unforgiven my grandparents, long dead, the Woodbury County court system, the whole goddamned Establishment, an antiquated usage of a word, almost forgotten, springing from a deep well of late 1960's cultural history.

I want to escape, find the hippies, now also aged, some even dead, who have sheltered me and given me dope, partied with me, fucked and fucked with me. I'm no longer a 53-year-old woman seeking answers to a problematic past, but I'm there, reliving everything as I smelled and felt it back then.

Get-me-out-of-here!

80

March 22-31, 1969

(Sioux City)

SATURDAY, MARCH 22, 1969

THANK GOD I'M OUT of that place, if only temporarily, though I'm worried about D.J. He seemed so sad.

Julie is so cool to let me stay here–I just hope Mo doesn't bug her too much. I don't want to cause my aunt and uncle any trouble.

I JUST GOT OFF THE PHONE with Jeff. Julie let me talk as much as I wanted–well, as much as my pocketbook could stand; I have to save any money I can for Pennsylvania.

No nurse looking over my shoulder. Far out! What a fantastic rap session!

Jeff says I act tough and worldly to cover up my insecurities, not because I'm on an ego trip, but merely to survive. Yes, I was a street chick, but not tough–

"Jennifer, you don't belong on the street," Eleanor once told me, "and if you're looking for someone to love you, you won't find him here."

She was right about the first part, but I did find Jeff on the street.

Maybe it's because Jeff doesn't belong on the street, either.

Sunday, March 23

I WENT SHOPPING with Julie; we had an interesting discussion about Mo. Looks like she's ruffled everyone's feathers in this family.

Mo makes her rounds around town—everyone must know my business by now. I might as well take out a full-page ad in the *Sioux City Journal*, and announce,

NEWSFLASH!

Jennifer Semple's in the Shrink House!!!

Mo must really be pissed off now at Julie—she would rather see me rot in Hell than have anyone, especially family, on my side.

I get the funny feeling I'd like to stay here for a while, after I'm released for good. But I just couldn't do that; Mo would never leave Julie alone.

Besides, I'd have to promise Julie that I'd stay in Sioux City for six months, and I don't want to break that promise to her.

One of these days, if I'm to have Julie's respect, I'm going to have to tell her the truth about what happened in L.A. I'm not sure how much she already knows, but I'll bet she's only heard Mo's version.

How much will I tell Julie? Will I tell her that I dropped acid at least 10 times and that I enjoyed it? How can I ever explain the groovy times I had with acid without her thinking I'm being contradictory? That my decision to quit was made after I nearly jumped out of that window on New Year's Eve? Who knew it was only tear gas? I thought I was about to die...

Okay, so I wasn't on acid that night, just bennies, but, still...

Will I tell her about Stoney and our one month living together, and how he degenerated into a heroin and acid freak?

Will she think less of me if I reveal these facts?

Monday, March 24

Mo has found out about my trial visit. I think that police matron Opal Casey snitched on me. If never see that bitch again, it'll be too soon.

"I'll help you," the police matron said. Yeah, right into the nut house.

Mo keeps calling here and asking for me; I always refuse. Maybe she thinks I'll answer the phone, but I don't, just for that reason.

I haven't had one flashback since I've been here; I seem to get them only when I'm upset. Here, I find it easier to laugh things off.

"Cry, and the world laughs *at* you; laugh, and the world laughs *with* you."

Tuesday, March 25

I might get to stay another week! Julie's going to ask Uncle George, and if he and the hospital say yes, I'm in; otherwise, I leave tomorrow morning for the institution.

If I get an extra week, I'll go back April 2. By that time, I hope they will have found a place for me. Sooner or later, I'll have to go back to the institution to pick up my clothes and mail, but I need to build up my resistance once again.

Returning will feel like being committed all over again.

Wednesday, March 26

I'm in! I get another week here. Hooray!

Sometime this week, I'm going to help Julie paint the kitchen. It's good to feel needed, that I'm doing something other than sitting around on my butt, taking up space.

Mo invited me over for Easter dinner.

"Forget it." I'll find something else to entertain me. I felt like saying, "If Jeff can come too," but who needs to cause an unnecessary hassle? Besides, Easter is the sixth, and I'll be back at Cherokee by the second.

Courtesy of you-know-who.

I've decided that I won't tell Julie everything, just a need-to-know basis. I want to confide in her, but it might not be a good idea to spill every detail–some of it is pretty ugly.

Julie says I was probably so shy during my early days because of Mo. She has a way of talking to people that makes them feel inferior, below her–hard on a child, especially a sensitive one. Mo didn't really want me–I was a duty, which is probably why she didn't take Robin–someone else offered, and Mo and Dee were off the hook.

No one ever came right out and said, "We don't want you," but I felt it. I *was* a very lonely kid, but now, with Jeff, I feel wanted and loved. I may feel lonely *for* Jeff, but that's different from being alone because of no love at all.

It helps having Julie and my cousins around; they create a lot of noise and chaos.

They kill the silence.

I feel especially close to my cousin Steve; we fought sometimes, but as we grew older, we became pretty good friends; he's smart like Jeff–and sensitive, too, in a family that doesn't reward sensitivity as a virtue. He's going into the Air Force, and I just hope he doesn't end up in Vietnam, like Peter. Steve should be in college, not acting as cannon fodder overseas–he earned a perfect score on his college boards, surprising the entire family, because Steve has never been the kind of guy to brag about being brainy. He just quietly goes about his business. If he can stay out of Vietnam, he'll have a great future.

Thursday, March 27

I GO BACK TO THE INSTITUTION on Wednesday. I'm not looking forward to seeing that place again. I hope I get lots of letters from Jeff–then I won't mind so much. Also, maybe Benson will have found a place for me.

I talked it over with Julie, and we both agreed that it would not be a good idea for me to stay here. Under other circumstances, this would've been a perfect setup for me.

But I was honest and told her that I plan to split Iowa as soon as possible. How could I lie to the only person in this nutty family who has listened and tried to understand my point of view?

Julie says she won't say anything to Mo and Dee–she'll just turn a blind eye.

And when I split, it will be from another foster home.

Then maybe Mo will leave Julie alone.

Friday, March 28

MY COUSIN PAT tells me I'm strange.

He's still in high school–so what does he know, anyway?

"I *like* being strange," I say.

He just shakes his head and walks away.

Why on earth would anyone *ever* want to be ordinary? I see people, unhappy, going about their work-a-day lives, only to retire when they are old and cranky like Mo and Dee. Why not be able to retire now, when we can actually enjoy it?

I do miss the scene, except for the drugs; maybe that's unrealistic–isn't the scene all about drugs?

It was fun while it lasted, even at the end when things got freaky with Stoney and his friends. And that thing with Rudy...

My favorite memory: dancing wildly and singing to "Love Street" with Jeff, Stoney, and Pam in the sitting room at the dorm.

Horton made them stub out their cigarettes. "You go outside for that."

So we did, where we carried on and sang even louder.

That was the last time I saw Jeff. Had I known he was going to split in two days, I would have stayed with him, talked with him one more time.

I HAVE THIS VISION:

A community in Colorado filled with freaks who have put down and cleared their heads.

We could get together with other like-minded people, buy up hundreds of acres of land, build our own houses, and plant our own crops. We would get our highs without drugs, just through music, meditation, psychedelic posters, and black and Strobe lights–a natural high. In this community, we would share the work–we would live close to the land. We would have families, but all the women would share in the child care and domestic chores, and the men would take care of the heavy manual work. Working wouldn't be so bad if we had a goal– you'd be working for the family, and there wouldn't be any particular boss.

Could it work? Can ex-drug users get it together enough to lead extraordinary and exciting lives without drugs and still thumb their noses at the Establishment?

Creating such communities could stamp out Establishment life–now it seems that people don't work for themselves, just for the Establishment. The hell with that.

JUST HEARD FROM DREW–he may be getting out on bail. He wrote about getting royally screwed over. I can't believe how much like Jeff he is. He, too, says, "Screw you!" to the Establishment.

President Eisenhower died today.

Saturday, March 29

Julie asks me about my job at the bank.

"Was it interesting?" she asks.

"Not really. Mostly grunt work."

"Well, everyone has to start at the bottom."

"I guess–though there were a few odd incidents."

I tell her about the bank being robbed–I didn't even know about it until after the fact–and John Lennon's Roll Royce being parked outside the bank. For what reason, I don't know.

But I save the weirdest for last.

It happened in September. Work started out routine enough, just making my regular calls. This guy, a stockbroker, applied for a loan on a Toyota, so I did all the scut work on him, calling the credit bureau, mortgage company, other banks holding his loans–so far, so good. The guy's credit is clean as a whistle, always pays "as agreed," a very positive report.

But, then, I called his employer.

"You might want to hold off on that loan," the guy's boss said. "He was arrested yesterday for murdering his wife."

I've always wondered why we had to call place of employment, especially when the borrowers submit a recent pay stub.

 Now I know.

I told my co-worker Carol about it.

She just laughed. "Yeah, that stuff happens more than you'd think."

I can see this dude writing up his list:

(1) Pick up dry cleaning.
(2) Apply for Toyota loan.
(3) Buy gun, Lysol, garbage bags, rags, and mop.
(4) Kill that bitch Susan.
(5) Clean kitchen.

"Wow," Julie says. "You could write a book about that guy."

I'll pass.

Sunday, March 30

THE ONLY THING I MISS about Cherokee is not getting my mail; I look forward to getting *lots* of letters from Jeff.

It's a lazy Sunday afternoon, and I'm hung over. I'm not even out of my pajamas, and it's already 12:30. Last night, my cousin Steve, Susie, and I went to The Loft in South Dakota, where the drinking age is 19. Susie and I got completely bombed. Steve and I got in early: 1:00 a.m. Early for me, that is.

I FIND AN OLD ISSUE of *Rolling Stone* in Tim's room, the one with naked pics of John Lennon and Yoko Ono (front and back!) from the *Two Virgins* album and interview with John. He told the interviewer:

> *I've never seen me prick on an album or on a photo before: "What-on-earth, there's a fellow with his prick out." And that was the first time I realized me prick was out, you know. I mean, you can see it on the photo itself—we're naked in front of a camera—that comes over in the eyes, just for a minute you go!! I mean, you're not used to it, being naked, but it's got to come out.*

What a far out thing to say; John must've been stoned out

of his gourd. I wish I would've bought a copy of that issue; for weeks, bums and freaks sold it on the street, near Wallich's–I could've picked it up any time.

Maybe Tim will give me his copy.

Another blow-up with Mo. Yesterday, she sent Glenn over to spy on me–imagine, using a 13-year-old kid for such devious purposes.

The report she got: I had loads and loads of makeup on; I was wearing long dangling earrings (?? I don't even wear earrings); I wore caked powder on my face (I don't wear face makeup, just eye makeup); I was dressed in weird clothes (the same clothes *she* sent to the institution); and I was sitting on the floor smoking. Said I called her a jackass. I don't think so–I've learned to keep my big mouth shut, and I'm not about to upset the cart by saying stupid stuff like that. I might *think* she's a jackass, but I'm not about to tell any spies what I *really* think. I don't want to make any unnecessary trouble–I just want to be left alone.

Mo calls Julie and says, *specifically*, that she does not want me to visit here anymore because *she* (Mo) wants to bring her friends around, and she *can't* because *I'm* there.

I must be a freak of nature, the girl to be kept hidden in the closet. She's really getting weirder and weirder, almost obsessed about me. I don't wish her any harm; I just want her to back down.

Julie just shook her head in disbelief–this would be funny, except Julie has to put up with all this, long after I've split. One more reason I can't stay here after I get out of Cherokee: Mo would pester George and Julie to death.

Monday, March 31

I'm half watching the Eisenhower funeral on T.V. and thinking how plastic it seems–all those delegates coming to pay their last respects. Man, what a plastic bunch of dudes and chicks. I kind of liked 'ole Ike and can't understand why all these so-called friends waited until he died to pay a visit. They knew he was going to die soon, anyway, so why not see him while he's still alive?

No luck with the *Rolling Stone* issue. A friend of Tim's already has dibs.

Damn.

LAST NIGHT, I tossed and turned the entire night; I had weird dreams about dueling with Mo and Dee. I couldn't stand all the bickering, so I split for New York, though that's the last place I'd go. I was running all around the city, like visiting museums and climbing all over the exhibits. Then, when I got tired, I couldn't find a hotel, so I knocked on the nearest convent door. Somehow, Peter (How did he get in the picture, anyway?), found me, but then he spied Cynthia's mother and went off with her, leaving me do my own thing. And, then, ta-da! Jeff comes in from the blue yonder and rescues me from the convent and from myself.

Far out dreams!

Speaking of Peter: *he got married!*

Strange. Just last month, I received a letter from him, declaring how much he still loved me and how he would fight to win me back.

Some fighter. Looks like he just needed to get married.

That guy's always been a bit strange anyway. I could never figure out *why* I got engaged to him. Maybe I thought I couldn't get anyone else.

Last spring, when he came home on leave from Vietnam, we decided to go out–we'd been pen pals. We dated a bit–he took me to see *The Graduate*, and we just sort of hung out together. Nothing serious, at least on my part.

He tried to putting the moves on me, but I wasn't ready. One night, he stood me up and just seemed to disappear–no sign that he wanted to split or break up. He didn't call.

What had I done to make him to make him reject me?

Later, Mo (everything seems to come back to Mo) ran into him downtown–he was with a girl. I didn't believe her; Mo tends to exaggerate and blow things out of proportion. I thought maybe the girl was his sister or cousin.

Mo called Mrs. Raskin, his grandma, who'd been in the hospital.

Peter had shacked up with some married woman, whose flyboy husband was in Vietnam.

Absolutely pissed me off.

I wasn't hung up on Peter–which is why, I think, he split on me–but now I didn't have a prom date, and it was too late to find another guy, except one of my cousins. I wasn't *that* desperate, and, besides, I'd hear about it for the rest of my life if I dated a cousin. Also, my ego was terribly battered. I cried and cried because I couldn't go to prom–it *is* supposed to be a big event in a high school girl's life.

But that's life.

I moved on, went to California, and started dating Frank, another soldier pen pal, this one from Beverly Hills. Again, a casual thing–a few dates, a few laughs, and a lot of Bali Hai. Nothing explosive. We remained friends, and, eventually, he, too, drifted away.

People seem to come and go in my life.

Peter was just doing his thing, and I was all right with that. So I wrote a friendly letter to him, explaining my new outlook on life.

I received the strangest letter back.

"I'm sorry about that woman and the way I behaved," he said. Then he declared his love.

I was taken aback, but flattered. The bombshell came in the next letter: he asked me to marry him.

Like an idiot, I accepted. It felt good to be wanted. But

after a month of being faithful–not dating other guys–I realized my mistake. I didn't love him; I was still pissed, and I wanted to break off the engagement like right away.

No delicate way to do it, but after moving in with Stoney, I *had* to do it.

Peter was, more or less, cool about it; we even stayed friends for a while, writing back and forth, and then he stopped writing.

I didn't think too much of it–he just sort of stopped existing for me.

I wrote him a letter from the institution, just to let him know where I was.

He wrote back, insisting he would win me back. Then, nothing. Now, I know why.

I'm *so* glad he's married; now he's someone else's problem.

81

April Fool
(Sioux City)

TUESDAY, APRIL 1

APRIL FOOLS' DAY:

Almost 550,000 soldiers stationed in Vietnam, 33,641 dead, exceeding the number of soldier deaths in Korea.

Some days, I just want to stop reading the newspaper and turn off the TV.

I want the war to stop before another person dies.

I'm going back to Cherokee soon–I'm not looking forward to that.

Mo called again, this time to tell me she's glad I'm leaving.

She can't seem to make up her mind.

JULIE SAYS that if I've been made ward of the state, I can't legally leave the state, without permission, until I'm 21.

But if I get married–funny how *that* keeps popping into the picture–I would no longer be ward of the state. So if I split with no intentions of getting married, just moving in with Jeff, I could be arrested and dragged back.

Maybe we should just get hitched.

I don't think that's Jeff's bag–he's got college ahead of him–but I'll accept his terms, though I expect to see a lot of problems from the Establishment.

I don't want to push him into something he's not ready for.

I wouldn't mind being Mrs. Jeff Brown, but I want him to feel exactly the same before I'd even consider getting married.

Now that I've been away from California for a few months, I see things a little differently. I did things I would not ordinarily do, so maybe Pam is right:

I *am* a prude, at least according to street standards.

Rick and Mel. At one time or another, I wanted to make love with them—but our relationships fizzled before I was ready, and they moved on.

In Rick's case, that was a good thing, but I've always wondered about Mel, how things might have been different had I been ready…

82

Mel's Room

November 1968

(Hollywood)

BIG PARTY AT MEL'S, a room at The Mission.

Actually, the entire place was happening, everyone there: Stoney, Syndi, Pam, Levi, Rudy, Jeff, Eleanor, Jim, Denny, Percy, Linda, Bob...even Caesar!

Stoney passed around Blue Cheer, free and easy with his dope.

He hugged me and planted a sloppy kiss on my lips. "Syndi and I have split for good."

I nodded and dropped the tab. I spied Mel, in an intense conversation with a girl, about 14, blond hair down to her waist. I'd never seen her before.

I threw my arms around Mel. "Let's go trip." I pulled him away from the girl. "She's jail bait," I said. "I'm legal."

"She'll give," Mel said. "She said so, you know."

"You're mine, at least for tonight."

"I'm yours," he said, allowing me to lead him away.

We went to his room, where we tripped and spent much of the night talking about sex, casual and otherwise. I tried explaining why I didn't want to have sex unless I was in love–

"I love you," he said.

What about the blond who nearly led him away, under my

nose?

"No, you don't."

He laughed. "Well, maybe I don't, but I sure dig you."

We started making love, kissing and fondling, and, then, I was naked, he was naked–

He pushed against me–

"No, please! Not yet!"

He stopped and sighed.

I offered to jerk him off.

"That's okay," Mel said. He jumped up out of bed, pulled on his jeans, and ran out of the room.

I threw on my clothes and found him in a corner, getting sucked off by Syndi.

Big deal. She's probably done just about everyone in Hollywood, so why not Mel?

She's made herself into a Hollywood joke.

It's not easy earning a reputation as a slut around here, but she has managed.

Stoney put his arms around my shoulders. "Sorry about your boyfriend."

I shrugged. "It's okay."

"That's why I broke up with Syndi." He shook his head. "That bitch is too much."

"She might as well do it for money."

"She does. That's her day job."

"Daytime hooker?"

"Yeah, she's got a business clientele. Straight dudes who want it on the job."

Hollywood is nothing like Sioux City, where businessmen go to work to conduct business, not get the business.

"I don't even want to know," I said.

Stoney laughed. "You haven't been around much, have you?"

"I guess not."

"Maybe I can show you." He rubbed my shoulders.

I broke away. "Later, maybe."

I stumbled toward Mel and Syndi. They looked like two merged amoebas, a high school science project, her head bobbing up and down on his crotch.

"Hey, Syndi," I said, laughing. "You enjoying yourself?"

Syndi looked so earnest–no, desperate–in what she was doing.

She looked up. "Go away."

"I think I'll watch."

Mel, red-faced, pulled away, zipped up his jeans.

"It's okay, Mel; she's not worth getting riled up about."

He pushed Syndi away.

She wandered off, hunting for another guy.

"Look, I'm sorry…"

I shrugged.

"I'm not that way. Really. Let's talk."

"Okay."

We went to Mel's room and locked the door.

"Why do you guys do all these ridiculous things?"

"I don't know."

We spent the rest of the night in his bed, rapping about the sexual differences between guys and chicks. I nestled in the crook of his arm; his curly red hair smelled like apples.

We dug back into basic high school biology and concluded it must be an evolutionary characteristic: men try to ball anything they can because they have millions of seeds to spread around, and women must be selective because they have only a limited number of eggs.

"Syndi's just a mutant," I said.

83

April 2, 1969

(Cherokee)

WEDNESDAY, APRIL 2

IT WAS KIND OF GROOVY Mel and I didn't make love that night.

It was the longest rap session I had with a guy without having to fight him off.

A comfortable night.

But within a week, he was back with his old girlfriend, the little blond who looked 14 but was actually 18, and three weeks later, I moved in with Stoney.

I still wonder, though, how my life could've been different with Mel, what might have been.

I WAS GOING TO LEAVE for the institution last night, but I decided to get up early this morning—why spend an extra night at the shrink house if I didn't have to? But it was hard getting going so early.

When I got back, I found four letters from Jeff—I hardly know where to begin...maybe in order.

Jeff's also Irish, about 1/16th, but also part Cherokee, Welsh, Scot, German, Dutch—Heinz 57, like me.

He included a short letter from his brother Keith, the one who wants to become a biker. He says, "I can't wait 'til you get here so I can see this Jennifer that Jeff is always talking about—you sound like a groovy chick to me."

My first friendly introduction to the family.

Jeff doesn't want me to wait two months, but he understands I might not have a choice. I'm still not sure how much he wants me to bop into Pennsylvania; I can't tell if he's just scared how we will survive on our own or if he's having some second thoughts.

Jeff also quoted some important dudes and chicks I have never heard of: Nietzsche, Koestler, Porter, Orwell. I have heard of Orwell, but I've never read anything by him.

Sometimes, Jeff seems way out of my league, so abstract and all, playing with numbers, something about two plus two equaling five. According to him, I'm an abstract idea right now because I'm not there, but I *feel* very real, and I know *he's* real, even if he's not with me at this moment.

I'm not very philosophical; I haven't read the right books—maybe I should have studied harder in school. The right answers can be found in the great books—at least that's what my English teachers always said—and I need to read some of those books, instead of pot boilers like *Gone with the Wind* and magazines like *True Story*. Otherwise, Jeff and I will have nothing to talk about.

Still, I tend to see the world as it is, not as an abstract concept. Math, as much as I hated it in school, is straight forward and dependable: two plus two will *always* equal four, no matter what the great thinkers say or how they try to tweak the numbers to fit some abstract idea.

Maybe it's time to take a look at the world through a prism instead of a window.

I had to look up two words: "nihilist" (one who believes in the destruction of social norms for the betterment of the future–sound familiar?) and "apocalypse" (great devastation and doom)–heavy stuff. I see that Jeff has a gloomy side, but his eloquent writing somehow transcends his gloom.

Peter was also gloomy, but his writing was blah and boring–no spark.

Frank's letters were fun and funny, but, in the end, they were filled with insignificant gab–very much like my letters.

Odd. I've no idea how Stoney writes–I don't even remember his handwriting, let alone any opinions and ideas he might have had. He could be brilliant, but I'd never know it–acid does *not* make you smarter than you already are–it just fucks you up–and, as for insights? I don't know. Timothy Leary and Ken Kesey seem to think acid can enhance your view on the world, but were they were talking about street acid?

I never really knew Stoney at all, except sexually, and even that is becoming a vague memory. I drew his face once, from memory, in an attempt to hang on to that part of my life. I wonder if things between us might have been different if we had written to each other before living together.

After all, I'm discovering a lot about Jeff through his letters, before we get sexually involved–maybe we can get the nitpicky stuff out of the way before we meet face-to-face again.

I like what he says about phone calls being atmosphere–it suggests the impermanent aura of the spoken word–that letters are more important because they act as a future history that can be referred to at a later time. Phone calls are cool, but their words float into the atmosphere, never to be retrieved, except as memory, and memory can be flawed. But letters are black and white, no room for dispute.

I admire Jeff's truthfulness; he's honest in a way that other guys aren't, even when the truth might hurt. Most guys, like Rick and Mel, would just tell you they love you because they want to ball you; Jeff lays out the undisguised truth–take it or leave it.

He was so comforting after Mel split up with me.

84

Logic

November 1968

(Hollywood)

JEFF CALLED and asked if he could come over to the Dorm.

I needed a good friend, but I wasn't in the mood to hang out on the scene that night. Pam was at Levi's–I'd have Jeff to myself.

"Sure, if you don't mind Horton chasing after you with an ashtray."

He laughed. "I'll just ignore her."

We sat in the parlor–no guys allowed in our rooms. Horton hovered nearby–to protect my virtue, I suppose, from the evil Rent-a-cop.

Ironic. I feel safer with Jeff than anyone else in the world. We could sleep in the same bed, and as long as I said, "no," he wouldn't violate me, so Horton's surveillance was wasted on the wrong guy.

I ranted on and on about Mel.

"In a way, you're fortunate," Jeff finally said. "You weren't that deep into the relationship, right?"

I nodded.

"You love him?"

"Not exactly."

"Then it's better to know now than later."

Who could argue with such dead-on logic?

"I don't think the dude set out to hurt you—it just happens the girl who got away came back. It's got nothing to do with you."

I hadn't thought of it in those terms. I felt much better, and we moved on to more interesting topics: the ongoing student strike at San Francisco State, communism (pros and cons), and the recent Supreme Court decision overturning Arkansas' ban on teaching evolution in public schools.

"Man," he said. "We missed a bullet there—could've been the Scopes trials all over again."

We talked until curfew, then he kissed me on the forehead. "Don't worry, little sister. You'll find the right guy. And he'd better know how lucky he is."

85

April 2-15, 1969
(Cherokee)

TUESDAY, APRIL 2

I LOOK FOR D.J.

I feel so bad leaving him in such an unhappy state—I'm worried about him. But when I find him, he's pulling last year's stalks from one of the gardens in the back, singing, off key,

"Don't sit under the apple tree with anyone else but me..."

"Hey, D.J.!" I wave to him.

He looks up. "Jennifer! You're back."

"Unfortunately. How's it going?"

"About the same. Middlin' good."

"You were so sad when I left."

"Well, I had a long talk with the fir, and he told me not to be sad. The waters will still come, and they will kill, but they'll also bring good things too."

"Small consolation for the plants in the path."

D.J. shrugs and wipes his brow. "Yep, but they're alive today."

I don't quite follow the logic of why he's happy today, when he was so sad last week, but I'm glad to see he's not in total despair.

"Where did you hear that song?"

"Song?"

"'Don't Sit Under the Apple Tree.'"

"My mom used to sing it all the time. When she was dusting the furniture. It was real popular during the war, you know."

"Really? I thought it was a depression song. My grandmother sings it all the time."

"I like it. Reminds me of my mom before she had to send me away."

"Do you miss being free?"

D.J. shrugs. "I dunno."

"I can't wait to be out of here."

"I don't know what I'd do if I was out."

A chill runs through me—even the remotest possibility of being in here long term absolutely terrifies me.

I ALMOST THREW A STAPLER at Benson today—I was *really* pissed at him. They *still* haven't found me a place, and I'm getting impatient. He called me emotional and impulsive—said I was being unreasonable.

Unreasonable?

They declared me sane weeks ago, and *I'm* being unreasonable? After we went around for an hour and half, that's when I picked up the stapler from his desk and said, "Mr. Benson, you know I feel like throwing this at you?"

He kind of looked at me, and said, "Yes, I can imagine that you do."

I *really* wanted to throw it then, but that would have landed me on locked ward.

ALONG WITH JEFF'S FOUR LETTERS, I also received one from Frank, Mr. Beverly Hills/Bali Hai himself. He's married now—I seem to have that effect on old boyfriends. But he's terribly unhappy; he had to get married, and wants a thing with me.

Yeah, right. Now I'm going to chase after married guys.

These guys want to play house; then they're shocked when they knock up someone.

I wrote back and said, "No dice."

Either a friendship or nothing at all.

Thursday, April 3

I just heard that there was a local TV show last Sunday about my case. No names were mentioned, but they had nailed every detail. The girl in question was 18 years old, from Sioux City, lived with her grandparents, was out in California working and suddenly split her job–definitely sounds like me–and dropped out. She was picked up by the heat a few times in L.A. (as was I, for stupid things, mainly). As the show progressed, they mentioned that the girl was in the Cherokee Mental Hospital, so that about narrows the possibilities.

It was a teen panel–kids about my age and a little younger–rapping about dope.

At the end, the commentator asked, "Would you ever do dope?" and they all said "No!"

No guts. Oh, well, their thing.

Besides, I don't believe them.

This place sure is empty without Drew–dead is more like it. We rapped about nothing much, and he was a lot of fun. One day at the canteen, he ate a cigarette.

Joyce *is* leaving–tomorrow, in fact. She's back on Ward 4, and told me herself. Actually, she seems much better, not quite so far into the depths of gloom or so high into the clouds of ecstasy. She's actually acting normal, which seems strange, because normal doesn't seem normal for her. Her face and hands are covered with a strange blotchy rash, though, like she's been burned, kind of the way we all looked a few weeks ago with our winter rashes, what with the dry, overheated, and crackling air.

"My family needs me," she says. "I'm glad to get out of here." She sounds a bit wistful, like she's not quite sure.

Even if I were bona fide insane, I'd be itching to split this joint. "I wish I were leaving, too."

"Don't worry, they won't keep you too much longer," Joyce says, her voice certain.

"I sure hope you're right."

"You don't belong in here, Jen."

"Tell that to Mr. Benson and my grandparents."

"They know it—the system's fucked up, not you."

Her dead-on assessment surprises me—I thought she was too wacky to know much of anything, let alone get how the system figures into the equation—I certainly haven't figured out why they keep perfectly sane people locked up while setting free a fragile Joyce loose to contend with two kids and a husband, who, apparently, hasn't been too understanding.

Maybe they've agreed to send Joyce home as a reward for never having done drugs—she's the way she is just because of something gone awry in her mind, not because of filling her head with dope.

Still, I'm jealous she's being cut loose, although I don't have a good feeling about it—like, maybe, they're releasing her before she's ready.

AFTER TWO WEEKS of ailing, Carrie's back on 4 from the infirmary.

When I ask her what had been wrong with her, she just shrugs. "They don't know, but it's not my heart. Probably panic attacks." She laughs like a fiendish little elf. "So you *didn't* save my life, Florence Nightingale."

Like I would hope for something serious so I could play the big heroine? "Well, it *could* have been serious."

"But it *wasn't*."

"Okay, I get it."

"You screwed up, and landed my ass in the tank for over two weeks!"

That's what I like about Carrie: her utmost gratefulness to a friend who was trying to help her when no one else gave a shit. "Yeah, I guess I screwed up."

Yeah, I screwed up, all right—the next time she has palpitations, I'll just look the other way. Actually, I'd like to distance myself from Carrie anyway; she has become obsessed not only with the idea of sticking a rat up her vagina, but now she's talking about larger animals, such as cats and dogs. Where does she come up with all this stuff, anyway? Sooner or later, she's going to end up on locked ward, or, worse, in isolation, which, I hear, is a padded cell.

I'll just hang out with Penny from now on.

PENNY AND I PAINT our cigarettes with nail polish again—only this nail polish is flammable (we didn't know it, though), and our cigs go POOF! Scares the shit out of us!

Gotta stop doing this stuff. If I get caught...

FRIDAY, APRIL 4

JIM MORRISON has been formally charged with public intoxication, open and public profanity, and indecent exposure.

The court freed Jimbo on $50,000 bond—for him, a drop in the bucket.

I sent Jeff an Easter card—he'll get it late because I couldn't find the right card and had to settle for a syrupy one with a bunny playing a saxophone.

I haven't heard from him since Wednesday—I told him to keep writing because even if I leave here, the letters will be forwarded.

I have to spend Easter in this place, but that's okay; by Christmas and next Easter, I'll be with Jeff.

Joyce went home today. I didn't get a chance to say goodbye to her–I overslept.

I like Joyce, but I don't want to see her in here again.

BENSON HAS ME PAGED from the canteen for an unscheduled talk.

I flit into his office, armed with a Dr. Pepper in my left hand, and a half-smoked Tareyton 100 in the other, and plop myself into the closest and most comfortable chair.

"Oh, oh, what did I do now?"

He offers me two choices: a dorm or a foster home.

"I don't care. I'm not staying around Iowa that long."

Again, we get into a huge hassle about my leaving the state. *Where is that goddamn stapler?*

Like he's read my mind, he pulls the stapler from his desk and thunks it in front of me.

A test? If so, I'll pass.

"Why do you smoke?"

"'Cos I'm nervous; this place is slowly driving me nuts."

My hands shake all the time; I'm getting frustrated, and I tell Benson so.

Oh, I love hassling him–I *thrive* on it.

On Wednesday, I asked him, "Are you happily married?" Caught him off guard–he couldn't answer. Once I told him that there was too much of a generation gap between us; he's only 25, but, sometimes, he acts like an old man.

After Benson's session, I'm sent to rehab to rap with Mrs. Williams about my future. She seems to be pushing Floriculture School–why, I don't know. Plants shrivel up and die under my watch. I tell her, in a nice way, that she can shove the Floriculture idea–that my place is with my boyfriend in Pennsylvania.

Then a flash: when I'm released, I'll have a mental health record, so I take it out on the poor lady who's just helping me find a career–the wrong career, but a career, nevertheless. I feel kind of guilty for giving her a hard time.

But, then, Williams tries pushing some Home Ec courses offered by the institution. I'd have to stay here another four weeks to complete the course–who needs that?

I blow a fuse. "I already know how to cook."

I make a groovy peanut butter and jelly sandwich.

I'm going to give Benson a bad time about this harebrained Floriculture idea, let him know I'm not interested in their little schemes to keep me here.

THE STAFF had a meeting about Penny and me skipping O.T.–a really bad scene–they're going to make us go, even if they handcuff us and drag us over.

Penny and I might have to go three times a day, instead of two to make up for the times we skipped. Will find out the outcome on Monday. We might get sent to locked ward and get our ground cards taken away–then again, nothing much might happen. Who knows? They schedule one of the O.T.'s at 8:30– ungodly hour–and I'm usually too tired to get my bottom out of bed at such a ridiculous hour, so I just skip. Yesterday morning, the R.N. came in and tried to get me up. I finally rolled out at about 9:30, got dressed, and ran into Penny in the hallway.

"You two are supposed to be at O.T.," the attendant said.

We go, "Oh, reeaaallly?"

I did go to O.T. yesterday afternoon and made a pair of moccasins, size 10, and they're much too big for me. I don't profess to having the world's smallest feet, but these things are definitely too big. I'll give them to Jeff and make myself a smaller pair when I get around to getting to O.T. again.

Except I don't know Jeff's foot size.

Penny and I get written up for yelling after 10:00 p.m., waking up the whole ward. Penny and I were writing this little nasty note (just for the hell of it), and she ran off with it and jokingly said she was going to give it to the attendant. I let out a hoot and chased her down the ward and collided head-on with the attendant. We both got chewed out.

I tell the day attendant I'm not going to O.T. anymore—they'll have to drag me there. At first, I also refuse to pick up linens, but then decide, for my own good, I'd better.

I should have never gotten out of bed today; I received an Easter card from Mo and tossed it. Then, tonight, I got mad because they wouldn't allow me to visit Carrie and Anna on locked ward. I told the O.T. nurse I didn't want to make anything, but she said I had to do something, so that's why I made the moccasins—mindless and stupid.

I hate this place more and more each day, so I just raise Cain for the hell of it. Ever since my trial visit, I've grown more impatient with Mr. Benson and Dr. Favis and the snail's pace of getting me out of here.

I feel as though I'm in Purgatory, waiting for entrance into heaven, which is almost worse than pure Hell; as long as there is a possibility of passage into the promised land, I wait.

If this place were true Hell, I'd simply get up and walk out—take my chances with the heat coming after me.

"I DON'T THINK it's right to have a 'shotgun' marriage that I'm not really ready for," Jeff said in his April 3 letter. "And I may lose you again (at least until you're twenty one), but I don't think it's right and won't say it is—because whether or not I'll be living with you, I'll always be living with myself, and I have a bad habit of insisting on internal harmony."

And more about *her* again: "I got rather pissed off with Miss Lizzie and wrote her the following letter: 'Dear Lizzie: Go Get Fucked! Love, Jeff.'"

I hardly know what to think.

I also received a letter from Drew today; I'm sort of falling for him. I don't love him, at least not in the way I love Jeff. Ever since Drew was released to police custody, we've been writing back and forth—and we just click. I thought we could be just friends, but he has hinted that he feels more than that, and I'm feeling something back. He's so much like Jeff—it's scary. There's something about his letters that echo Jeff's love for important subjects. But he doesn't know how long he'll be in jail. Even if there weren't any complications, I couldn't see being involved with him *and* Jeff.

I thought I was over the new-guy-every-week phase.

Apparently not.

SUNDAY, APRIL 6

IN LAST NIGHT'S LETTER to Jeff, I tried explaining the Drew dilemma, but I'm not sure if I'll send it—maybe I'll just sit on it for a while.

Why Drew? Why now? Is it because Drew is closer geographically?

And I used to accuse Pam of being shallow?

Like I don't always agree with Pam about her relationships, but she has such a big heart, and she never holds my moralizing against me.

I'm concerned, though; Pam keeps alluding to some problem, but she doesn't specify what it is. I just hope she's okay and hasn't hooked up with some really bad ass.

I wish she'd write more; I miss our long talks.

MONDAY, APRIL 7

The Little Sioux River overflows its banks, cresting at 23.90 feet, resulting in major flooding of roads and the extreme Southeast corner of Cherokee, with some water flow reaching the Northwest corner of 2nd and Beech Streets in Cherokee.

To date, this is the third highest crest in history.

THE SNOW is melting very fast now, the river overflowing; D.J. is very sad again. I don't know how to console him about Cherokee plants dying along the river and low-lying areas.

I find it hard to get all worked up about plants, mostly weeds, perishing from the flood, but I do hate seeing D.J. upset.

I sent Jeff my April 5 letter about Drew, reminding him that my running out to Pennsylvania is not something to be taken lightly.

In his last letter, Jeff revealed something Stoney told him last fall: "Sure, I *like* Jennifer. But I'm not the kind of guy who gets married. A couple of months'd be cool, but I sure wouldn't want to get married!"

I'm not sure why Jeff waited until now to tell me–why not back in November when it might have done some good?

I could have gone my entire life without knowing; it wouldn't have matter–I've already figured out that Stoney's a piece of shit; he didn't care if I got pregnant–he was going to leave me, no matter what.

I wonder if Drew will be getting out of prison any time soon?

TUESDAY, APRIL 8

I'M THINKING about calling Jeff to warn him about my April 5 and April 7 letters; I wish I hadn't sent them. Later today, I'll write him and try to patch up things. If I can't call, at least in a few days, he'll get a letter.

I'm *so* impulsive at times–I should have known that any feelings for Drew were transitory; today, he hardly seems a threat. I'm still a slightly bent about Jeff's pompous April 3 letter, but, in a way, I did ask for it. I did come on a little strong about the marriage bit.

Still, Jeff's telling me about Stoney's cruel remark really stings.

I can't think of anything I'd rather know less.

Penny and I don't have to make up any more O.T. sessions, as long as we behave and start attending regularly.

It's like, "Why bother?" I'm out of here soon.

I talk with Benson tomorrow; I made an appointment because I want to hassle with him. I'm going to tell him where I'm at–that is, if I still feel sure about it then.

I received a sweet letter from Mo. She promised she'd respect my wishes–maybe she's figured out that the only way to fix our relationship is to accept my moving to Pennsylvania.

I'm going to hold her to that promise.

WEDNESDAY, APRIL 9
(Akron, Iowa)

The Big Sioux River overflows its banks, cresting at 22.99 feet, resulting in major flooding of the town, roads, and farms. The river's crest at Akron is the highest to date.

(Cherokee)

Carrie's on locked ward again. I don't know what she's done this time because I've been avoiding her. Maybe she talked a bit too much about rats and other mammals.

D.J.'s in a funk because of all the floods, the worst in history. I feel so helpless; I don't know how to console him.

Benson and I had a run-in today–he tried to make me promise that I'd stay in Sioux City for a while.

"I don't make commitments I can't keep," I said.

THURSDAY, APRIL 10
(South Dakota and Iowa)

In Sioux Falls, South Dakota, the greatest flood of the century occurs. The Big Sioux River gauge on highway 38A crests at 19.80 feet, 7.8 feet above flood stage.

Fast melting record snowfalls have caused waterways in the area to swell past flood stage. On March 12, 30 inches of snow blanketed the ground but had decreased to 10 inches by the end of the month and one inch by April 8, which saw warm temperatures in the high 60's.

In Sioux City, Iowa, the Big Sioux River reaches a historical top crest of 108.30 feet.

(Cherokee)

ANNA IS OFF LOCKED WARD and wants to try splitting again and wants me to go with her.

I'm thinking about it–she's 19, so I can't get my ass racked for contributing to the delinquency of a minor, which is why Penny can't go with us. Thank God she understands how uncool it would be if Anna and I were caught with a minor.

The plan is to head for the West coast first–let things cool down a bit before I head east to Pennsylvania–that's the first place the heat will look.

But now I'm having second thoughts. For one thing, Anna's a bit of a flake; her first attempt at escape was unsuccessful–I was surprised she was released from locked ward so soon. I doubt if a second attempt would yield much more success.

If Penny weren't a minor, I'd risk it with her–for all her silliness and playfulness, she's got a solid head on her shoulders.

I've become very close to Penny, even though she's so young. In many ways, she's older than me–having lived an entire adult life in a few short years. I'm amazed at her resilience and survival skills. To her, this place is just a nuisance, a detour to her real life, even though she's been here for over a year–her sense of humor is contagious; if it weren't for her, I would've gone mad long ago. It's too bad that she has such a stinker for a doctor; he won't allow her to go home on trial visits, and she actually ended up on locked ward for a day, just for the same kind of pranks that I have played.

I'M REALLY WORRIED about Pam. Have I pissed her off? Does she think I snatched Jeff away from her? I never got the sense she even wanted Jeff, except maybe as a conquest. I'm not judging her–she does her thing the way she sees it.

I keep writing to her, asking her if I've done anything to hurt her, but no answer.

Maybe her feelings for Jeff are deeper than I thought. But I never got the feeling she was particularly hung up on him as a permanent thing. For her, planning a trip to Pennsylvania seemed more like a lark than a serious endeavor.

She did tell me once that she'd like to get Jeff–I felt slightly jealous, even though I was still with Stoney.

I've never asked Jeff this, and I really wouldn't want him to answer, anyway, but did he ever make love to Pam?

I'll never ask–I'm too afraid of the answer.

Maybe I'm reading too much in the Jeff thing. One other possibility: perhaps she's still deeply involved with the dope scene, and, here I am, lecturing her about putting down. I probably sound like her mother, and who needs that?

I'm not jealous if Jeff extends his friendship to Pam.

Actually, I'm more concerned about that Lizzie creature– she's more of a threat than Pam ever was, and I will continue to keep my eye on *that* friendship.

MR. BENSON SAYS he will know something by tomorrow about my foster home, so I've got to be cool, or I'll get nothing. I'm in hot water as it is.

I gave Bonnie, one of the night attendants, the finger last night–very unladylike. I shouldn't act so juvenile, but she gets to me.

It was after midnight, and Bonnie just walked by–I was supposed to be in bed, so she gave me a dirty look. Watch me get written up again.

Sioux City and Cherokee was on the national news because of the awful flooding–I hope Jeff isn't worried.

This hole's on a hill, and I'll be damned if *I've* seen any water.

D.J. IS STILL IN MOURNING, though he seems to recover very fast. Once this flooding stops and the sun comes out, he'll be his same cheerful self.

For a retarded guy, he seems to have an innate understanding of how the world works and just accepts it.

I can't do that.

FRIDAY, APRIL 11

JEFF TOLD ME to disregard his last letter's mention of April 13-19 as the time to arrive in Pennsylvania.

"Play it by ear," he said. "*You* decide when it's cool to come out. Any time is fine with me (sooner the better, though)."

It looks as though the institution will decide, at least indirectly, when I go to Pennsylvania, and it certainly won't be in the next few days. Jeff hasn't even found an apartment yet, and that scares me.

He said, "We'll work out what happens when you get here."

Really? Where am I supposed to live when I get there? On the street?

No thanks. Done that already.

I know Jeff worries about money–I do too–but shouldn't a place to live would be a top priority? I know I'll have to get a job, but I can't get one in Pennsylvania before I get there, so he'll just have to save harder, or I'll have to get a job in Sioux City, and earn enough for an apartment before going to Pennsylvania—

What *does* a pad cost, anyway?

Maybe I should take some of Jeff's letters with a grain of salt—in his way, he does love me, but he flip-flops so much. One minute, he's talking about not wanting to get married because he's not ready—and absolutely refuses just because the Establishment requires marriage for sex—and the next, he's discussing baby names: Eric and Andrea as faves. How strange is that?

Question: If the Establishment suddenly banned marriage, would Jeff whisk me off to the altar in protest?

Maybe he thinks too hard about the future—the future will come, no matter what he thinks, and it will happen the way it's supposed to happen—maybe I'm a little bit of a Calvinist.

Or maybe he's just trying out new ideas in his letters, and I'm the logical recipient, the person he thinks will understand the most. I do the same thing in my diary, but I don't send my thoughts to anyone—I'd die first. But maybe guys don't keep diaries, so they have to write their thoughts somewhere and share them with someone.

The thing is, if I wait a day or two, another letter arrives, contradicting his previous letter. I hardly know what to think. Confusing.

What if I'm not making the right decision? Part of me says I shouldn't run out to Pennsylvania—that I really don't have any idea what I'm getting into. Jeff has even warned me that he's not 100% sure about us, and who's to say I'm so sure about him?

I ASKED D.J. to go to the dance tonight; I might get released soon, and I'd like to dance with him, even if he does have lead feet. I want the other patients to see what a nice guy he is.

He said, "I dunno," which really means no.

I tried. He's been such a good friend to me; I'd like to see him meet someone nice here, maybe another long timer.

He's never going to get out of here—

Who's to say that's necessarily bad?

SPRING IS HERE! Hardly any snow on the ground—what's left is nestled under the pine trees or where the sun rarely hits. The grass is green now, and it's actually hot out.

I spent the entire day outdoors, where I had a run-in with two snakes—at the same time. Each was about two feet long; both had yellow streaks on their slimy bods. Ick! I went off screaming; I hate snakes—I have a dreadful fear of them. Even seeing one from afar is enough to make me want to faint.

I tell D.J. about the snakes, and he just laughs. "Nothin' to be afraid of. Probably just garter snakes."

"They were too big."

"They can get pretty big, but they won't hurt no one."

"A boyfriend once teased me with a snake. I nearly passed out."

Stoney, who else? God, was I ever pissed off at him.

D.J.'s face reddens. "I hope you dumped the jerk!"

"We've split up."

"Good. He's bad. Anyone who teases a woman is bad."

"I gave him a piece of my mind. No boyfriend will ever tease me like that again."

"Better not."

"I mean it, too."

Anyone who ever teases me with a snake is liable to get his ass knocked into blocks.

I STILL CRINGE at a long-ago nightmare about the crescent moon and snakes.

I was only four. Mom worked nights as a cocktail waitress

and cigarette girl; she boarded me at Madge Marin's day/night nursery.

I remember little from that time–just my terror of snakes and other slimy creatures...

*

I wake up, wet and cold.

"Auntie Madge!"

She stomps into the room. "What's your problem?"

"I pee pee."

Auntie Madge slaps me. She picks me up and pulls off my wet PJ's.

She pushes me into the bat'room.

"I'm going to flush you down the hole, you rotten kid!"

She stuffs me into the potty, bare rudy first; my feet up...she flushes and flushes and flushes....

Cold and wet.

I'm going down the hole!

–A scary place.

"I'll be good, I won't pee the bed again, please let me out!"

She laughs and flushes some more. "You'll go live where the snakes and lizards live, and they'll eat you alive!"

"NO, PLEASE! I'LL BE GOOD!"

She yanks me out. "I'll let you go this time, but"–poking her finger in my chest–"next time, down you go!"

Auntie Madge dunks me in the tub...cold water...

Scrub! Scrub! Scrub!

New sheets and nightie. "I don't want to hear a peep from you until morning."

Auntie Madge goes away.

Hide...under my sheet.

Hot tears.

The skinny moon follows me. Does it follow everybody? Does it follow only little bad girls who wet the bed? Is it going to tell on me if I think naughty things?

What are *naughty things?*

I'm so tired.

"*Little girl.*"

I sit up.

"*Little girl Jennifer.*"

The skinny, curly moon. Bright.

It wiggles. "*I'm going to get you, eat you alive, Jennifer Lee.*"

NO! I can't yell. Sticky in my throat.

"*I'll chase you down the potty, follow you until the snakes eat you alive, you dirty little spalpeen.*"

DEE DEE?

"*Your Dee Dee can't hear you. He's in Sioux City, a trillion zillion miles away.* YOU BETTER RUN, LITTLE GIRL JENNIFER."

That old moon cackles and shows two big sharp teeth.

I jump out of bed.

"*You can't hide!*"

I run out of the room and down the hall and down the hall and down the hall and down the hall...I run past open doors, and in each window, there he is, laughing and chasing me, and there's no end to the hall, just open doors and open windows, and I'm running and running, and the open doors and the moon is a blur, and I'll never stop running, because I'm running in a circle now, whirling around like a dark merry-go-round, when, suddenly, I'm outside, and the sun shines and smiles, and the scary moon is gone.

"*Mr. Moon had to go to sleep,*" *Mr. Sun says.*

"*I want my mommy.*"

"*Not now.*" *He points at some sunbeams.* "*Look over here.*"

I look, and it's a playground, filled with water. I like water. "*I want to play in the water.*"

"*Okay. But stay inside the lines.*"

I see the lines, two skinny black lines, and I'll have to walk tippy-toe like a ballerina to doggy-paddle from here to the end of the world.

"*Bad things will happen if you don't stay inside,*" *Mr. Sun says.*

I doggy-paddle and the lines are squished together, and I can't even walk tippy-toe, and I can't turn around. I have to keep going forever and ever. "*I want my mommy.*"

"*Ha, ha,*" *Mr. Sun laughs, and it's dark again.*

It's not Mr. Sun!

The scary moon plays a mean trick.

"*Look down, little girl.*"

The water's gone. There's nothing but snakes, licking at my feet, rattling and hissing.

Snakes crawl up my legs.

"*MOMMY!*"

*

CHEROKEE REMINDS ME of Madge's place, with its long hallways, dark alcoves, and spooky grounds, although the playground has been replaced with tall, gloomy trees that cut the sunlight from the ward, even in winter.

I'm frightened at night, which is why I don't like to go to bed any sooner than I have to; I see and hear things, ghostly clicks, bumps, wind whirling around the turrets–this place catches a lot of wind, being on a hill–and hisses, almost as if the ghosts of past patients roam the hall–

I wonder if anyone has ever died here? Probably, like in the old days, when getting committed was a one way ticket into this hole–

My new nightmare: I'll die an old lady in here, or, worse yet, I'll be in here for an eternity–that this is the real Hell that the nuns and priests warned us against.

Somehow, I'd rather endure the pain of fire and brimstone than much more of this.

God, this *is* Hell.

TWO BOTHERSOME THINGS:

(1) Jeff bought Buffy Sainte-Marie's *Spin and Spin, Little Wheel*. He loves it–and I must admit, the lyrics are groovy–but I can't stand her singing–her voice wavers and rasps at the same time. Kills my ears.

Our first disagreement about music.

(2) Bali Hai Frank keeps writing me–I can't believe his audacity! He's not even subtle. He keeps telling me that he wants me–he doesn't get that I love Jeff. All I have to offer Frank is platonic friendship, nothing more, and he has to tell his wife. I don't care why he had to get married, but, the fact is, he is married, and I don't want to come between a married couple. If she doesn't like the idea, then that's it.

I have enough problems dealing with my own life, like Jeff. Back in February, I was so sure about him–I was already packed up and ready to jump on the bus to York, Pennsylvania, but now–

Am I *fleeing from* something, rather than *running to* a lover?

God knows I want out of Iowa in the worst way–even if Jeff weren't in my life, I'd still have my eye on the next bus back to L.A.–anywhere but here.

Hell, even if it's all wrong, Pennsylvania has got to be better than this and more of Mo and Dee Dee's preaching and old ways.

Right?

I AGREE WITH JEFF: I like the name Eric very much, but I don't dig Eldridge at all for a middle name. I do like Andrea, but prefer Melanie.

I like Antonia because I'd like to call my daughter Tawnie– I dig that so much!

Tawnie Brown. Outasight! I also like Stephanie, so...can't think of many guys' names, but I've always been partial to Jeff, though I don't dig naming boys after their fathers. Too many Jeffs around could be confusing.

I don't believe that bullshit about acid wrecking chromosomes, and even if it were true, neither of us have dropped enough acid to make any great physical changes.

When the time comes, maybe we should ask a doctor about the after effects of acid. Jeff definitely wants to wait until 25 to have kids, but I don't want to wait that long. Maybe hold off until after he finishes college, but 25?

That's almost middle age.

A chick can only take The Pill for two years—40 years from now it might be different—and I don't think either of us would relish male contraceptives too much.

Where did Jeff ever come up with, "I would even love you, even if you didn't shave your legs"?

Penny thought it was hilarious, and announced Jeff's declaration to the entire ward.

Everybody laughed. Hairy legs could become a reality; then I'd have to hold him to his promise.

Once, in high school, a few of us decided, for the hell of it, to let the hair grow on our legs to grow in for a whole month, just to see how it would feel. Knee socks were in, so we didn't have to suffer any teasing, but it sure felt weird.

All that prickly hair pushing through.

After the month was up, we revved up our razors and got ready for the Great American Shave-in.

The whole issue of body hair is kind of strange, actually. Why are women expected to shave their underarms and legs, and men are not? In fact, the hairier the man, the better. Does that make any sense? Why not just keep all hair?

In Europe, women don't seem to worry about body hair. Hans, a high school pen pal, once sent me a picture of a pretty German girl in a bathing suit, and her underarm hair was thick and black, about four inches long, but she was all smiles and didn't seem self-conscious at all, but, if we dare to go hairy, we get teased and called Lesbians.

Back in eighth grade, there was a girl, Gerilyn O'Hoolihan–

she was kind of boyish and liked to play real baseball (with wooden bat and hard ball, instead of the plastic stuff that the rest of the girls liked). Her parents wouldn't allow her to shave her legs, and I'm not so sure she really wanted to, anyway. Behind her back, all the kids called her Gerry O'Hairy Legs and called her other names that weren't very nice, but she didn't seem to notice, or, if she did, didn't care.

Still, it goes to show how all-powerful the Establishment is when it comes to deciding what's acceptable and what's not.

Come to think of it, I've been rather lax lately in the shaving department.

I HAVE NOTHING to wear for the dance tonight. I own three pairs of slacks: one pair is ridiculously stained (from sitting on the grass); one pair just plain dirty; and the other torn. All my dresses and blouses are also dirty. Anyway, what good are tops without bottoms?

I dig deeper into my meager wardrobe, and find a shorts outfit that I had all but forgotten. Actually, it's a real short dress with bloomers and a sash that ties in back–very in last summer in L.A. (I bought it at Zayres near Mom's house). It's light blue, tiny raised white polka dots. It's clean, but in bad need of ironing and repairs, so I get out the iron and needle and thread. For not being too handy in those departments, I come up with something that looks kind of cute.

Feeling saucy and groovy, I wear it to the dance.

Everyone laughs.

They say my outfit looks like pajamas.

A few years ago, I would've been embarrassed and upset, but now it's hilarious.

Besides, how many girls get to wear pajamas to a dance?

Then the biggest surprise of all.

D.J. shows up, hair all slicked up and in place. He's decked out in a new pair of overalls, a new shirt (solid blue, not plaid!), and new shoes. Clod hoppers, of course, but all shined up.

"You wanna dance?" he asks, bowing and offering me a daffodil.

I accept the flower and tuck it behind my right ear. "You bet I do."

Definitely beats Wolfie and some of the other animals I've encountered in the past few months.

The Righteous Brothers' "Unchained Melody" strikes up: a good, old-fashioned slow dance. Somehow, it seems fitting that my best male friend here would take me into his arms, and sweep me onto the dance floor.

Maybe sweep isn't exactly the right word.

We're both awkward, and, mostly, we clunk around on the dance floor, his clod hoppers stepping onto my feet, I grabbing the lead.

We're the only ones on the dance floor; the rest of the patients root us on.

I can only imagine how we might look to outsiders, to normal observers: I in pajamas and D.J. in his gardening clothes, working hard at ballroom etiquette and failing horribly.

But we don't care; this is D.J.'s debut, maybe the first of many dances–perhaps a future girlfriend.

It all fits.

If I close my eyes, I'm no longer on the dance floor, but gliding among the clouds and looking eastward, to my future.

Sunday, April 13

Everyone's raving about the *Hair* album, but I think it's awful. When I was on trial visit, my cousin Pat played it constantly–I thought I'd go completely out of my head.

I do like the song "Hair," but that's it.

In L.A., the play *Hair* was playing at the Aquarius, across from Wallich's, but Stoney and I were too broke to see it.

Why can't I get Stoney out of my mind? Part of me still

misses him very much—maybe it's because we never broke up officially.

End of story—sort of.

Our breakup was inevitable—no doubt. Yet our relationship remains in suspended animation, frozen at that moment when he kissed me goodbye, and said, "See you in two weeks."

My feeling for Jeff is comfortable and warm—and I love talking with him—but, with Stoney, sex was hot. We didn't have much to talk about, now that I think about it, and I don't even know if he was that smart—he didn't really talk that much about anything, except dope, and toward the end, not even the sex was all that great.

But what if Stoney showed up, in full armor, galloping up the Cherokee hill on a white steed, totally off dope and no longer dealing, ready to rescue me? Would I go with him?

I honestly don't know.

It's not a likely scene, even without armor and white horse; Stoney will be entrenched in the drug scene for many years, and then he'll end up in jail.

Now that I think about it, he really isn't a very nice person; he didn't treat me with much respect.

Still, I miss him; whenever I think about him, I get this little knot in my stomach.

Monday, April 14

FANTASTIC NEWS! That young old goat Benson *finally* found me a place!

Outasight!

It's a dormitory setup in Sioux City. I leave Wednesday morning, but unless I find a job right away, I return to the hospital on Friday night, and I'll get discharged the next week—otherwise, they'll just discharge me while I'm gone and send my stuff to me.

I phoned Jeff tonight, to tell him the good news. But he's still hung up over the Drew debacle; my explanation didn't quite satisfy him. I explained again why I wrote that letter.

I finally got up the courage to ask him why he told Lizzie "To Go Get Fucked." She must have done something totally horrible.

He said he'd tell me in his next letter.

I still worry about that little twit.

And this anti-marriage crap?

Marriage is a "security trap"?

"Dreadfully permanent"?

"Details unimportant"?

"Trial marriage?"

And what happens if *I* end up with a baby, and he decides he doesn't love me anymore?

I don't know...

I may be flighty, impulsive, and silly sometimes, but even *I* can see who ends up with the short end when a relationship fizzles and a baby is involved. At least in a marriage, the girl is protected somewhat...I want my future children to be protected financially–*I* want to be protected.

In a trial marriage, a man has all the advantages of marriage, but without the responsibility, and a woman has all the responsibility but without the advantages...

Maybe I *am* more Establishment than I thought...

Yet Jeff's idea of starting a commune in rural Pennsylvania appeals to me, especially if it's a stable and drug-free one. He's right about choosing our family carefully, though; we don't need the Stoneys, Rudys, and Levis messing up the social structure with their drugs, laziness, wild behavior, and crazy friends.

Advantages of commune living: people around all the time to help out; no one starving because of unforeseen hard times; built-in babysitters; more hands, fewer chores; money not an issue–no one would be rich, but everyone would have enough dough. Jeff seems to worry about money all the time–he's always complaining how much he has spent on phone calls, gasoline, and car insurance–

His family must be poor, but I get all uptight when he obsesses about money all the time.

Most 18 year olds are cash-poor, aren't they?

Disadvantages of commune living: people not pulling their weight, fakers who might take advantage and steal from the commune bank account, lack of privacy–everyone would know your business and might ask you to do something (like babysit) when you didn't feel like it–

Lines would need to be drawn...

And I'm not sure about natural childbirth; in my book, "natural" equals "pain." I have also read that some communes reject the notion of having birth certificates for babies. Too strange.

I don't want some government official coming around and saying that my kids aren't citizens of the U.S.–I want proof. Kids eventually grow up and have to go to school, though a commune school might be possible.

Also, I have heard about some communes that require you to swap mates for sex. That doesn't appeal to me at all–I want only one man in my life. I envision a commune that dictates monogamous relationships–married or living together–and expels anyone caught breaking the monogamy rule. A form of divorce should be allowed–after all, there could be unusual circumstances, like dumping a mate who has broken the monogamy rule, or if a man beats on his old lady and kids–those details would have to be worked out in a charter.

Any children would need to be protected, both physically and financially, from squabbling mates. No child should have to go through what Robin and I had to. Siblings would never be separated. Custody issues would be clearly spelled out, and the parent most capable would get custody of all the children. If no parent is capable, then the children will go to a stable, willing commune family.

Members could not personally own guns–communal rifles would be used for hunting game for food–but not for sport–and then locked up. Guns for sport cause nothing but trouble, and, besides, animals shouldn't be killed just for fun.

The extended family would live on a compound, but individual families would live in their own homes, owned by the commune. Each family would pay rent, either through cash payments or barter, maybe a combination of the two.

Women would care for the children and do the domestic work–cooking, sewing, household chores–while the men did the heavy work–hunting, farming, heavy construction. Maybe some men and women would be allowed outside jobs, depending on their skills and education.

Though I haven't quite worked out the job issue–should commune members be allowed to work outside the commune, or will they be required to work on the compound, as teachers, doctors, farmers, accountants, etc.? Haven't quite figured that out–I see advantages and disadvantages, though making people stay within a limited compound seems a bit strange.

Would a family be allowed to take trips away from the compound? I, for one, would like to see more of the world, but if everyone took their vacations in the summer, then no one would be left to take care of the compound–something else to be worked out.

Jeff's idea sounds so cool, but a lot to think about.

Commune living isn't something to be jumped into lightly, without some major planning.

And a wedding ring.

Okay, so it may be too soon for a wedding ring, but I get so tired of hearing from men about marriage being a trap; I don't see it that way, but as a commitment between a man and a woman. I'm not quite sure how I feel about getting married right now–18 does seem a bit young, but I don't want to discount the idea entirely.

During our phone conversation, out of the blue, Jeff suggested I make peace with Mo and Dee Dee. After all they've put him and his family through–quite generous and forgiving.

I'd like to bury the hatchet, once and for all, but will they let me live my life the way I see fit?

If not, then I don't see how we can patch things up.

But I said I'd try because, for Jeff, it seems to be important.

In today's letter to him, I tried explaining how I feel about our relationship: "Right now, I'm sure of myself, but will I feel that way tomorrow or the next day? I'm not afraid to love you in a physical way–I may be rusty, but certainly not afraid. I still want to live with you, but it might be a good idea to let things cool down–play the Establishment's stupid game until they tire of it. What do you think?"

I just assumed that my relationship with Stoney would evolve into a marriage. I didn't think about it–I just jumped into the relationship without considering Stoney's point of view.

So, now, I'm being cautious. The Stoney thing stung me. The old adage, "Love everyone, but trust no one," seems especially appropriate.

Still, when the time does come to make a decision, I will not accept the marriage trap argument as valid.

I want my children to have a name, and I will want a husband who is fully committed to me, loves me enough to say, "I do," and mean it.

Jeff's not ready to hear that yet.

IT'S AFTER MIDNIGHT, and I'm kind of beat. I washed my hair at 11:00 p.m., and then noticed the horrendous mess left in the ward kitchen; I devoted an entire hour and 15 minutes cleaning up. Whoever made the popcorn tonight obviously didn't clean up. I'm not really that ambitious, but guess who'd get the rap if no one cleaned up?

I'm not popular with the older set on this ward. I'm young,

so I like to run around. Just because I get written up about every day doesn't mean I do everything that goes wrong. At every ward meeting, I sort of sit there and flinch at the long list of transgressions.

I do flush the toilet, however. Some chick—we still don't know who—never flushes. When the ward finds out who, she'll surely get mugged.

Also, the people here display an utter lack of boundaries, always poking around in your business—sometimes when you're doing your business. It's so gross having a nurse or attendant barging in on you when you're in the bathtub and even on the toilet. I'm very freaky about strangers seeing me naked and doing very personal things.

So I do understand Jeff's need for privacy, but with him it almost seems like an obsession. Freaking out when his mother's in the same room, but 20 feet away? Seems extreme. She doesn't sound like the nosy type at all.

Maybe he's exaggerating to make a point; I can't imagine feeling so self-conscious around someone you love. Around strangers, yes. Lovers, no.

I can't stand when some stranger comes into your room in the god-awful morning to wake you so that you can hurry up and eat a lousy breakfast of lukewarm coffee, cold eggs, undercooked bacon, and warm orange juice and then rush to make some pointless doodad in O.T.

One attendant, Bonnie, reminds me of Mo, with her incessant, "Rise and shine, the early bird gets the worm."

One day, I just answered, "No, the early worm gets the bird." I gave her the finger and rolled over to go back to sleep.

Some of the other patients, Carrie especially, don't seem to care that you might want to be alone—they just barge in, even when it's obvious that you're writing a letter or in your diary, and start yakking at you. I just want to bop them! This is why I stay up so late; I can grab some privacy while everyone else sleeps. It's quiet then, but not a scary quiet, like when you're already in bed and can't sleep–it's only then that the night fills me with terror.

Otherwise, I embrace the late night.

I like when Monica, another night attendant, is on duty. She's my age, and totally cool. I can talk with her about nothing much, and she doesn't hassle me about going to bed before midnight. She doesn't act like Establishment, either, with all their nosy and judgmental ways. She seems to know when I want to be alone, and disappears into the office to do paperwork.

She has the most beautiful long blonde hair I've ever seen. While they're on duty, the nurses and attendants with hair hanging below their shoulders are required to keep their hair up in a knot or bun, but once Monica came to visit when she was off duty, and her long, flowing hair reached almost to her waist, thick and shining.

"Should I cut it?" she once asked, playfully.

"No way."

She just laughed.

I hope she doesn't cut it–ever.

Tuesday, April 15

In less than 24 hours, I'll be getting out, hopefully for good. Then I have to think seriously about my plans for the next few weeks. I'm a bit anxious about leaving; as much as I hate it here, it *is* safe, and I have made some friends: D.J. and Penny especially.

I don't have to worry about where I'll sleep tonight and when I'll eat. I can see how people can get stuck here for years, why D.J. doesn't want to leave.

I called Jeff again, just to make sure everything is okay; he seems a lot happier about my discharge, so maybe I'm being paranoid about his flip-flopping.

Still, Jeff's April 11 letter suggests an unsettling option: living apart at first and just dating. I'm not quite sure what to think. On the one hand, it might be a good idea, a sort of getting reacquainted before jumping into something super heavy.

And, yet...I sense a reluctance. Maybe a part of him doesn't want me to come out.

Once I get an idea in my head and make up my mind about something, I want to forge ahead, even if it doesn't feel quite right. It's like I can't turn back, no matter what.

Maybe it's the same with Jeff.

The idea of living apart and not having sex sounds silly–over the past few months, we have gone beyond the point of just dating and holding hands. We've revealed our deepest secrets.

Well, most of them.

I'm not all that sure about getting into a heavy scene again, especially without some safeguards; I've never been to Pennsylvania–what's it like? I've never heard of York; just Philadelphia and Pittsburgh come to mind. If I needed help, where would I go? Jeff's parents wouldn't help–his mom has made that clear, and I couldn't turn to Mo and Dee Dee; they'd say, "I told you so," and I'd have to live with that for the rest of my life.

No, I have gone too far to *ever* go back.

BUMMER. Joyce is back, this time, according to Carrie–who somehow manages to find out all the scuttlebutt–she's really freaked out and has been in a padded cell for the last 48 hours, screaming her head off. Maybe her responsibilities were too much...

Carrie herself has been back on 4 for only about a day, which probably explains how she knows so much about the people in locked ward. She likes to gossip about people who are worse off than her.

I knew it was too soon for Joyce—this screwed up place really pisses me off. Her doctors had to know it, too, but they chose to look the other way. Why couldn't they talk some sense into Joyce's husband?

He has to be the most selfish person in the world...

I'LL BE SO GLAD TO SPLIT this joint—

But not until I say goodbye to D.J.

I find him watering the fir tree, our mutual friend. "Hey, D.J."

He nods.

"Well, this is it; I leave tomorrow."

"I know."

"I just want to say goodbye."

"I hate goodbyes."

"I do too."

"Will you visit me?"

"I'm going to Pennsylvania, D.J., and it's far away."

"Yeah, I know. To see Jeff."

"That's right."

"Thanks for inviting me to the dance. It was fun."

"Yeah, it was."

"I'm gonna miss you."

"Me too."

He continues watering the fir, lightly shaking the hose as if to nudge the water out faster. Then he puts the hose down and hugs me, a tentative, holding back hug. I'm going away, after all, out of his sphere, and he has already begun the process of disconnecting.

My life is about to take a dramatic turn—how it eventually plays out, I'm not sure—but I'll be out of here and into the world, doing my thing.

But D.J.'s day-to-day life is here, always to be the same, following the seasons, nurturing new plants, mourning the dying and dead.

If I were to return 25-35 years from now, I might find D.J., an old man, in this same spot, the fir tree a mighty sage.

V

Leaving Cherokee

86

April 16-30, 1969

(Sioux City)

WEDNESDAY, APRIL 16

I'M ALL SETTLED in Shesler Hall, courtesy of the state.

Another dorm, more rules.

In two weeks, I'll be responsible for paying my own way. Starting now, I must buy my own clothes, soap, shampoo, cigarettes, stamps, paper, etc. I've found a job, which means I don't have to go back to Cherokee on Friday! Denise's Diner on West 7th, a small, dilapidated joint, 7:00 a.m-3:00 p.m. shift.

Balls!

But I would have agreed to any job, even shoveling shit, if it meant not having to go back to Cherokee. If I *never* see that nuthouse again, it'll be too soon. Still, slaving at Denise's Diner will be as close to shoveling shit without actually having to shovel it.

Denise, the owner, is about the hardest, wrinkliest woman I've ever met, a nervous, bird-like chain smoker. She's old, probably in her late 50's, maybe early 60's, and all skin and bones. Her hair, red with purple highlights, is teased into a rather large bouffant, overshadowing her tiny body, and her teeth are yellow with dark specks between them. Her voice is deep and raspy, like a man's–she could out-cuss a sailor.

"You're gonna work your goddamn ass off around here, for shit wages," she said when she interviewed me. "But you can earn some good tips." She took a drag on her cigarette. "Just play along with the guys–they like giving the girls a hard time–and don't get all fuckin' women's lib on 'em."

I can do that, at least for a few weeks.

"And get your ass in gear, and don't poke. I do most of my business at lunch–these men gotta get fed fast and back to work."

I'm glad this job's temporary. A shitty buck an hour, plus tips, to start. But I'm just interested in staying out of Cherokee and splitting this town. Soon, I'll be getting that $116.00 refund from the government, and I'll save every spare penny.

"Lazy bitches don't last here," Denise said as I headed out the door. "Be here, at 7:00 sharp, or don't bother comin' at all."

Thursday, April 17

My first day at work wasn't so bad, though I wouldn't want to do this for the rest of my life. Actually, I'm not sure *what* I'd want to do. I like art and writing, but I don't see much of a career path in either.

Maybe I shouldn't worry–a good home life is what's really important; work is just that: a daily grind, something to keep body together and roof over head. Go to work; forget about it at quitting time. Jeff's right that we shouldn't become so work-a-day that we forget each other, though it would be cool to find jobs we liked.

I can't see Jeff working at that flour mill for the rest of his life–he's much too smart, a thinker, not a hard laborer. I hope he can work in college–maybe I can help put him through. I doubt very much if I'll ever go to college–I don't have the desire. School is such a drag.

I hate getting up so early, but do like getting off at 3:00– plenty of day left! I have time to do other things, like have fun.

I had so much time in Cherokee, but with so little to do; now I have so little time, it seems, with so much to do. Why can't there be a happy medium?

I hope my time in Sioux City passes swiftly.

Jeff wants me to come out now, but leaving right now is not a good idea, though as soon as I earn enough bread and get my refund, I'm splitting, no matter what they do. If they want to keep me in this fucked town, they'll have to lock me up and chain me to the wall–

No matter. I'd find a way out.

Friday, April 18

Mrs. Lundeen, a social worker–they seem to butt a lot into my life lately–came by the dorm and informed me that if I wanted the rest of my clothes and stuff from Mo and Dee Dee's, I'd have to fetch them myself.

I wasn't thrilled by the prospect, but, on the other hand, if I wanted to make sure I got everything, it was a necessary evil.

Mo *never* keeps her word. She and Dee Dee agreed to return all my letters, but they only gave back one letter from Jeff; I know for a fact that they have at least one other letter from him, and some from Pam and others, as well.

I confronted Mo about the missing letters, including Pam's.

"Those letters were so filthy I hid them so the grandkids wouldn't find them," she said. "And I don't remember where I put them."

"Liar! You have those letters, and I want them back now!"

"Go away! I didn't ask you over here!"

She's the one who told the social worker I'd have to pick up my stuff myself.

"You have no right to keep my things."

She then rooted through some drawers and came up with some letters from Pam and other friends. I doubt if I got them all back.

"Where's Jeff's letters?"

"Dee Dee has one at the office."

"Where's the other one?"

She just shrugged and turned away and started humming.

I hate when she puts on the big freeze and gets that glassy-eyed, blank stare.

She acts like she's ignoring everything around her, but I know better.

"I'm splitting here in about a month, and don't try to stop me."

"You go do whatever you want. You're just like your mother, and I've washed my hands of her."

"I'm not ever coming back, either!"

"Get your things, and get out!" she screamed.

I gathered what I could carry and went to Dee Dee's office.

After some discussion and arguing, he pulled a letter out of a drawer and handed it to me.

I grabbed it. "I knew it," I said. "You've been lying to me."

He shook his head. "I give up trying to help you."

"I don't need your kind of help. I just want to do my thing."

"Well, we won't stand in your way."

I turned away and left.

THE RESCUED LETTER is postmarked February 14, 1969, a lifetime ago. On the front of the envelope: a drawing of an American soldier shooting a Viet Cong, the back with a long-haired Uncle Sam raising the peace sign, reciting "My Country, 'Tis of Thee..." and a message, "Could it Even Happen in America?"

Another note to Mo and Dee, letting them know that he never promised to stop writing to me. The letter raps about nothing much, just about running into an old girlfriend at a basketball game; now she's engaged to some straight dude.

Jeff managed to cover the important things in later letters, but, still, it pisses me off that certain people can't keep their hands off my personal belongings. This letter looked like it had never been opened, but I'm sure that Mo and Dee have read and resealed it.

The January 20 letter is still missing, and I suspect I'll never get it back, no matter what they've promised Dr. Favis and Mr. Benson. I suspect Jeff accepted my offer of more than friendship, and that's all. At that time, he had no reason to sass Mo and Dee. I doubt if there was anything pornographic in it, maybe a few cuss words, but that's all.

I received a $50.00 check from The Bank of America today, and when I get my $116.00 back from the government, I'll have almost $170.00. I also have some loose change around. I'll stay here long enough to earn about $80.00 more. Since the state is paying only my first two weeks room and board, I'll have to save a lot from my first two paychecks. I should be able to save about $40.00 per paycheck, that is, until I have to start paying my room and board. With tips, I'll probably make only about $48.00 a week.

At the latest, June 1st for Pennsylvania.

God, if I hadn't found this job, I'd be going back to Cherokee about now—for the whole weekend.

Saturday, April 19

My job isn't that hard—it takes no brains waiting on horny old men with nothing better to do than hang out at Denise's Diner, smoking cigarettes and drinking coffee or beer.

Yes, I have to serve beer. I'm not old enough to conduct my own life, but, apparently, I'm old enough to serve alcohol. It seems that being of age depends on what the Establishment wants from you.

My boss Denise is really strange; she's trying to scare me by saying how this is such a hard job. Physically, maybe. My feet are killing me—I had to soak them in hot water, they hurt so badly—and the customers are extremely rude. To them, I'm just a fixture, created to wait on them hand and foot, or they treat me like I'm their mother or girlfriend. I felt like telling a couple of those asses to back off, but Denise says we have to suck it up.

"Part of the job, honey," she said.

I'm glad this is temporary.

I have already earned $20.65, including tips. I bought two new tee-shirts, one red and one with daisies. I also bought a pair of blue jeans and Cream's *Wheels of Fire* album. Stoney used to go around singing, "Spoonful, Spoonful, Spoonful," and I used to think, "Man, what a freak going around, singing about cereal." But, then, Pam played the song, and, wow, I really dug Cream's version.

But Stoney made it sound like a cereal commercial.

I CALLED JEFF tonight, but he wasn't home; then I called Susie and Isabelle—they weren't home either. So I called Cynthia. I can't stay mad at her forever, but we'll never be the close friends we once were. I can't trust her; she's one of the reasons I got stuck in Cherokee in the first place. Besides, she's just too Establishment.

We hung out for a bit, but, already, she's trying to talk me out of going to Pennsylvania; she'd rather see me die and wither here in Sioux City, just like her.

Besides, if I wanted a lecture, I'd go visit Mo and Dee.

Sunday, April 20

I SLEPT IN LATE TODAY, until 11:50. God, only one day a week off. Now I understand why Jeff's letters are shorter now. It seems like I can think of a million things to tell him, but by the time I get home, I can't sit still long enough to write a coherent thought, and then I'm so tired, I'm stupid. All the physical work and then walking the six or seven blocks back and forth is helping to keep the weight off, but it saps all my energy.

In many ways, this job is better than Bank of America–that job was so stressful, and I always had a knot in my stomach from having to call all those straight people to check the credit of other straight people. Always had someone on my back about rushing some important loan application.

Monday, April 21

I'm so dead-assed tired, I can't even muster up enough energy to write any letters.

I can't *wait* to quit this job. Denise is such a two-faced bitch, jabbering about working hard, but she lounges around, chewing the fat with the guys, and chain-smoking those god-awful Camels without filters. If there was ever a reason to quit smoking, she's it. I don't want to grow old looking like a dried up prune.

Even when it's super busy, she doesn't hustle her butt any–she just barks at the help to move faster. What kind of an example is that?

The guys talk dirty to her, she thinks it's hilarious, but it's just gross. Customers or not, I'm not taking that kind of crap. After one creep pinched my butt, I told him off.

"You better watch your step, honey," Denise said.

I'd like to tell her to go to Hell, but I need this job, at least for a few days. But, damn it, no old fart had better touch me, unless I give him express permission.

Tuesday, April 22

I go to National Industries, to find Dee Dee. I must talk to him and Mo about my leaving. I get the strangest feeling he's under the impression that I've forgotten about going to Pennsylvania.

I need to set the record straight.

I think Mo knows—she should—I've made it plenty clear to her. But I'm going to try to have a rational talk with them both, and if that doesn't help, nothing will. At least I will have tried.

I still haven't received my things from the hospital—it's all Benson's fault. He's doing this on purpose, testing me.

After work, I went downtown to buy some suitcases. I found a footlocker for $12.00; I should be able to fit all my worldly possessions in that. I dragged it back to the dorm and started packing my things.

I can feel it in my bones: spring is definitely here, and I'll soon be on my way to York, Pennsylvania!

WEDNESDAY, APRIL 23

I RECEIVED A LENGTHY LETTER from Jeff, written from April 15-20—my favorite so far. Lots of little stuff: a date with his cousin Karen, making $30.00 a week more, seeing Caesar on TV, the meaning of Pennsylvania (Penn's Woods), rapping on the phone, jobs (present and future), Buffy Sainte-Marie on TV, enforced abstinence, wheat harvest at the flour mill, pet names, a sweet story about the Little Red Hen loving Jennifer during rough times, old girlfriends—another explanation why old feelings about Lizzie came back and how I'm so much like her—oh, yeah?

—Speaking of Lizzie: Jeff hasn't yet revealed what she asked about me that wasn't any of her business. I wonder if he's heard from her since his "Go Get Fucked" letter—

He also wrote a form-free, freak-out poem about me. No one has *ever* written me a poem, and a good one too, not silly like my stuff. Well, maybe "Whirling bats/And catamounts" is a bit odd, but I'm not about to question Jeff's gift, worth more than all the mansions and fancy cars in the world. When I knew Jeff in L.A., I really didn't know this side of him very well. I knew he was smart, but not quite as deep. Maybe these months of writing back and forth–before getting together–have been good for us. It's easier to reveal feelings in a letter; I can hear Jeff's voice and sense his presence. I *feel* his letters.

He still worries about money, even with extra money coming in; if I get a part-time job, it should help. He wants to be the main provider, and that's cool. When I have children, I want to stay home with them, at least until they're in school. I'd feel much better if Jeff got a pad, though–even if he lives at home for a while.

Jeff goes back and forth about the living together issue. He proposed the idea of living apart for about 4-5 days, just to get re-used to each other. Seems kind of strange, but it's up to him to figure out the right time to leave home.

IN HIS APRIL 19TH LETTER, Jeff reveals his views on the draft and the war:

> *My 1-A scares me. I think the draft board will be glad to get its hooks into me, anyway–and I will not serve as a combatant; I don't care what they say! I'll have to check over my appealing rights and see if I can stall anymore before I can sneak into college (I'm not exactly anxious to go to jail for my beliefs), but whatever I do, it will have to be quick.*
>
> *Shooting holes in North Vietnamese isn't exactly my idea of "making my country a better place in which to live."*
>
> *And getting holes shot into me by North Vietnamese seems equally purposeless (and a bit more painful). A kid I used to know in high school was shot through the head last week, and it destroyed his memory and his muscular coordination. If I ever have to go, I at least want it to be for something more worthwhile. I'd rather go to war against the Chicago Police Department than the Viet Cong–at least there I would know what I was*

fighting for.

I'm scared, too; I can't see him fighting in a war, rifle in hand. No one should be forced to go to war against his will. It seems unfair that only men are drafted.

Although I'd hate it, why not women, too, like in the Israeli Army? At least the burden would be shared. If we must have a draft, women could be required to do behind-the-lines duties, unless they wanted to fight at the front.

On second thought, the draft should be abolished altogether.

The more I read about this war, the more pointless it seems—the South Vietnamese don't really want us there, and the Viet Cong fight dirty, what with all their underground tunnels and hideouts. In their own territory, they hold the upper hand: the Cong know all the nooks and crannies, and our boys have to navigate around hidden land mines and other traps. Why should men my age be forced to carry a rifle and grenades and kill complete strangers who aren't bothering us at all? From what I could tell, this war fucks up guys really bad, or, worse, kills them off like they were clay pigeons.

Mo and I do agree on this one issue.

"Just old men sending young men in to die," she says all the time. Mo then gets this faraway look in her eye, like she's remembering something sad from long ago. I know Dee Dee was in France during World War I, but I think that was before she knew him. Maybe she had a beau who died...

Otherwise, her utter hatred of war doesn't quite fit; usually she's so Establishment, but not on this issue. She's always trying to think of devious ways for my cousins to get out of going to war.

She's especially worried sick about Steve Semple going to Vietnam.

I'm worried, too. Jeff's schoolmate was shot in the head: too horrifying. Sooner or later, someone I know is going to die by some Viet Cong's hand.

Please, not Steve or Jeff.

I don't know what Dee Dee thinks about the war; I'm sure he has his own ideas, but, to keep the peace, plays along with what Mo thinks.

I dread it, but I have to talk with them tomorrow. Set Dee Dee straight about my plans. Mo knows, but those two don't talk to each other much.

The other day, when I told Mo I'm definitely going to Pennsylvania, she reluctantly said, "Okay"–after a big argument, of course. Now she seems resigned.

But she keeps sending me these "Dear Abby" articles about relationships that don't work out.

I MISSED SEEING CAESAR on *The Monkees Special.* On national TV, too!

Even narks get featured on TV; I'll bet the L.A.P.D. was thrilled to see its main Hollywood and Vine undercover detective whooping it up with the Monkees and their teenybopper groupies.

Makes me feel a little homesick for L.A.

THURSDAY, APRIL 24

I HATE THIS JOB.

Denise is not only a bitch, but also a crook.

I was about to clear the counter in my station–it was a mess because lunch had been busier than usual, so I was behind in my cleanup–when, a bit too sweetly, Denise said, "Honey, you take a short break."

I got a bad feeling–it just didn't fit; usually, she's yelling at me to get my ass in gear. Still, I like to give people the benefit of the doubt, so I got myself a Coke and sat in a booth.

You can tell Denise has been at this job a long time: she

had that counter cleared and cleaned in five minutes, but she wasn't quite fast enough with her sleight of hand: from the counter she slipped a dollar bill, *my* dollar bill, into her pocket.

A measly one buck an hour, and your boss fucking rips you off. If this is the Establishment, then you can have it.

"You took my dollar," I said.

"What dollar?"

The gall.

"My tip."

"Lazy girls don't *get* tips."

I wanted to strangle that woman, but if I confronted her, she'd deny it, and then fire me for false accusations and insubordination.

Call the police? Right.

I'm going to quit as soon as possible and split this godforsaken town.

Where *is* that tax refund, anyway?

I HAVEN'T HEARD FROM PAM lately. Something's definitely wrong. Has she gone off the deep end?

I did get a letter from Ray, a patient still in Cherokee. A real head, drugs his lifeline. I feel sorry for him, but he's made his own Hell. Divorced, four kids, busted for dealing–

It's weird. He's so much like Stoney. Ray and I talked a lot, but he came on too strong. It took Stoney a week to ask me about living with him; Ray asked after two hours, even after I told him about my problems with Stoney and my relationship with Jeff. His type never understands; they're too intent on screwing whatever moves, dropping acid, and shooting up. I can't hate those kinds of people–only pity them. I could never love a guy like Ray.

I've dealt with too many Stoneys and Rays to affect me the way such B.S. once did.

Ray's letter was short–not very informative and not emotionally penetrating, just words on paper. In fact, it took me longer to explain about Ray than what he wrote.

Penny's home on trial visit this weekend, to attend a wedding, so she called me. Lots going on at the institution. Drew might beat the narcotic rap on some technicality, and his new girlfriend is on locked ward, freaked out, hallucinating, and screaming her bloody head off. Penny thinks she'll have to go on shock treatments.

Other gossip: Ray might come to Sioux City on trial visit, and that 16-year-old guy still has it bad for me. I feel sorry for him, but he'll just have to get over it. Why is it that when you pay any attention to guys, they assume that you want to go with them?

I really like Penny, but now that I'm away from the institution, I realize how little we have in common. Before, we had our hatred of the shrink house to moan about, but now, not much at all. I can't imagine her life at all–past or future. Her boyfriend's in prison; she won't tell me what he's in for, so it must be super serious. Maybe if she could finish high school, she could pull herself away from these bad relationships and find someone who would love and protect her. She couldn't help what happened to her when she was 11, but she can determine what happens in the next few years...

But I don't see it happening. She may think she loves that jailbird, but he'll use her and then split.

Friday, April 25

When I first read Jeff's April 21 letter, I was ecstatic: "I *everything* you," he said.

No one has ever everythinged me before, and I was soaring like an eagle–

Then I turned the page, and there it was, my worst fear:

"Lizzie wrote...she asked me to visit her, two hundred

miles away...I don't everything Lizzie, but I love her—more than a friend, less than an old lady—"

Why did he have to ruin such a perfect declaration of love?

I hate the idea of Jeff's going to Altoona to see that little bitch. She's playing with his head.

"I feel like a coward," he said. "It would be so nice if I could tell Lizzie to 'go get fucked' and then mean it a week later. I can't detest a person who doesn't detest me, and Lizzie is too much like you to simply ignore."

Why are guys so stupid about girls who play silly little games? Girls like Lizzie dangle candy canes in front of their prey and then yank them away. Yet guys keep chasing after them because the chase is everything. If Jeff ever catches her, she'll just laugh in his face and move on, and the whole thing will feel hollow and cheap.

If she's the virgin she says she is, he won't even get a sample. Quite frankly, I have my doubts—maybe technically—but there are other ways of having sex without actually having intercourse—I'll bet she knows them all.

I hate her; I wish she'd go away and never be spoken of again. It's so unfair that she gets to see him before I have my chance with him. He says he will stay faithful to me, and I believe he means it, but I know how women can dangle sex in front of a man to snare him. She doesn't even want him; she just doesn't want me to have him.

I *must* get myself out to Pennsylvania as soon as possible, before it's too late.

Now I wish Jeff and I were getting married instead of just living together. Perhaps a marriage certificate is just a piece of paper, but it's still important.

I CUT WORK today; I was on my way to the diner, about two blocks away, when I decided I didn't want to go. I couldn't stomach that bitch yelling at me all day and stealing my tips and feeling helpless about it.

Denise represents everything bad about the Establishment: greed, immorality, gaudiness.

Yet, if I try to get what's mine, I'll be the bad guy, just like when I asked for help back in February. It's best to take care of matters on your own.

So what if she's a person short today? Let her and those creepy men rot. I'll never go back there again.

Any time now, I'll be getting my tax refund from the IRS and possessions from the institution; then I'll split for good.

I don't need Denise's Diner or anything else in Sioux City, Iowa.

BAD NEWS.

Jeff received an invitation, announcing the May 8 nuptials of Pamela Lynn Matthews and Leonard George Whitaker.

"No wonder we haven't heard from Little Sister!" he said. "Anyway, I'm sort of glad to hear about that–Pam always needed more than just an 'old man'–she belonged on the street even less than you did."

Obviously, Jeff doesn't realize that Leonard George Whitaker is the one and only Levi. Stoney once told me Levi's real name.

Pam marrying him shakes me up–a lot.

I SAW TERI from high school today–does she ever look different–I just couldn't believe it; her hair is so long and straight, not frizzy and short any more. People change so much in a year. Teri was so friendly to everyone in high school, but she didn't exactly strike me as being that way now. Actually, she acted kind of snobby and stuck up. Maybe she got wind of Cherokee, and now she thinks she's too good for me.

It's going to be like that from now on. Kids from high school have changed, many of them pursuing college, career, or marriages; I'll eventually drift away from my closest friends–I see it happening already.

Some will even move away from Sioux City.
Some of the guys will be drafted and sent to Vietnam.
Some will die there.

All my clothes and other belongings, including the Melanie painting, arrived from the hospital tonight. So, once I get that refund, there'll be nothing to stop me from leaving for Pennsylvania, except, maybe, for whatever happens this weekend in Altoona.

Maybe I shouldn't be so worried about it; if Lizzie is as featherbrained as I think she is, Jeff'll see through her. I'll keep my fingers crossed and hope that refund comes, like, tomorrow. And get my ass to York, Pennsylvania.

No matter what, I'm splitting for *somewhere*, whether it be east to Pennsylvania or west to California.

I'm hoping it's Pennsylvania.

Saturday, April 26

I will not return to Denise's.

Besides, she'd probably fire me on the spot. So, like the rest of the unemployed, I slept in today, until 9:30. I probably should have given her proper notice, but when I get uptight, I really don't stop to think about what's right. I just couldn't face that creepy broad again.

Besides, she's probably figured out by now that I'm not coming back.

Tuesday, April 29

Pennsylvania, here I come.

I got tired of waiting for Jeff's decision in a letter, so I called him, money well-spent.

The verdict's in: me!

Jeff seemed tired, almost let down, like coming down from super acid or speed. We didn't talk long, just enough to find out:

(1) He had a fantastic time in Altoona
(2) Lizzie is more than just a friend, but less than an old lady
(3) I'm still definitely number one.

My instincts tell me to watch out for that little bitch. I went to school with girls like her–cock teasers who play with men's emotions. They don't want the guys they flirt with–they just don't want anyone else to have them. It's almost like they keep spare guys around, just in case. The maddening thing: these guys hover in the wings, willing to be manipulated by some cute nymphet who bats her eyes at anything with a penis.

Last night I had a nightmare: Jeff and I were sitting in front of Wallich's, just grooving. He was wearing his Rent-a-Cop hat and I my brown felt hat.

Like the first time we met, but now we were old, at least in our mid-fifties and gray-haired, leaning on identical canes, each intricately carved, right down to the skin, as a coiling snake about to strike.

"Hey Jude" was playing on Eleanor's radio–why I still had Eleanor's radio, I don't know. Paul's voice was tinny and distant–like he was winded and tired.

Jeff turned to me. "Lizzie, could you please turn up your radio?"

I *must* get out to Pennsylvania–as soon as possible.

Wednesday, April 30

Hopefully before we're really old, I'd like to go back, with Jeff, to Wallich's Music City.

Were Jeff and I destined to meet? So many things worked against our ever meeting that I have to think that a powerful force drew us together for a reason. Our lives were too much like parallel lines–trekking on similar paths, never to intersect.

Anything could have gone wrong:

(1) Not being at Wallich's at the same time–
(2) Or not talking at all–
(3) Both forgetting to get the other's address–
(4) A lost address–
(5) Stoney working out (at least in the short run)–
(6) Mo succeeding at stealing all of Jeff's letters–

Any one of these events would have broken the link between us.

Love *is* fragile, and–

I *still* don't have my tax refund.

87

May 1-6, 1969

(Sioux City)

THURSDAY, MAY 1

MAY DAY!

A nice fat $116.41 refund check from Uncle Sam arrived this morning.

I'll be leaving soon, real soon. My first thought, "Gotta leave tomorrow." Then I get hold of myself–I'm not even ready to leave yet. I thought it would be at least another month.

Monday, May 5, 1969.

That's when I'll leave.

I'll meet Jeff on May 6, at 7:25 p.m. at the York bus station.

Isn't spring groovy?

I GIVE NOTICE at this place; it's like pulling teeth. God, Mrs. Ashton, the housemother here, insists I'm running from something.

After paying all my debts and buying my bus ticket, I'll have $50.00 left–not much, but it's better than the last time I tried splitting–I would have had about $3.00 left.

Now I have all my important belongings, and Jeff has a job.

My itinerary: I leave Sioux City at 9:15 Monday morning.

Three changes: Des Moines, Chicago, Pittsburgh, and, finally, York.

Ray stopped by tonight, but I was visiting Aunt Julie. Mrs. Ashton probably thought he was a bit weird.

I kind of like Mrs. Ashton, but she gets to me. She misinterprets me a lot. Maybe I'm not the typical chick, but why does the Establishment always try to make you like the rest of the world? If you don't fit into the mold, wow! They brand you. Life isn't fair if you don't fit in with the rest of the flock.

I don't want to be like the rest.

Going away party tonight, complete with Vietnamese Red!

Friday, May 2

Jeff is high on spring, reaching what he calls "a Great Plain of Joy"—how cool is that?—just like a little kid, all without drugs! It's like everything has fallen perfectly into place for us—he's even considering marriage!

Last night's party was okay, though the Vietnamese Red was disappointing, not that much kick, or is it me? Maybe I'm just plain sick of the drug scene.

My friends were glad to see me, but it's clear that when I leave Sioux City, their lives won't be all that different.

For them, my existence will be just a blip.

Saturday, May 3

Jeff's April 29 letter is *so* strange—about the sky always being out of reach:

> *Time is so short: all I want to do is everything. Nobody ever does everything they want to do—that's why death is terrible. To die before you've reached the sky is tragedy— the sky is always an inch away from our fingertips—no*

matter how high we may reach.

Pretty heavy stuff. Sometimes I wonder why he can't embrace the present instead of always looking back or ahead.

His novel today has to be better than yesterday and not as good as tomorrow. I like the idea of doing my best today, because if you take care of today, tomorrow will, more than likely, follow, and yesterday's already gone–can't change what was.

I could lament about mistakes I made in L.A. and how I ended up in the institution–maybe if I had done things differently, I wouldn't have gone to Cherokee, but I did, and that's that. I can't go back and change what happened, but, maybe, I can learn from yesterday's mistakes and not make them again–not end up in Cherokee again.

April 30 letter. I don't understand what Jeff means about bypassing love. How does one bypass love? Isn't love the ultimate goal in life? Even he admits that he doesn't know what else he's looking for life.

Fame? Fortune? Renown? How important are those things if you don't have someone to share them with?

I don't know where Jeff got the idea of my leaving him–maybe I was a little pissy about his Lizzie visit, but I don't remember saying anything about leaving him.

In fact, I'm changing my whole life to be with him–I'm not about to leave him now. And I may be losing my family forever, if earlier today is any indication.

I finally had that talk with Mo and Dee Dee together–not pleasant. Mo blew up–said she'd disown me if I left and not to come running to them for help or money if I got into trouble.

I'm definitely on my own.

"Look," I said. "I have to do this. It doesn't mean I don't love you, but I love Jeff, and I want to go to him."

"That dirty hippie," Mo said.

"He's *not* a dirty hippie!"

"You'll stay here and meet a decent Catholic man," Mo said. "And raise a pious, Catholic family."

I shook my head.

"What can we say or do to convince you to stay here?" Dee Dee asked.

"Nothing. My boyfriend is 1,200 miles away, and I want to be with him. That's all."

"We can stop you," said Mo, reaching for the phone. "I'll call the police."

Dee Dee knocked the receiver out of her hand. "Knock it off, Olive."

"Don't try it," I said. "I'll go to court, but I'll do it right this time–I'll hire my own lawyer."

"Nobody's going to try and stop you, Jennifer," Dee Dee said, tears in his eyes. "What have we done to drive you away?"

What can I say? I don't want to go into all that nasty stuff of the past few months because it will just start another fight, and the accusations will fly back and forth, and I don't have the stomach for it anymore.

What would be the point?

"Look, I'm going away, but that doesn't mean I won't come back–"

"If you leave, don't bother coming back–ever!" Mo said.

Mo, always riling shit up.

"That's it! I'm leaving. I can't have a civilized conversation with you people!"

"When you end up barefoot and pregnant, don't come running to us for money!" Mo yelled as I slammed the front door behind me.

Don't worry: I won't.

SUNDAY, MAY 4

TOMORROW. I leave. Finally.

I managed to fit all my possessions into the footlocker, but it was tight; the thing weighs a ton. My whole life's there.

A knot in my stomach—for the first time in my life, I'll truly be on my own, a scary thought.

In their own way, Mo and Dee were good to me—after they took me in, I never lacked for anything: food, clothes, shelter, education—even love.

But now I'll be responsible for myself. Even when I was on the street, my family was always a fallback—I knew I could always go back. No longer an option. Mo has made that clear.

So I'll have to move forward, not look back.

I am truly a woman now.

Monday, May 5

I wake up at 6:00 a.m., ready by 7:00. I splurge and take a taxi to the bus station, there by 7:30—this is one bus I don't want to miss.

I'm not angry with Mo and Dee—well, maybe a little with Mo, but only because she was so ridiculous the other day. I wish they understood that this is something I have to do and would do eventually anyway. I'm not running away to get even with them for the Cherokee bit—

I'm running *to* my new life.

Once, when I was four, I ran away because I wanted to be in the movies, and I thought that one had to run away to do that. I was not angry at anyone—it was just something I had to do. Hours later, when Dee Dee and Dude found me wandering around in the dark, they snatched me from the street, and slid me into the car.

It was deep into an Iowa winter. I wore only a red snowsuit; they must have felt relieved to find me alive and okay.

I bawled and pitched a fit; I was so angry with them for thwarting me. They couldn't understand I wasn't running away to leave them but to find something else.

I would come back.

Obviously, I was too young back then, but not now...

I show my ticket to the agent and check the footlocker at the counter–fortunately, no one questions my business.

I sit and wait.

Dead time, but, nonetheless, necessary.

At 8:45, Dee Dee, alone, slips through the station door.

Oh, oh.

Dee Dee spies me and slides toward me.

Before I can even open my mouth, Dee says, "Before you say anything, just hear me out."

"Okay."

"I'm not going to stop you from going."

"That's good."

"I just want to make one more plea–"

"My mind's made up."

"You're breaking our hearts–"

"I'm sorry about that–"

"No, you're not–you wouldn't be leaving if you knew how much this was killing us."

"I have to go."

Dee Dee sighs. "Stay a few months, get a good job, save up some money–think about what you're doing."

"I've had several, long months to think." Like I'm going to fall for *that* ploy again. "I've made up my mind."

"You know, your grandmother was going to call Cherokee and report you as a runaway, but I told her it wouldn't do any good."

"Thanks."

"She might still do it. Once she's decided something, you know how she is."

"I know."

"I was hoping to reason with you."

"Dee Dee, I'm leaving in a few minutes."

"I see. You know, you'll always have a home back here." Dee pauses. "If you ever need a bus ticket back to Sioux City, just call."

"I'll keep that in mind."

"I despise Jeff Brown with all my heart; he has only one thing on his mind…–"

"Goodbye," I say, turning away.

Without another word, Dee Dee disappears, through the crowd and out of the terminal.

(Greyhound bus)

THE BUS has just pulled out of the station.

I'm headed out of town, toward Des Moines–

Where I'll pick up my first connection to York, Pennsylvania.

A long journey:

> Sioux City.
> Des Moines.
> Chicago.
> Pittsburgh.
> York.

Goodbye, Sioux City and Woodbury County–
Good riddance to Cherokee and all of Iowa.

TUESDAY, MAY 6
(Driven to Pennsylvania)

I NOW UNDERSTAND how Pennsylvania got its name: I've never

seen so many trees in my life. All kinds of trees: pines, firs, oaks, conifers, maples—lots of maples—old, stately trees, with thick trunks, not like the scraggly ones dotting the Iowa landscape. Even the mountains are tree-covered, not like the bare, naked ones out west.

The trip from Pittsburgh to York should only take about 4½ hours, but this leg will total about 7-8 hours; we are scheduled to stop in about every small town along Route 30, weaving on mountain roads, curvy and dangerous.

It's hot today; the air-conditioning doesn't work, so I've slid open the window—hot air blows in, but any moving air is better than motionless, sticky humid air—still, I feel half sick to my stomach, and I need a shower. Spending a night on a bus next to a woman holding her bawling two-year old in her lap is not exactly my idea of great fun—probably not hers, either. This bus, thankfully, is practically empty, so I have two seats to myself—I stretch out.

Somewhere between a town called Breezewood and York, the bus breaks down, and we wait about 45 minutes for a replacement. Even the bathroom doesn't work—all clogged up—and I have to pee.

It seems like I always have to pee, whether I'm being hauled off to somewhere where I don't want to be or fleeing from it.

Jeff expects me at 7:25.

It's like the Establishment's getting one more lick in before Jeff and I can finally be together.

The replacement bus doesn't have air-conditioning either, but at least it has a working bathroom, and it's moving in the right direction:

Chambersburg.
Fort Louden.
Gettysburg.
I study my map and count off the towns.

Around Gettysburg, the road switches to three lanes, the middle one flip-flopping back and forth between east- and westbound. I have never seen a set-up like this back home–a bit harrowing as the bus passes cars and slips back into the right lane just before the passing lane switches back to westbound.

Gettysburg is an important Civil War battlefield, but I see nothing from the road, except restaurants, hotels, souvenir shops, and gas stations. Maybe Jeff and I can visit some of the historical places together–we'll have a lifetime together to explore many fascinating places.

We pass through Gettysburg.

New Oxford.

Abbottstown.

Thomasville.

And, finally–

York.

A strange city, its houses, many of them brick, crammed in rows, running for whole city blocks; Iowa homes are mostly separate, only a few duplexes.

Thirty minutes late, the bus rolls into the station.

Jeff waits in front. He's slightly taller than I remember, maybe a little heavier, but in a good way–in L.A., he was pale and thin, skin and bones. Now he looks slightly muscular, decked out in bellbottoms, print shirt, and suede vest; his skin is slightly bronzed. His hair is shorter–his concession for getting a job–but it looks fuller, almost blond. He wears a light brown cap.

Suddenly shy, I wish I could have had a shower and a change of clothes before this first meeting. My clothes feel grungy and my hair oily and gross, but I'll have to do.

As I step off the bus, he moves tentatively toward me. Our embrace and kiss feel awkward, strange.

It's one thing to imagine this first encounter, but quite another to really know it.

But I'm finally here, and that's what matters.
It's been a long, long journey.

VI

Released

August 30, 2004

88

A Journey Ends
(Leaving Cherokee)

YES, A LONG, LONG JOURNEY.

I fled, carrying most of my worldly possessions and what felt like an ultimatum: either my grandparents' love or my youth.

I chose my youth. What I didn't know back then:

Mo and Dee Dee still loved me. They just didn't know how to let go of a child who was obsessed with leaving.

It's now time to forgive these people who drove me to Cherokee, to involuntary commitment, time to leave the institution for good.

Jerry guides me away from the sundial, toward the front portico. "You okay?"

"I think so. I went back."

"To the past?"

"Yes." Sudden chill in the air. "The other side of the sundial."

Jerry places his arm around my shoulder and pulls me close. "Well, now you're back in 2004."

Finally.

We return to the receptionist, who asks, "Find what you need?"

"Well, I'm looking for the centennial book about the institution. The owner of The Bookseller said you might have a copy left to sell."

Yes...a few copies left, had to reprint it, due to popular demand, but this is it now, no more print runs.

The young receptionist unlocks a cabinet, seizes a book from the shelf, and hands me *Cherokee Mental Health: 100 Years of Serving Iowan's*, a spiral-bound booklet, published in 2001.

I flip to the first page:

This book is dedicated

To the employees of the

Cherokee Mental Health Institute

Who have proudly been serving

Iowans for 100 years.

The spiral-bound booklet feels bulky and awkward in my hands, its dedication too ironic.

What about the ones who drive this place, the patients?

Despite my misgivings, I buy the book.

Jerry and I leave the building and hurry to the car.

As we loop around the grounds, I can almost see them as they were on my last day as a patient. That April day had been chillier, perhaps, and the greenery not quite as lush–Spring in Iowa emerges reluctantly–but the ghosts are still here. Perhaps a few of the same patients are also here. I'm fairly certain that Penny, Carrie, Drew, and Anna have moved on, but I wonder about Wolfie and D.J.–if he's still alive, he'd be almost 80 now.

And then there's Joyce, a Sylvia Plath without the artistic gifts. I'd lay money on her long-term return to Cherokee–she was so fragile and edgy.

As a patient, I spent a lot of time walking these grounds. Even back then, I knew I was different from the other patients; I was not on any drug protocol and, after the first few days, was granted some latitude to wander around on the grounds, so they feel familiar to me, even in 2004.

I took a lot of walks, to think, to escape. In those two months, I watched winter inflict her full fury, the floods of early spring rushing through the lower parts of the city, and, just before I was discharged, the sudden calm of leaves and grass sprouting, birds chirping–noticing, for the first time, how quickly nature adapts. Between April 7 and April 16, this hill transformed from a gray, foggy slush pile to a bucolic Spring scene.

Halfway down the hill, we pull away from the official blue sign introducing The Cherokee Mental Health Institute–we now leave 1251 West Cedar Loop, pick up West Cedar Street, then right on North 3rd St., which turns into U.S. 59 South, toward Sioux City, away from Cherokee.

On the road back, I flip through the book. I wasn't expecting a great masterpiece, but I assumed that a centennial edition would cover all the years through 2001, but it doesn't. Most of the photographs are from the early 1900's, the latest from the 1950's and early 1960's. The text consists largely of supply lists and bills, circa 1902-1903, from businesses and old news clips describing the characteristics of incoming patients, bearing very little relevance to my time there.

I slam the book shut–little help here.

Will secrets embedded in memory, letters, and journeys strike like a bolt of insight? Will the pieces of my story fall neatly into place? Or will it be more complicated than a passive expectation for clarity?

I suspect yet another journey will need to be undertaken, another structure to be built.

We are near Correctionville, about halfway to Sioux City.

The book drops to the floor.

Rooting through Jerry's briefcase, I find today's edition of the *Chronicle Times*. Cherokee's newspaper is a slim publication, one section, 14 pages. Top news: a lengthy success story about attracting Bogenrief Studios, a family of stained and blown glass artisans, to Cherokee and the fire department's unveiling of a new aerial platform.

No obituaries reported for today, one birth announcement, one engagement, and three police reports: a domestic violence incident, a female juvenile charged with theft of items from a private residence, and a 25-year-old male charged with driving while intoxicated.

No national news.

Featured in the social section, a story about local writer and news correspondent Barbara Ann Derksen, honored by The Iowa Business and Professional Women for her novel:

Mind Trap.

No section called "Cedar Loop News" for the institution. On this day, as it was for me in 1969, these are two distinct towns, one wide open and transparent, the other shadowy and secret–just a no-name outline on the map.

As we cruise into downtown Sioux City, I fold the newspaper and slide it back into the brief case.

VII

Final Diagnosis

89

May 9, 1969

(Cherokee, Iowa)

SINCE THE DICTATION of the initial summary the patient had remained stable with no significant changes. While she was waiting for placement in a foster home she was sent on a trial visit at her aunt's place in Sioux City. Again in this trial visit she was pestered by her grandparents. The patient's trial visit went well and she went along well with her cousins and aunt. On her return from her trial visit a group living situation had been found for this patient. This would offer a housemother and a dormitory type living arrangement. She was sent on a one-week trial visit to this place during which she was able to find a job. This patient, therefore, is now being discharged.

FINAL DIAGNOSIS:

Adjustment Reaction of Adolescence.

–Dr. Mariano A. Favis, Jr.

Epilogue

A Final Update
And a Short History
The Cherokee Mental Health Institute

DECEMBER 2012

(York, Pennsylvania)

IN LATE SEPTEMBER 2004, I gathered my laptop, notes, photocopies of old letters to and from my ex-husband, the Cherokee centennial book, maps of Iowa and Cherokee, and the August 30 issue of the *Chronicle Times*. I carried them to Skopje, Macedonia, where I spent October 2004 - May 2005 cranking out a 700-page draft.

A stranger in a strange land attempting to codify an unresolved past. Still, writing that first draft was exhilarating: I had few distractions: for eight solid months, I simply wrote.

Often tapping away eight hours a day, five days a week, I became 18 again, an odd space for a 21st-century baby boomer. Not only did old issues and angers rise up again, but after rereading my ex-husband's letters, I even developed a slight (albeit temporary) crush on him–also compounded by the impending birth of our granddaughter Rhia, born late 2004.

As of late 2012, she is eight and feisty–an echo of my grandmother, who, within her great-great granddaughter, has returned to usher me into my old age.

In 2009, I returned to Macedonia, completed manuscript on my hard drive and my own Fulbright as a creative writer and teacher–perhaps another story to be written at a later time.

AFTER MY JULY 2005 RETURN to the U.S., the revision process presented a rocky road, ordinary life often interfering and my trying to decide what to delete, add, and rewrite. Because this is my story, every detail seemed important, but I eventually deleted about half the manuscript, including the following short history of the institution, out of place in the main narrative, but still an important piece to my story.

*

THE EXTERIOR of the Cherokee Mental Health Institute does not resemble a state hospital.

The grounds, on a gentle slope leading up to the main buildings, are stunning and kept pristine by the grounds keepers and not walled or gated from the community. In summer, lush greenery dominates–the carpet grass is cut and watered regularly, and several varieties of trees, including conifers and deciduous types, majestically dot the landscape. Iowa trees in general tend to be sparse and scrubby, so these grounds offer an oasis, a gift to Sioux Valley Iowans, perhaps explaining their broad appeal.

The buildings are over 100 years old, some of them resembling red stone and brick castles, with spires and circular annexes, but in good exterior condition.

If there is anything forbidding about the place, it can be found in its history and my commitment there. According to *Cherokee Mental Health: 100 Years of Serving Iowan's*, the institution was founded in 1902 as the "Cherokee State Hospital for the Insane." It is not a stretch, then, to view the long shadows cast by the trees and spires as sinister. Also, the red brick portion is somewhat an anomaly in Iowa, not indigenous to this area, known more for its black, loamy earth.

The facility resembles a private secondary school or even a college campus, except for one section, now used as a sex offender unit and housing 35-80 inmates. According to a Department of Human Services press release from then-Governor Thomas J. Vilsack's office, the Civil Commitment Unit for Sexual Offenders (CCUSO), dedicated on September 8, 2003, has been designed to treat "dangerous sexual offenders."

"The litmus test for everything we do is safety," said Kevin Concannon, Director of the Iowa Department of Human Services. "We've gone the extra mile to make sure this facility is safe for patients, safe for staff, and safe for the community."

CCUSO is housed in a remodeled wing of the institution, the sex offenders having "no contact with patients at the mental health institute." The section does resemble a maximum security prison, cordoned off with steel fences and barbed and razor wire, incorporating "security cameras and locks," and mandating "special training for security personnel."

At 18, I would have been upset about having a sex offender unit housed on the same grounds. Safety is a relative term, "safety and sex offenders" an oxymoron, no matter how many security cameras, bars, locked doors, and razor wire used. In a 2005 blurb on *Online Highways*, the sex offender unit is not mentioned:

> *The Cherokee Mental Health Institute (MHI) is a state of Iowa psychiatric facility, operating under the Department of Human Services. The institute provides psychiatric inpatient and outpatient services. Forty-one counties in northwest Iowa are served for adult patients and fifty-five counties for children and adolescents.*
>
> *The MHI is proud of its campus, The Cherokee Human Resource Center offers patients, as well as the Cherokee community, access to a hiking trail and nature study. In addition to the MHI, the campus is also home*

> *to other agencies including Synergy (Chemical Dependency) Center, The Boys' and Girls' Home, the YES (Youth Emergency Services) Center, Job Service of Iowa, Vocational Rehabilitation, Juvenile Court Services, and the Ecumenical Institute.*

Traditional psychiatric inpatient admissions have dwindled since involuntary commitment of patients for frivolous reasons was struck down by two significant Supreme Court decisions: Humphrey v. Cady, 405 U.S. 504, 509 (1972), which ruled involuntary civil commitment to a mental institution as "a massive curtailment to liberty," and O'Connor v. Donaldson, 422 U.S. 563, 574 (1975), which ruled that there is "no Constitutional basis for confining such [mentally ill] persons involuntarily if they are dangerous to no one and can live safely in freedom" and that the presence of mental illness "does not disqualify a person from preferring his home to the comforts of an institution."

In late 2012, shortly after the Newtown, Connecticut, mass murder tragedy, the mental health community and law enforcement agencies would do well to remember these two powerful Supreme Court decisions before embarking on a witch hunt against people who are suspected of being mentally ill or are actually mentally ill.

Evidently, incorrigible minors at Cherokee are still not accorded the same rights as adults. A 2002 *Des Moines Register* article reveals that

> *An 11-year-old boy with extreme behavioral problems is subjected to enemas, made to wear diapers and forbidden to bathe at the DHS-run Cherokee Mental Health Institute until a judge orders the procedure halted. DHS promises an investigation into the boy's treatment. Another state agency later finds that the DHS staff implemented treatments that were "conducted in accordance*

with doctor's orders."

Fortunately, I wasn't incorrigible enough to be subjected to such indignities.

At the time of my involuntary commitment, my only protection was the Supreme Court decision Specht v. Patterson, 386 U.S. 605, 608 (1967), which offered legal protection at the mercy of the court system itself: "...involuntary commitment to a mental hospital, like involuntary confinement of an individual for any reason, is a deprivation of liberty which the State cannot accomplish without due process of law." Even a neophyte can see how a lower court could (and did) interpret that decision; my court record speaks for itself.

Back in 1969, I met some of the employees, many of them dedicated to serving Iowans. But Cherokee owns a sad history of warehousing the mentally ill, the incompetent, and the incorrigible. Before the two important Supreme Court decisions, people not fitting into conventional boxes prescribed by the dominant culture were often punished and hidden away.

Forgotten.

Cherokee itself simply fulfilled a mandate created by an antiquated judicial system mired in nineteenth-century wild west justice.

My residual anger lies with Woodbury County, Iowa, and the police officers, lawyers, judges, and doctors who pushed through sloppily prepared paperwork and trumped up reasons without considering a person's constitutional rights.

I came out of my experience fairly well-adjusted, though my "inclination to conflict with social convention," as predicted by R. Lowenberg, has persisted, for I have always believed that so-called conventional wisdom is vastly overrated. Ralph Waldo Emerson articulated the herd mentality best:

"A foolish consistency is the hobgoblin of little minds."

The world needs people who would flout conventional wisdom, not warehouse and silence them.

The Cherokee book does offer some interesting history about the institution's origins. The first superintendent, Mathew Nelson Voldeng, M.D., was hired in 1902–his beginning salary $250.00 a month. He served from 1902 to 1915 and died in 1934.

One would not suspect Cherokee as being a hotbed of feminism, but, surprisingly, Iowa's first female physician, Dr. Lena Beach, served there, starting in 1902, for which she was paid, as Woman Physician, $100.00 a month, less than the 1st and 2nd Assistant Physicians (presumably men), who were paid $133.33 and $116.66 respectively, but more than the 3rd Assistant Physician, paid $91.66. Somewhere, there exists a biography of Dr. Beach, this pioneer spirit who started the wheels of women's rights rolling in Iowa.

In the early years, many of the staff lived on the campus; however, children were not allowed. Children born to employees were "farmed out to foster homes within the community to be raised."

Now *that's* workplace loyalty.

The first eight Cherokee patients were admitted between August 15 and August 26, 1902. In late August 1902, 563 patients arrived via two trains: 310 from Independence and 253 from Clarinda. In Independence, curious citizens looked on as the stronger patients walked two miles from the hospital and the weak and sickly were transported by trolleys or hay wagons to the Cherokee train. According to the 29 August 1902 Cherokee newspaper, Clarinda offered a higher class of patient: "better dressed, better behaved and showed a little more intelligence." More patients, 777 from Clarinda and 144 from Mt. Pleasant, were expected in the next few days.

BETWEEN 1933 AND 1951, Cherokee boarded over 1,400 patients. At its peak, the institution housed over 1,700–no date is given for this number, but with the 1954 introduction of Thorazine, patient population began declining. The book offers no figures for 1969, but the population must have still been fairly substantial, for most of us had roommates.

Throughout the years, patients have been subjected to insulin and electric shock therapies, integral parts of Joyce's treatment. Straitjackets were discontinued in the early 1950's, but lobotomies were performed into the early 1970's. Had I known what a lobotomy entailed, I would have been terrified that if I didn't behave, the procedure would be in my future. However, lobotomies were done as a last resort, reserved for the most violent patients. To my knowledge, I did not meet any lobotomy patients at Cherokee, but, at that time, I would not have been cognizant of their characteristics. I suspect that these patients were kept segregated from the general population.

Years later, I met a person who had endured a lobotomy; it was frightening to witness the damage done to him. He would simply turn on and off like a light switch, talking one minute and then drifting off into some kind of trance and then coming back, picking up exactly where he had left off.

DURING WORLD WAR II and post war, from February 1944 to May 1946, the Civilian Public Service Company #131, made up of conscientious objectors, served at the facility in lieu of military service. This company consisted of 25 conscientious objectors, 10 of their wives, and one sister. They served as nurses' aides, kitchen workers, drivers, lawn and garden assistants, housekeepers, and stenographers. I would have appreciated knowing this bit of history, given my own objection to the Vietnam war and my fears for Jeff and my cousin Steve.

At its peak, the hospital, on its 840 acres on the hill, was, in itself, a small functioning town, boasting its own coal-burning power plant; a complete working farm; hospital facilities, including a dentist's office, lab, geriatric ward, and morgue; a cemetery; a full restaurant; a butcher shop; laundry facilities; residences; carpenter and machine shops; a sewing factory; a bakery; an "amusement hall" and orchestra, made up of staff, who were often "hired on their ability to play an instrument"; a softball team; a pharmacy; and a barber and beauty shop.

Certainly, if the rest of the world disappeared, the institution could have survived, taking care of its patients and following the standard drug and psychological therapies.

The book does clarify one matter that, for years, has puzzled me: in April 1969, I spoke with a Mrs. Williams about job training in Floriculture; I could never figure out why she was pushing this career so hard, but the book reveals that Cherokee, in addition to its working farm, complete with vegetable fields, flower gardens, orchards, and beef and dairy cattle, also maintained an extensive greenhouse, overlooking the southeast section of the grounds, where the institution grew flowers and vegetables year round, even exhibiting some of their products at various state fairs. I don't remember seeing or even hearing about this greenhouse, but I might have embarked on a career because of its existence. At various points in its history, several other training programs were offered to patients: bakery and butcher schools, to name two, and a physician residency program, for doctors just out of medical school. Currently, the facility offers a physician assistant specialty training program.

I complained bitterly about the food; in my mind, a good Cherokee meal consisted of roast beef, mashed potatoes and gravy, and peach cobbler, reserved for Sunday dinner. However, most of the time, we were served such delights as instant scrambled eggs (with a green tinge), overcooked vegetables (mushy cauliflower comes to mind), a strange meat—which I suspected was liver—and wicked coffee, often served lukewarm, so I was surprised to read about the T-bone steaks and oyster stew served during the 1960's. I don't recall such meals, but I do remember losing a lot of weight there.

One odd, though darkly humorous, note: 100 years ago one group of female Cherokee sewing factory workers were scrutinized very carefully, for "...some medical authorities warned that professional seamstresses were apt to become sexually aroused by the steady rhythm, hour after hour, of the sewing machine's foot pedals." Had I known that, I would have happily taken up sewing as a career path, but then the next part of this equation might have given me pause: "[These same medical authorities] recommended slipping bromide–which was thought to diminish sexual desire–into the women's drinking water."

The hospital also had its own morgue, but this building was torn down in 1966, well before my time as a patient. Interestingly, the morgue was located near the Kinne Building, demolished in 1972, where the tuberculosis patients were kept. The morgue may have disappeared, but a cemetery remains on the grounds–831 patients interred between 1907 and 1962, the last a 62-year-old woman. The deceased, unclaimed by family members, were placed in wicker baskets in graves marked with numbers, for being a mental patient was considered too shameful to be made public, even after death. I never saw or heard about this cemetery–and D.J. never mentioned it.

In 1969, I knew nothing about the morgue and cemetery, but I must have suspected something; on April 11, after recounting a frightening nightmare I had at age four, I asked, "I wonder if anyone has ever died here?"

I'm glad I didn't know; I was frightened enough about the possibility of being incarcerated for a long time and then dying in the institution.

Chronicle-Times (Cherokee) journalist Ken Ross noted that "The cemetery is down a road beyond a locked gate. Trees surround the cemetery and Beacon Hollow Creek runs nearby." So I wouldn't have stumbled upon it during my walks.

In 2001, as mental illness became less of an embarrassing secret and more visitors asked to see the cemetery, the institution decided to create a memorial and formed a committee to plan the cemetery reconstruction, offering a dignified resting place for the 831 patients. In the past, when descendants visited the graveyard grounds, they were disappointed.

"We were apologetic about the condition of our cemetery," said Mike Thompson, plant manager for the institution.

The project was completed in 2002 and slated for dedication in time for Cherokee's 100th anniversary celebration, which took place on August 15, 2002, denoting the 1902 arrival of the first patient.

I don't know how much *Cherokee Mental Health: 100 Years of Serving Iowan's* really explains in terms of my time in Cherokee, but it does reveal some of the ingrained attitudes toward mental patients that still persisted in 1969. I would have liked more information about the history of the institution, including the subsequent superintendents, psychiatrists, and psychologists who practiced there, and more detail about the therapies, but confidentiality issues might have hampered the committee charged with pulling this history together.

Perhaps my story will reveal something important about Cherokee and other similar state hospitals.

Special Thanks & Apologies

To Dr. Mariano A. Favis, Jr., for being one of the good guys.

Your wisdom changed the course of my life.

Thanks to Michael Klein, author of *Track Conditions* and *The End of Being Known* and my former Goddard advisor, for his careful comments on my draft; he helped me to decide what to add and delete–mostly delete. Thanks, also, to York College of Pennsylvania's Faculty Development Committee for a much-needed grant so that I could complete this book. Last, but definitely not least, thanks to my husband Jerry Siegel who read several drafts and offered me many valuable comments and insights.

Apologies to Jeff Brown, a starring player and still my friend, for his immense understanding. I can only imagine what it might be like to have one's past life dragged out and exposed to the world by an ex-spouse. Also, thanks to Jeff for reading the drafts and commenting on them.

Apologies to one bit player: although my husband Jerry had no role in my life during the late 1960's, he has patiently accompanied me in my various quests for information. It must seem strange to read about that other Jennifer, not quite the Jennifer he met, courted, and married.

Additional apologies to three offstage players: Eric, my son by Jeff; Casey, Jeff's wife; and Rhia, my granddaughter–Eric's daughter. They have absolutely no role in this drama, and yet, by association, they are a peripheral part of it.

About the Author

JENNIFER SEMPLE SIEGEL is author of *Are You EVER Going to be Thin? (and other stories)*, *The Trash Can of L.A.*, and *Memoir Madness: Driven to Involuntary Commitment*.

She has taught Creative Writing and Literature at York College of Pennsylvania and Ss. Cyril and Methodius University of Skopje (Skopje, Macedonia).

Her fiction and non-fiction, including scholarly articles, have been published in various national and regional journals, magazines, and anthologies. From 1993-1996, she edited *Onion River Review*, a literary journal.

She earned her M.F.A. in fiction from Goddard College (Plainfield, Vermont).

In 2009-2010, Semple Siegel served as a Fulbright Scholar in Skopje, Macedonia.

In addition to her teaching and own writing, her Fulbright project included helping to develop a new American Studies program at Ss. Cyril and Methodius University.

She currently lives in Pennsylvania with her husband Jerry.

For more information about the author and her books:

www.Jennifer.BanMyBook.com

Acknowledgments, Sources, and Notes (Chronological)

Original Sources

Jeff Brown, Personal Correspondence (January-May, 1969) (Quoted/paraphrased throughout the book, most notably *Sections IV ["Cherokee"] and V ["Leaving Cherokee"]*).

Jennifer L. Semple (Personal Correspondence, January-May, 1969) (Quoted/paraphrased throughout the book, most notably *Sections IV ["Cherokee"]and V ["Leaving Cherokee"]*).

Cherokee Mental Health Institute Court Records for Jennifer L. Semple. Woodbury County, Iowa. (February 18-19, 1969) (Quoted/paraphrased throughout the book. All available records in entirety presented [as a special insert] in the middle of *Chapter Fifty Five*).

Cherokee Mental Health Institute Hospital Records for Jennifer L. Semple. (February 19-May 9, 1969) (Quoted/paraphrased throughout the book, most notably in Sections IV ["Cherokee"] and V ["Leaving Cherokee"]).

Harley D. Semple. Personal Correspondence (Two letters, February 1958). (*Chapter Seven*).

Jennifer L. Semple's Greyhound Ticket Stub (One-way to York, PA, from Sioux City, IA, via Des Moines and Chicago, $43.35). Date of Issue, 5/1/69. Actual dates of travel: May 5-6, 1969. (*Chapter Eighty Six*).

Other Sources

Jennifer Semple Siegel. "Cherokee Mental Health Institute Photograph." 30 August 2004. *(Canvas for Book Cover Image)*.

"Earth's Moon: Overview" [Photograph], via spacecraft Galileo. NASA. http://solarsystem.nasa.gov/planets/profile.cfm?Object=Moon. *(Book Cover, The Moon superimposed on the image)*.

William Blake. "The Marriage of Heaven and Hell." The Alchemy web site on *Levity.com*. http://www.levity.com/alchemy/blake_ma.html. *(Front Matter)*.

Peter Koestenbaum. "Existentialism: Philosophical Anthropology." *Manas: Exploration in Ethical Thought*, 1948-1988. Vol. XXI, No. 51 (18 Dec. 1968). (http://www.manasjournal.org/pdf_library/VolumeXXI_1968/XXI-51.pdf. *(Front Matter)*.

"Crazy." Lyrics by Willie Nelson. Recorded in 1961. Performed by Patsy Cline. *Wikipedia*. http://en.wikipedia.org/wiki/Patsy_Cline.

("*Caged*").

Reference to the song "They're Coming to Take Me away, HA HAAA." Lyrics by Jerry Samuels. Recorded in 1966. Performed by Napoleon XIV (Jerry Samuels). *Wikipedia*. http://en.wikipedia.org/wiki/They're_Coming_to_Take_Me_Away,_Ha-Haaa! ("*Caged*").

"The Apollo 8 Christmas Eve Broadcast (Reading of Genesis)." *NASA*. http://nssdc.gsfc.nasa.gov/planetary/lunar/apollo8_xmas.html. (*Chapter One*).

"Apollo 8 Timeline." *NASA*. http://history.nasa.gov/SP-4029/Apollo_08i_Timeline.htm. (*Chapter Two*).

"Apollo 8: Christmas at the Moon." *NASA*. http://www.nasa.gov/topics/history/features/apollo_8.html. (*Chapter Two*).

Reference to Cecil's Stand, a small outdoor café that served typical street food: hamburgers, hotdogs, French Fries, etc. Note: Based on personal memory; however, the author has not been able to corroborate the existence of this business. (*Chapter Two*).

"Apollo 8: Description." *NASA*. http://nssdc.gsfc.nasa.gov/nmc/masterCatalog.do?sc=1968-118A. (*Chapter Two*).

"See the Funny Little Clown." Lyrics by Bobby Goldsboro. Recorded in 1964. Performed by Bobby Goldsboro. *Wikipedia*. http://en.wikipedia.org/wiki/Bobby_Goldsboro. (*Chapter Two*).

"John Steinbeck." *Wikipedia*. http://en.wikipedia.org/wiki/John_Steinbeck. (*Chapter Two*).

Mission Hotel (Also known as "The Mission"). (*Chapters Four and Six*). Note: This hippie hotel may have had another name and only known as The Mission to its transient residents. However, the author has no memory of another name. At this time, the author is unable to corroborate definitively the existence of this locale. The only reference found to a Mission hotel in L.A. county: The Mission, 950-958 Mission Street, located in South Pasadena, California. http://www.nhm.org/site/sites/default/files/seaver_center/pdf/GC%201323%20Historic%20Sites%20Surveys.pdf, page 50 of 58 (?). The author has her doubts, though; the exterior does not match her memory, admittedly flawed.

Voice of Harley D. Semple, extrapolated from the summary of Jennifer L. Semple's Mental Health Records and her subsequent conversations with Mr. Semple. (*Chapters Five, Seven, Thirteen, Twenty One, Fifty Two, Fifty Four, and Fifty Five*).

"Fire." *The Crazy World of Arthur Brown*. Lyrics by Arthur Brown. Recorded in 1968. Performed by Arthur Brown. *Wikipedia*. http://en.wikipedia.org/wiki/Arthur_Brown_(musician). (*Chapter Six*).

"Disasters: The Chicago School Fire." *Time Magazine*. (15 Dec. 1958) http://www.time.com/time/magazine/article/0,9171,810717-1,00.html. (*Chapter Six*).

"History of Los Angeles: Restaurants That are Old or Extinct, S-Z (Tick Tock)." *L.A. Time Machines*. http://www.latimemachines.com/new_page_43.htm. (*Chapter Eight*).

"The Loco-motion." Lyrics by Gerry Goffin and Carole King. Recorded in 1962. Performed by Little Eva. Info from *Wikipedia*. http://en.wikipedia.org/wiki/The_Loco-Motion. (*Chapter Twelve*).

"Same Expectations at Hungry Tiger." *Los Angeles Times* (17 May 1985). http://articles.latimes.com/1985-05-17/entertainment/ca-9087_1_hungry-tiger. (*Chapter Seventeen*).

Voice of Olive Semple, extrapolated from the summary of Jennifer Semple's Mental Health Records and her subsequent conversations with Mrs. Semple. (*Chapters Twenty Two, Twenty Nine, Forty Three, Forty Five, Forty Seven, Forty-Nine, and Fifty Five*.)

Gospel Themes. Jehovah's Witnesses. *The Watchtower*. http://gospelthemes.com/denom10.htm. (*Chapter Twenty Three*).

"Purple Haze." Lyrics by Jimi Hendrix. Recorded in 1967. Performed by The Jimi Hendrix Experience. *Wikipedia*. http://en.wikipedia.org/wiki/Purple_Haze. (*Chapter Twenty Five*).

"Jan Durrell" [the author's mother]. About the Book Cover. *Devils Dance in Me*, Lee Shepard. http://javasbachelorpad.com/dvldance.html. (*Chapter Twenty Six*).

"All Along the Watchtower." Lyrics by Bob Dylan. Recorded in 1968. In 1969 performed by Jimi Hendrix and Bob Dylan. *Jimi Hendrix*. http://www.jimihendrix.com/encyclopedia/document,19690114,1.html. (*Chapter Thirty*).

United Airlines Flight #266 Crash. Info from *Wikipedia*. http://en.wikipedia.org/wiki/United_Airlines_Flight_266. (*Chapters Thirty Two and Forty*). Note: It cannot be said with 100% certainty that the author had been on the Thursday #266 flight [the crash occurred two days later, on Saturday], but she did note it in a letter to Jeff. She was, however, an 18-year-old girl prone to drama and exaggeration.

"Dear John" [Entire poem, reprinted with permission]. Jackson H. Day. http://jacksonday.home.comcast.net/~jacksonday/john.htm. (*Chapter Thirty Five*).

"Richard Nixon: Presidency." *Wikipedia*. http://en.wikipedia.org/wiki/Richard_Nixon. (*Chapter Thirty Six*).

Hewlett-Packard 9100A Personal Computer Ad. *Science News*. "History of the 9100A Desktop Calculator, 1968." *Hewlett-Packard*. http://www.hp.com/hpinfo/abouthp/histnfacts/museum/personalsystems/0021/0021history.html. (*Chapter Thirty Eight*).

Wild Man Fischer. "Merry-Go-Round." *An Evening with Wild Man Fischer.* *Wikipedia.*
> http://en.wikipedia.org/wiki/An_Evening_with_Wild_Man_Fischer). (*Chapter Forty Two*).

"1969: U.S. Statistics." *Info Please.*
> http://www.infoplease.com/year/1969.html. (*Chapter Forty Four*).

"Turn-On." Wikipedia. http://en.wikipedia.org/wiki/Turn-On. (*Chapter Forty Four*).

"Douglas Hoffman." Sioux City Soldier Killed in Vietnam. From the Virtual Wall Website.
> http://www.virtualwall.org/dh/HoffmanDE02a.htm. (*Chapter Forty Four*).

"Sp4 Carroll Paul O'Neill." Sioux City Soldier Killed in Vietnam. From the Virtual Wall Website.
> http://www.virtualwall.org/do/OneillCP01a.htm. (*Chapter Forty Eight*).

"Eight of our finest state [Iowa] legislators..." Note: Jeff Brown wrote this in a February 13, 1969, letter, which the author did not receive until *after* she was released from the institution. However, it is likely she read the same newspaper article–she was, and remains, an avid reader of newspapers. (*Chapter Fifty*).

Note about Chapter Fifty Four, "A Possible Scenario": This chapter is not presented as solid fact, but as a recreated dialogue based on textual evidence found in the author's court and commitment papers, presented as a special insert in Chapter Fifty Five. (*See also* "*Original Sources*" and Copyright page, both located in *Front Matter*).

Arthur Blessitt. "Sunset Strip 'His Place' and the Late 60's."
> http://www.blessitt.com/MediaPressInfo/SunsetStripHollywood60s/SunsetStripHollywood60s.html. (*Chapters Sixty and Seventy Four*).

"Two Hippies" [counterculture joke]. Originally from L.J. West's *Psychotomimetic Drugs* (1970); quoted in Oliver Sack's "Speed." *The New Yorker.* 23 Aug. 2004: 64. (*Chapter Sixty*).

Mass Marketing (Cincinnati, OH). "Map of Storm Lake and Cherokee, Iowa." Funded by KCHE, Sioux Valley Broadcasting Company (92.1 FM and 1440 AM), Cherokee, Iowa. Published 2001. (*Chapter Sixty One*).

Jan E. Morris. Text adapted from "The Miami Incident" [Jim Morrison's genital exposure, which allegedly occurred in Miami, Florida, on March 1, 1969]. *The Doors Collector Magazine* (www.Doors.com). Direct quotes are Jim Morrison's.
> http://www.doors.com/miami/one.html. (*Chapter Sixty Four*).
> Note: The other Doors claim that while Morrison was, indeed, very inebriated, he never exposed himself at all. Doors' member Ray Manzarek has described the "Miami Incident" as a "mass religious hallucination." "The Doors." *Wikipedia.*

http://en.wikipedia.org/wiki/The_Doors.

Walt Whitman. "Song of Myself" (from Part 48). *Leaves of Grass.*
http://www.infoplease.com/t/lit/leaves-of-grass/ch03s48.html. (*Chapter Sixty Seven*).

John Durham Peters. Partial quote from an excerpt of *Speaking into the Air: A History of the Idea of Communication.*
http://www.press.uchicago.edu/Misc/Chicago/662764.html. (*Chapter Sixty Seven*).

Paulette Herrmann and Tony Morris, Chief Production Editors. *Cherokee Mental Health: 100 Years of Serving Iowan's: A Pictorial History.* Iowa Department of General Services Printing Division: November 2001. (*Chapters Sixty Nine, Eighty Seven, and Epilogue*).

Chronicle Times (Cherokee, IA). (30 Aug. 2004), 1-14. (*Chapter Sixty Nine*).

Cuba Hijacking. March 6, 1969. Note: In a March 7 letter to Jeff, the author referred to a *Sioux City Journal* news story about a March 6 Cuba hijacking, a fact confirmed by "List of Cuba-United States Aircraft Hijackings." Wikipedia: "Black Panther Tony Bryant (d. 1999 at 60) hijack[ed] a National Airlines plane en route from NY to Miami and directed it to Cuba. He was arrested in Cuba and spent 10 years in a Cuban prison after being suspected of being a CIA agent. The US Government pardoned Bryant after his return in 1980. His 1984 book *Hijack* described his experience in Cuban prisons."
http://en.wikipedia.org/wiki/List_of_Cuba_%E2%80%93_Unite d_States_aircraft_hijackings. (*Chapters Seventy and Seventy Three*).

An earthquake mentioned in passing: most likely the Borrego Mountain Earthquake (5.4), which occurred on April 9, 1968.
http://earthquake.usgs.gov/earthquakes/recenteqsww/Quakes/ci1 0736069.php. (*Chapter Seventy Two*).

"Nixon's Hard Choice in Viet Nam" [over 450 soldiers killed]. *Time* Magazine (14 March 1969).
http://www.time.com/time/magazine/article/0,9171,839817,00.ht ml. (*Chapter Seventy Two*).

Arthur Blessitt. "Turned On To Jesus" [Toilet Service at His Place].
http://www.blessitt.com/E_Books/TurnedOnToJesus/Jesus_Pag e26.html. (*Chapter Seventy Five*).

Dwight D. Eisenhower [Death: March 28, 1969].
http://en.wikipedia.org/wiki/Dwight_D._Eisenhower. (*Chapter Seventy Nine*).

Jonathan Colt. From "John Lennon Interview. *Rolling Stone."* (23 Nov. 1968).
http://www.dmbeatles.com/interviews.php?interview=67. (*Chapter Seventy Nine*).

Vietnam War Death Stats. PBS website.
http://www.pbs.org/battlefieldvietnam/timeline/index3.html. (*Chapter Eighty*).

The Free Source http://www.thefreeresource.com/vietnam-war-1969-1975-

timeline-facts-and-resources. (*Chapter Eighty*).

"Don't Sit Under the Apple Tree (With Anyone Else But Me)." Lyrics by Lew Brown, Sam Stept, and Charles Tobias. Recorded and Performed in 1942 by The Andrews Sisters and Glenn Miller. http://www.cosmic-kitchen.com/song.php?id=andrews.sisters_DontSitUnderTheAppleTree. (*Chapter Eighty Four*).

Bob Cannon. "A Door Nailed." *Entertainment Weekly* (30 Oct. 1992). http://www.ew.com/ew/article/0,,312183,00.html. (*Chapter Eighty Four*).

United States. *Climatological Data.* [April 7, 1969, Cherokee flood]. Weather Bureau, National Atmospheric Administration, National Environmental Satellite, Environmental Data Service, and Information Service, National Climatic Center, 1969. 235. http://books.google.com/books?id=bDickvNHnCgC&pg=RA1-PA235&lpg=RA1-PA235&dq=%22April+1969%22+%2B+%22Cherokee,+Iowa%22+%2B+Flood&source=bl&ots=SUm2KHEGKo&sig=QhxMVneYslN7cknk2A-A-JwlG3Y&hl=en&ei=kepXTo7vLKTY0QGN-YGbDA&sa=X&oi=book_result&ct=result&resnum=6&ved=0CDwQ6AEwBQ#v=onepage&q=%22April%201969%22%20%2B%20%22Cherokee%2C%20Iowa%22%20%2B%20Flood&f=false. Digitized: 11 July 2005. (*Chapter Eighty Four*).

Bret Hayworth. "Akron Flood Expected Monday: Big Sioux River Historical Highest Stages." [Left Sidebar] [April 9, 1969, Akron floods]. *Sioux City Journal* (21 Mar. 2011) http://www.siouxcityjournal.com/news/local/0c07f261-783b-5096-b335-bed3ddff5389.html. (*Chapter Eighty Four*).

Perry Groten. "Sioux Falls Flood Anniversary" [April 10, 1969, Record floods in Sioux Falls and Sioux City]. *Keloland Television,* 10 April 2009. http://www.keloland.com/News/NewsDetail6371.cfm?Id=83140. (*Chapter Eighty Four*).

"Birth Announcements." *Chronicle Times* (Cherokee, IA). (30 Aug. 2004), 2. (*Chapter Eighty Seven*).

"Police Reports." *Chronicle Times* (Cherokee, IA). (30 Aug. 2004), 2. (*Chapter Eighty Seven*).

Ken Ross. "Aerial Platform is Now in Service." *Chronicle Times* (Cherokee, IA). (30 Aug. 2004), 1-2. (*Chapter Eighty Seven*).

"Social: Area Author Honored by IBPW." *Chronicle Times* (Cherokee, IA). (30 Aug. 2004), 8. (*Chapter Eighty Seven*).

"Social: Engagement Announced." *Chronicle Times* (Cherokee, IA). (30 Aug. 2004), 5. (*Chapter Eighty Seven*).

Paul Struck. "The Fruits of Labor: Local Effort to Recruit Bogenrief Studios to Cherokee Unrivaled." *Chronicle Times* (Cherokee, IA). (30 Aug.

2004), 1, 3. (*Chapter Eighty Seven*).

"Civil Commitment Unit for Sexual Offenders." *Iowa Department of Human Services*.
http://www.dhs.state.ia.us/Consumers/Facilities/CCUSO.html#search='CCUSO'. (*Epilogue*).

"Sex Offender Unit Moves" (Kevin Concannon, Director of the Iowa Department of Human Services, quoted). *Storm Lake Pilot Tribune* (9 Sep. 2003).
http://www.stormlakepilottribune.com/story/1511453.html. (*Epilogue*).

"Speaker Information: Health and Human Services Appropriations Subcommittee, January 23, 2007–Kevin Concannon."
http://www.legis.iowa.gov/DOCS/LSA/SC_MaterialsDist/2007/SDSLL015.PDF. (*Epilogue*). NOTE: I was unable to find the original Tom J. Vilsack press release about CCUSO online. It was on the internet in 2004, but had disappeared by 2011.

"Mental Health Institute." *Online Highways*.
http://www.ohwy.com/ia/m/md164002.htm. (*Epilogue*).

"alt.support.foster-parents." (Re: a 2002 *Des Moines Register* article). *Google Grupos* (Groups)
https://groups.google.com/group/alt.support.foster-parents/msg/e8696b584410bfc3?hl=es. (*Epilogue*). (NOTE: I could no longer find the original article online, which appeared online in 2004 but had disappeared by 2011).

"Chlorpromazine (Thorazine)."
Wikpedia.http://en.wikipedia.org/wiki/Chlorpromazine. (*Epilogue*).

WORKS CITED AND CONSULTED
(ALPHABETICAL)

"1969: U.S. Statistics." *Info Please.*
    http://www.infoplease.com/year/1969.html.
"alt.support.foster-parents." (Re: a 2002 *Des Moines Register* article). *Google Grupos* (Groups)
    https://groups.google.com/group/alt.support.foster-parents/msg/e8696b584410bfc3?hl=es.
"Apollo 8: Christmas at the Moon." *NASA.*
    http://www.nasa.gov/topics/history/features/apollo_8.html.
"The Apollo 8 Christmas Eve Broadcast (Reading of Genesis)." *NASA.*
    http://nssdc.gsfc.nasa.gov/planetary/lunar/apollo8_xmas.html.
"Apollo 8: Description." *NASA.*
    http://nssdc.gsfc.nasa.gov/nmc/masterCatalog.do?sc=1968-118A.
"Apollo 8 Timeline." *NASA.* http://history.nasa.gov/SP-4029/Apollo_08i_Timeline.htm.
"Birth Announcements." *Chronicle Times* (Cherokee, IA). (30 Aug. 2004), 2.
Blake, William Blake. "The Marriage of Heaven and Hell." The Alchemy web site on *Levity.com.*
    http://www.levity.com/alchemy/blake_ma.html.
Blessitt, Arthur. "Sunset Strip 'His Place' and the late 60's."
    http://www.blessitt.com/MediaPressInfo/SunsetStripHollywood60s/SunsetStripHollywood60s.html.
Blessitt, Arthur. "Turned On To Jesus."
    http://www.blessitt.com/E_Books/TurnedOnToJesus/Jesus_Page26.html.
"Borrego Mountain Earthquake" (5.4), April 9, 1968.
    http://earthquake.usgs.gov/earthquakes/recenteqsww/Quakes/ci10736069.php.
Brown, Arthur. "Fire." *The Crazy World of Arthur Brown.* Recorded in 1968. Performed by Arthur Brown. *Wikipedia.*
    http://en.wikipedia.org/wiki/Arthur_Brown_(musician).
Brown, Jeff. Personal Correspondence (January-May, 1969).
Brown, Lew, Sam Stept, and Charles Tobias. "Don't Sit Under the Apple Tree (With Anyone Else But Me)." Recorded and Performed in 1942 by The Andrews Sisters and Glenn Miller.
    http://www.cosmic-kitchen.com/song.php?id=andrews.sisters__DontSitUnderTheAppleTree.
Cannon, Bob. "A Door Nailed." *Entertainment Weekly* (30 Oct. 1992).
    http://www.ew.com/ew/article/0,,312183,00.html.
Cherokee Mental Health Institute Hospital Records for Jennifer L. Semple.

(February 19-May 9, 1969).

"Chlorpromazine (Thorazine)." *Wikipedia*.
http://en.wikipedia.org/wiki/Chlorpromazine.

Chronicle Times (Cherokee, IA). (30 Aug. 2004), 1-14.

"Civil Commitment Unit for Sexual Offenders." *Iowa Department of Human Services*.
http://www.dhs.state.ia.us/Consumers/Facilities/CCUSO.html#search='CCUSO'.

Colt, Jonathan. "John Lennon Interview to *Rolling Stone* (1968, 23 November)."
http://www.dmbeatles.com/interviews.php?interview=67.

Concannon, Kevin. Quoted from "Sex Offender Unit Moves." *Storm Lake Pilot Tribune* (9 Sep. 2003).
http://www.stormlakepilottribune.com/story/1511453.html.

Day, Jackson H. "Dear John" [Entire poem, reprinted with permission].
http://jacksonday.home.comcast.net/~jacksonday/john.htm.

"Disasters: The Chicago School Fire." *Time Magazine*. (15 Dec. 1958).
http://www.time.com/time/magazine/article/0,9171,810717-1,00.html.

"Douglas Hoffman." Sioux City Soldier Killed in Vietnam. From the Virtual Wall Website.
http://www.virtualwall.org/dh/HoffmanDE02a.htm.

Dylan, Bob. "All Along the Watchtower." Recorded in 1968. In 1969 performed by Jimi Hendrix and Bob Dylan. *Jimi Hendrix*.
http://www.jimihendrix.com/encyclopedia/document,19690114,1.html.

"Dwight D. Eisenhower."
http://en.wikipedia.org/wiki/Dwight_D._Eisenhower.

"Earth's Moon: Overview" [Photograph], via spacecraft Galileo. NASA.
http://solarsystem.nasa.gov/planets/profile.cfm?Object=Moon.

The Free Source. http://www.thefreeresource.com/vietnam-war-1969-1975-timeline-facts-and-resources.

Goffin, Gerry and Carole King "The Loco-motion." Recorded in 1962. Performed by Little Eva. Info from *Wikipedia*.
http://en.wikipedia.org/wiki/The_Loco-Motion.

"Goldsboro, Bobby. "See the Funny Little Clown." Recorded in 1964. Performed by Bobby Goldsboro. *Wikipedia*.
http://en.wikipedia.org/wiki/Bobby_Goldsboro.

Greyhound Ticket Stub [One-way to York, PA, from Sioux City, IA, via Des Moines and Chicago, $43.35]. Date of Issue, 5/1/69.

Groten, Perry. "Sioux Falls Flood Anniversary" [April 10, 1969, Record floods in Sioux Falls and Sioux City]. *Keloland Television*, 10 April 2009.
http://www.keloland.com/News/NewsDetail6371.cfm?Id=83140.

Hayworth, Bret. "Akron Flood Expected Monday: Big Sioux River Historical Highest Stages." [Left Sidebar] [April 9, 1969, Akron floods]. *Sioux City Journal* (21 Mar. 2011). http://www.siouxcityjournal.com/news/local/0c07f261-783b-5096-b335-bed3ddff5389.html.

Hendrix, Jimi. "Purple Haze." Recorded in 1967. Performed by The Jimi Hendrix Experience. *Wikipedia.* http://en.wikipedia.org/wiki/Purple_Haze.

Herrmann, Paulette and Tony Morris, Chief Production Editors. *Cherokee Mental Health: 100 Years of Serving Iowan's: A Pictorial History.* Iowa Department of General Services Printing Division: November 2001.

"History of the 9100A Desktop Calculator, 1968" (Hewlett-Packard 9100A Personal Computer Ad in *Science News*). *Hewlett-Packard.* http://www.hp.com/hpinfo/abouthp/histnfacts/museum/personalsystems/0021/0021history.html.

"History of Los Angeles: Restaurants That are Old or Extinct, S-Z (Tick Tock)." *L.A. Time Machines.* http://www.latimemachines.com/new_page_43.htm.

"Jan Durrell: About the Book Cover." *Devils Dance in Me*, Lee Shepard. http://javasbachelorpad.com/dvldance.html.

Jehovah's Witnesses. "Gospel Themes." *The Watchtower.* http://gospelthemes.com/denom10.htm.

"John Steinbeck." *Wikipedia.* http://en.wikipedia.org/wiki/John_Steinbeck.

Koestenbaum, Peter. "Existentialism: Philosophical Anthropology," *Manas: Exploration in Ethical Thought*, 1948-1988. Vol. XXI, No. 51 (18 Dec. 1968). (http://www.manasjournal.org/pdf_library/VolumeXXI_1968/XXI-51.pdf.

"List of Cuba – United States Aircraft Hijackings: March 6, 1969." http://en.wikipedia.org/wiki/List_of_Cuba_%E2%80%93_United_States_aircraft_hijackings.

Mass Marketing (Cincinnati, OH). "Map of Storm Lake and Cherokee, Iowa." Funded by KCHE, Sioux Valley Broadcasting Company (92.1 FM and 1440 AM), Cherokee, Iowa. Published 2001.

"Mental Health Institute." *Online Highways.* http://www.ohwy.com/ia/m/md164002.htm.

"Mission Hotel." http://www.nhm.org/site/sites/default/files/seaver_center/pdf/GC%201323%20Historic%20Sites%20Surveys.pdf, page 50 of 58.

Morris, Jan E. Text adapted from "The Miami Incident." *The Doors Collector Magazine.* (www.Doors.com) and http://www.doors.com/miami/one.html.

Nelson, Willie. "Crazy." Recorded in 1961. Performed by Patsy Cline.

Wikipedia. http://en.wikipedia.org/wiki/Patsy_Cline.

"Nixon's Hard Choice in Viet Nam." *Time* Magazine (14 March 1969). http://www.time.com/time/magazine/article/0,9171,839817,00.html.

Peters, John Durham. *Speaking into the Air: A History of the Idea of Communication.* http://www.press.uchicago.edu/Misc/Chicago/662764.html.

"Police Reports." *Chronicle Times* (Cherokee, IA). (30 Aug. 2004), 2.

"Richard Nixon: Presidency." *Wikipedia.* http://en.wikipedia.org/wiki/Richard_Nixon.

Ross, Ken. "Aerial Platform is Now in Service." *Chronicle Times* (Cherokee, IA). (30 Aug. 2004), 1-2.

Sacks, Oliver. "Two Hippies," quoted from "Speed." *The New Yorker.* (23 Aug. 2004): 64. Originally from L.J. West, *Psychotomimetic Drugs* (1970).

"Same Expectations at Hungry Tiger." *Los Angeles Times* (17 May 1985). http://articles.latimes.com/1985-05-17/entertainment/ca-9087_1_hungry-tiger.

Samuels, Jerry. "They're Coming to Take Me away, HA HAAA." Recorded in 1966. Performed by Napoleon XIV (Jerry Samuels). *Wikipedia.* http://en.wikipedia.org/wiki/They're_Coming_to_Take_Me_Away,_Ha-Haaa!

Semple, Harley D. (Two letters, February 1958).

Semple, Jennifer L. (Personal Correspondence, January-May, 1969).

Siegel, Jennifer Semple. "Cherokee Mental Health Institute Photograph." 30 August 2004.

"Social: Area Author Honored by IBPW." *Chronicle Times* (Cherokee, IA). (30 Aug. 2004), 8.

"Social: Engagement Announced." *Chronicle Times* (Cherokee, IA). (30 Aug. 2004), 5.

"Sp4 Carroll Paul O'Neill." Sioux City Soldier Killed in Vietnam. From the Virtual Wall Website. http://www.virtualwall.org/do/OneillCP01a.htm.

"Speaker Information: Health and Human Services Appropriations Subcommittee, January 23, 2007–Kevin Concannon." http://www.legis.iowa.gov/DOCS/LSA/SC_MaterialsDist/2007/SDSLL015.PDF.

Struck, Paul. "The Fruits of Labor: Local Effort to Recruit Bogenrief Studios to Cherokee Unrivaled." *Chronicle Times* (Cherokee, IA). (30 Aug. 2004), 1, 3.

"Turn-On." Wikipedia. http://en.wikipedia.org/wiki/Turn-On.

"United Airlines Flight #266 Crash." *Wikipedia.* http://en.wikipedia.org/wiki/United_Airlines_Flight_266.

United States. *Climatological Data.* [April 7, 1969, Cherokee flood]. Weather

Bureau, National Atmospheric Administration, National Environmental Satellite, Environmental Data Service, and Information Service, National Climatic Center, 1969. 235. http://books.google.com/books?id=bDickvNHnCgC&pg=RA1-PA235&lpg=RA1-PA235&dq=%22April+1969%22+%2B+%22Cherokee,+Iowa%22+%2B+Flood&source=bl&ots=SUm2KHEGKo&sig=QhxMVneYslN7cknk2A-A-JwlG3Y&hl=en&ei=kepXTo7vLKTY0QGN-YGbDA&sa=X&oi=book_result&ct=result&resnum=6&ved=0CDwQ6AEwBQ#v=onepage&q=%22April%201969%22%20%2B%20%22Cherokee%2C%20Iowa%22%20%2B%20Flood&f=false. Digitized: 11 July 2005.

"Vietnam War Death Stats." *PBS* website.
    http://www.pbs.org/battlefieldvietnam/timeline/index3.html.

Whitman, Walt. "Song of Myself" (from Part 48). *Leaves of Grass.*
    http://www.infoplease.com/t/lit/leaves-of-grass/ch03s48.html.

Wild Man Fischer. "Merry-Go-Round." *An Evening with Wild Man Fischer.* *Wikipedia.*
    http://en.wikipedia.org/wiki/An_Evening_with_Wild_Man_Fischer).

Woodbury County, Iowa. Cherokee Mental Health Institute Court Records for Jennifer L. Semple. (February 18-19, 1969).

Note about online sources: Unlike print sources, online sources, for various reasons, can (and do) disappear. The author apologizes if any of her online sources are no longer available for verification.

www.ingramcontent.com/pod-product-compliance
Lightning Source LLC
Chambersburg PA
CBHW071258110426
42743CB00042B/1087